A HISTORY OF
MODERN
BRAZIL

STATES AND REGIONS OF BRAZIL

VENEZUELA

GUYANA

SURINAME

FRENCH GUIANA

COLOMBIA

ECUADOR

RORAIMA

AMAPA

AMAZONAS

PARA

MARANHAO

CEARA

RIO GRANDE DO NORTE

PARAIBA

PIAUI

PERNAMBUCO

ACRE

PERU

ALAGOAS

TOCANTINS

RONDONIA

SERGIPE

BAHIA

MATO GROSSO

BOLIVIA

GOIAS

MATO GROSSO
DO SUL

MINAS GERAIS

ESPÍRITO SANTO

PACIFIC

CHILE

SAO PAULO

RIO DE JANEIRO

OCEAN

PARAGUAY

PARANA

SANTA CATARINA

ATLANTIC

RIO GRANDE
DO SUL

OCEAN

URUGUAY

ARGENTINA

N

200   0   200   400   600   800
miles

NORTH REGION

CENTER-WEST REGION

SOUTH REGION

SOUTHEAST REGION

NORTHEAST REGION

OTHER COUNTRIES IN SOUTH AMERICA

Map by Robert E. Schultz

A HISTORY OF
MODERN
BRAZIL

The Past against the Future

COLIN M. MacLACHLAN

A Scholarly Resources Inc. Imprint
Wilmington, Delaware

© 2003 by Scholarly Resources Inc.
All rights reserved
First published 2003
Printed and bound in the United States of America

Scholarly Resources Inc.
104 Greenhill Avenue
Wilmington, DE 19805-1897
www.scholarly.com

Library of Congress Cataloging-in-Publication Data

MacLachlan, Colin M.
  A history of modern Brazil : the past against the future / Colin M.
MacLachlan.
      p. cm.
  Includes bibliographical references and index.
  ISBN 0-8420-5122-8 I(cloth : alk. paper) — ISBN 0-8420-5123-6
(pbk. : alk. paper)
    1. Brazil—History—1822– I. Title.
F2535.M298 2003
981—dc21

2003000607

For my two sons

Keith and Alexander MacLachlan

About the Author

Colin M. MacLachlan is the John Christy Barr Distinguished Professor of History at Tulane University and former chair of the History Department. He is the author of numerous books and articles on a wide range of Latin American topics.

CONTENTS

ACKNOWLEDGMENTS

Acknowledging those who have contributed to my understanding of Brazil's history is an enjoyable task. My mentor, the late E. Bradford Burns, a splendid man, to use his own generous term, deserves much credit and none of the blame. As a student at UCLA, I well remember his tolerant consideration of new ideas. I have been assisted by many colleagues willing to share their thoughts and offer support. Roderick Barman read a partial draft and made straight-to-the-point suggestions on the politics of the empire. Andrew Chesnut more than once responded with much-appreciated advice and encouragement. Leslie Bethel, whose busy schedule precluded his reading drafts, nevertheless has always been a good-humored inspiration. Gregg Bockett, busy with his dissertation, took time out to review my notions of soccer. Darién Davis helped place a number of issues in context and suggested excellent modifications. Darién also guided me through the maze of racial terms. Paul Lewis read the entire work, commented on it, and suggested useful sources. Tony Pereira read a draft and suggested additional helpful sources as did Chris Dunn, who had just finished his own work on Brazil. Israel Beloch called my attention to the importance of the *Revista do Rádio*. Bob Toplin, a filmmaker but first a historian, made several helpful comments. Michael Warren, manager of Latin American Research for Toyota Motors North America, gave me excellent advice on the automotive industry. Michael Polushin provided access to books and offered interesting insights on a wide variety of topics. Daniel Castro, a student of guerrilla wars, also offered assistance. Bill Ratliff read the completed draft in much-appreciated defiance of his busy travel schedule. Tom Smith, a colleague and historian as well as a medical doctor, reviewed the public health material. Michael Boardman, over many enjoyable brunches at Pensacola's Seville quarter, went into every last aspect of the work. Bill Nañez offered the help that only a first-rate librarian provides. Alfredo da Mota Menezes forced me to reconsider certain views. Alfredo also kept an eye open for material that should be included.

A number of scientists helped place the country's environmental history in context. Members of the Tulane-Boot Chemistry Round Table, Harry Ensely, Dean of the Graduate School Mike Herman, Chemistry Chair Bill Alworth, Earth and Environmental Sciences Chair George Flowers, Brent Koplitz, and Liberal Arts and Sciences

Associate Dean Gary McPherson provided guidance. Ed Lyons of the Army Corps of Engineers, New Orleans District, also passed on useful environmental information. Dick Nabor provided insights into missile technology as well as the economic importance of space hubs.

In my department, colleagues and friends have been helpful and supportive, particularly Ken Harl, Dick Latner, Linda Pollock, Sam Ramer, Susan Schroeder, and Trudy Yeager. A former departmental colleague, Bill McClay, helped me refine my ideas of political history, as did Dick Latner. Donna Deneen dealt with unexpected computer problems and offered valuable assistance. Finally, to ensure instructional clarity, each section underwent field-testing in my Modern Brazil and Inventing Brazil classes, so the students also deserve thanks.

In the category of treasured cohorts, Professors Chris Archer, Bill Beezley, John Hart, Jaime Rodríguez O., and Paul Vanderwood have over the years encouraged me as needed (often the case). Institutional support, always greatly appreciated, came from Dean Teresa Soufas. The Tulane Latin American Center and its director, Tom Reese, stood ready to help. Copy editor Colleen Trujillo did an excellent and thorough job. Jeff Deutsch with skill and patience put the illustrations in user-friendly form. Alex Coles developed the map. Tom André shared his Jambalaya Jazz experience and lent me photos. At Scholarly Resources, Michelle M. Slavin guided the manuscript through the editorial process and offered advice and encouragement —all greatly appreciated.

A book like this could not have been possible without the labors of generations of talented scholars. My thanks and admiration go to them all.

Colin M. MacLachlan
New Orleans

CHRONOLOGY

Independence and Empire

1788–89
Tiradentes Conspiracy to establish republic

1808
Portuguese monarchy arrives in Brazil

1815
Brazil elevated to a kingdom

1821
Uruguay annexed as Cisplatine Province
João VI returns to Portugal

1822
Pedro declares independence of Brazil

1824
Constitution of 1824 promulgated
Brazil recognized by United States

1828
Uruguay created as independent buffer state between
    Brazil and Argentina

1831
Pedro I abdicates
Regency formed

1840
Regency ends and Pedro II becomes constitutional
    emperor

1850
Slave trade ends

1854
First railway constructed

1865
Brazil, Argentina, and Uruguay join in Triple Alliance to
    fight Paraguay

1870
Paraguay's defeat ends War of the Triple Alliance
Republican Party founded

1871

Law of the Free Womb frees children born to slave mother

1888

Golden Law abolishes slavery

1889

Emperor dethroned by army and republic declared

The Republic from 1889 to 1930

1891

First Republican Constitution of 1891 promulgated

1894

First civilian president takes office

1897

Destruction of Canudos settlement

1906

Valorization of coffee

1907

Unions win legal recognition

1910

Indian Protective Service established

1914

Eclética, first advertising agency, opens in São Paulo

1917

Brazil declares war on Germany

1918

Assembly of God (Assembléia de Deus) mission church
    founded

1919

Ford Motor Company establishes subsidiary

1922

Intellectuals support Modern Art Week in São Paulo
Copacabana revolt by dissident army officers
Radio broadcasts introduced

**1924–
1927**

Three-year trek of Prestes Column through backlands

1925

General Motors markets its cars in Brazil

1926

VARIG airline begins operations

1930

Revolution of 1930 brings Getúlio Vargas to power

The Republic from 1930 to 1963

1930

Getúlio Vargas assumes power

1932

Revolt in São Paulo
Literate women receive the vote

1937

Estado Novo announced

1942

War declared on Axis powers

1944

Expeditionary Force sent to Italy

1945

Army forces Vargas out of office

1946

Constitution of 1946 promulgated

1948

Revista do Rádio begins publication

1950

Vargas elected president
Television introduced

1951

Telenovelas introduced

1954

Vargas commits suicide

1960

Brasília becomes capital

1961

Election and resignation of Janio Quadros
Parliamentary system introduced

1963

Parliamentary structure replaced by presidential system

1964 to the Present

1964

Military regime established by Revolution of 1964

1965

TV Globo begins operations

1967

Constitution of 1967 legitimizes authoritarian regime

President Humberto Castelo Branco promulgates
National Security Law

1970–1974

Dirty war rages at its most intense

1972

International Environmental Conference held
in Stockholm

1978

Censorship relaxed
Habeas corpus applied to political detainees

1980

Partido dos Trabalhadores (Workers' Party) founded
José Lutzenberger publishes *The End of the Future? A
Brazilian Ecological Manifesto*

1985

Civilian rule reestablished
Movimento Sem Terra (MST, Landless Movement)
founded

1986

Xuxa moves to TV Globo

1988

Constitution of 1988 ends voter literacy requirement

1991

Treaty of Asunción creates Mercosul

1994

Real Plan and new currency introduced
Fernando Henrique Cardoso elected president

1998

President Cardoso reelected

2000

Fiscal Responsibility Law enacted

2002

Civil Code of 1916 replaced
Luiz Inácio Lula da Silva elected president

2003

Lula takes office

Glossary

Ação Integralista Brasileira (Brazilian Integralist Party)
A party established in 1932 and loosely modeled after European fascism

Afro-Brazilian
The term can include negro, mulato, or pardo, in Bahia *moreno*, and in some places *mestiço*. The term *negro* may, but not always, include *mulato* and *pardo*. To some extent, usage is situational, thus making it difficult to capture the proper term in each instance

Assembléia de Deus (AD)
Assembly of God, the largest Pentecostal group in Brazil

bossa nova
Fusion of samba and jazz to create a distinct Brazilian sound

Brasília
Capital of Brazil built in the interior of Goiás; completed in 1960

Carioca
A native of or pertaining to the city of Rio de Janeiro

Constitution of 1891
First republican constitution; ended property qualifications for voting

Constitution of 1988
New constitution introduced after the end of the military regime; notable for ending literacy qualification for voting

Côrtes
Portuguese parliament

dirty war
Counterterror campaign conducted by the state whose tactics included torture and disappearance; particularly intense from 1970 to 1974

Encilhamento
Period of excessive financial speculation in the early 1890s

Escola Superior de Guerra (ESG)
Superior War College, founded in 1949

Estado Novo (New State)
Term used by Getúlio Vargas to characterize his authoritarian regime after the auto-coup of 1937

Favela
Makeshift urban settlement of shacks illegally built by its inhabitants

Fazenda; fazendeiro
Large farm or plantation; its owner

Força Expedicionária Brasileira (FEB)
Brazilian Expeditionary Force that fought in Italy during World War II

Frente Negra Brasileira (FNB)
First black rights group, founded in 1931

Fundos de Participação de Estados e Municipios
Revenue sharing with states and municipalities by the federal government

Green Shirts
Popular name for Integralists, derived from their green uniform shirts

Imposto sobre Productos Industriais (IPI)
Tax on manufactured products, the most important source of federal revenue

International Monetary Fund (IMF)
Lender of last resort in a major economic crisis

Itamaraty
Brazilian diplomatic service

Macumba
Any Afro-Brazilian-influenced folk religion

Mercosul
Established in 1991 by Brazil and Argentina and others in the Southern Cone as a common trade zone

Movimento Negro Unificado (MNU)
Unified Black Movement; founded in 1978 to unite groups and keep them abreast of international events of importance to the African diaspora

Movimento Sem Terra (MST)
Landless Movement; established in 1985 as a grassroots peasant organization to seize unproductive land

Partido dos Trabalhadores (PT)
The Workers' Party; founded in 1980. Proposed by Luiz Inácio
Lula da Silva, elected president of Brazil in October 2002

Paulista
A native of or pertaining to the city or state of São Paulo

Policia Militar (PM)
The largest police force, with some 400,000 members. While
usually not under military control or part of the active military,
it serves as an army reserve

Revolution of 1930
Armed movement that ended the old republic; led by Getúlio
Vargas and the *tenentes*

Revolution of 1964
Military coup that established an authoritarian regime controlled by the army

Second Vatican Council (Vatican II)
Convened by Pope John XXIII in October 1962; empowered lay
Catholics to aggressively aid the poor; changed the relationship
between the Church and the state

Sertão
Backlands or interior, particularly of the northeast

Superior Tribunal Federal (STF)
Federal Supreme Court

Tenente
Army lieutenant

Torcida
Soccer fan club

INTRODUCTION

If there is one country Americans should study and understand, it is Brazil. As the diplomatic corps in Washington, DC, constantly reminds us, we have many things in common. They are correct in ways that are important, inspiring, and troubling. A significant number of the same formative elements shaped both countries. While not sharing twin histories, the two nations faced problems created by their common roots in colonialism. The need to invent a country, develop its economic and social base, then struggle to modernize and secure a respected world role has occupied the energies of both nations. Solutions differed, but the roots of many problems are remarkably similar.

This is my interpretation of Brazil. It reflects my belief in what is interesting and useful in order to understand a complex history and its continuing impact. As Brazilians are quick to point out, "Brazilianists"—foreigners who study Brazil—see the country through their own cultural prisms. They may well be right. Yet, is it an incorrect view? In our own context, the astute French observer Alexis de Tocqueville, who toured the then immature United States in the early nineteenth century, left a critique, warts and all, that rings true almost two hundred years later. Tocqueville's analysis went beyond restrictions imposed by his own culture to leave us with a human assessment of great value.

Britain and Europe had a guiding hand in modernizing Brazil as they did in the United States, but in a different way. Their surplus capital flowed through the hands of entrenched agricultural oligarchies. Railways and ports served an external export economy. Immigrants entered Brazil in general as replacements for slaves, not as an economically stimulating addition to a fully utilized and productive native-born labor force or as potential voters for a mass democracy. Eventually, although in a much-delayed process, immigrants dispersed throughout Brazil and stimulated the urban economy. As a result, a patriarchal thread runs through the country's institutions and social relations.

The United States, much closer to Europe and hence more accessible, found itself on the front lines as British and European capital sought an outlet for surplus wealth. The productive and expansive use of capital depended on workers. A responsive flood of immigrants supplied the labor, the market, and the desire, leading to the early victory of materialism. The United States, a largely immigrant creation, lost the ability to mold itself somewhere around 1850. In contrast, in Brazil the cultural paradigm absorbed outside influences without undergoing deep fundamental modification. The immigrant flow, much less than that to the United States, did not overpower the old Brazil.

The impact of immigration in the United States resulted in a partial severing of historic cultural roots. Tammany Hall, the Democratic Party machine in New York City, efficiently moved immigrants from the docks into the voting booth. Corrupt politics and political machines effectively blocked elite control but distorted the nature of mass democracy. As it emerged, mass democracy led to corruption, bribes, and all sorts of unsavory activities.

Immigrants in Brazil did not drive the movement toward mass democracy as they did in the United States. A shift toward mass politics became evident with the Constitution of 1891, which eliminated the property qualification for voting. After a brief period, the republican ideal succumbed as the oligarchy returned to power. The struggle between the radical republicans and the oligarchies depended to a large extent on middle-class army officers. The actual middle class, still small and powerless, could only applaud from the sidelines. The Revolution of 1930, fashioned by young officers, began to redeem the delayed promise of 1891. In 1932 literate working women joined the electorate and finally, under the Constitution of 1988, all adults (at least sixteen years old), including illiterates, were granted the vote. The movement of the electorate from property, literacy, and gender restrictions laid out in the 1824 charter to the mass electorate provided by the Constitution of 1988 required 164 years.

Slavery's heavy historical burden and race are issues of mutual concern. Both Brazil and the United States endure the self-inflicted stain of slavery and its lingering consequences. Shared experiences, from the relatively static condition of bondage to the fluid one of race in a free society, challenge both countries. The Brazilian myth of a racial democracy, now on its last legs, sharply contrasted with the now defunct American myth of separate but equal. Of the two, Brazil's projected a positive ideal.

Brazil territorially expanded from east to west, as did most transatlantic inventions. In the process, a frontier tradition emerged, and a certain approach to the land and what can be wrung from it became ingrained. The physical conquest of the interior is only now essentially complete. A growing awareness of environmental issues indicates that development has entered a more sophisticated stage.

Technology and industrialization, as in the American case, favored the middle class and workers—a process that is well advanced but still incomplete. Brazil remained caught in an agricultural cycle that created a dangerous dependence on world markets and an economic vulnerability to external events.

Brazil must struggle with one of the world's most unbalanced distributions of wealth. Creation of a mass-market economy is retarded by poverty. Nevertheless, Brazil should not be seen as a Third World country. A vital, energetic middle class exists in every way comparable to Europe and the United States. The country has a recognized international presence. During World War II, Brazilian soldiers fought side by side with the U.S. Army against Hitler. What happens in Brazil has an impact throughout the hemisphere and beyond. Its economy is the largest and most technologically advanced in Latin America.

All of this indicates that Brazil is different, yet subject to many of the same forces that shaped the United States. A fascinating comparative relationship, irresistible to thoughtful readers of history, ties both countries together. The historical evolution of Brazil is exciting, rich, and enlightening. The reader's personal reward is that of a time traveler able in some fashion to participate in a country's unfolding. Brazil is a wonderful journey.

While this work has been written with an American audience in mind, like the observations of Alexis de Tocqueville, I hope that I have transcended my own cultural restrictions. Readers should understand that Brazil is an important nation with a history worthy of study and respect. It must be approached accordingly.

CHAPTER ONE

The Imperial Experience

Drifting Toward Independence

B razil's independence in 1822 occurred almost as a formality.
Rather than a sharp break with the past, a long evolutionary journey with roots at least as far back as the sixteenth century can be
identified. Economics, almost the sole motivation of the pragmatic
Portuguese for establishing a presence in Brazil, in the end pulled
the colony from the mother country. The drift away from Portugal's
economic orbit began almost at the same moment when the Portuguese landed on the coast of Brazil in 1500. Early in its development, the need to market sugar in Europe forced the Portuguese to
rely upon the Dutch carrying trade and distribution network. Prolonged, weak demand for Brazilian sugar, beginning in the 1680s,
modified the socioeconomic structure. Previously unappreciated
activities and groups appeared to be vital to survival.

The skills, money, and credit of merchants moved to center stage
sustaining the now humbled sugar elite. In spite of laws to protect
seizure of land for debt, inevitably merchants became part-time sugar
planters, among their other interests. In Bahia the mixed economic
activities of merchants made survival possible and mitigated social
tensions. In Pernambuco a more rigid social division between merchants and planters, coupled with the disastrous decline of sugar,
led to violence as merchants and planters engaged in a bloody civil
war known as the War of the Mascates (1710–11). In the end, sugar
producers could not reverse economic reality. To the displaced agricultural elite, the merchants, many of whom were Portuguese born
and commonly dismissed as New Christians (Crypto-Jews), represented the triumph of predator traders over those who struggled to
wring wealth from the land. Even the still profitable tobacco industry failed to preserve the dominance of Brazilian producers over
Portuguese traders. Tobacco growers worked small plots of land
along with only a few slaves. Their production, in great demand as
far away as China, Europe, and Africa, sustained them at a relatively

comfortable level but did not transform them into an agricultural aristocracy. In a similar fashion, alcohol distillers depended on merchant activity. Primary goods producers faced ever more competition as the century progressed. British and French imperial systems favored their own colonies, while Portugal appeared weak and unable to help or even protect its colony. Overseas marketing became more important than producing.

Almost simultaneous with the rise of merchant power, a new group—the miners, soon to be incredibly wealthy—emerged. The discovery of vast deposits of gold and diamonds at the very end of the seventeenth century rescued the Luso-Brazilian economy but turned everything upside down, from society in general to the institution of slavery, to relations between the inhabitants and the state. Within Portuguese America itself, the vital center moved from the declining northeast to the southeast, where it remains today. Merchants, gold, and diamonds, along with unpredictable change, created wealth and instability, almost in equal measure.

The War of the Emboabas (1708–09), even more than the somewhat later War of the Mascates, exposed the tensions of a colonial world in transition. Gold in the backlands attracted immigrants from Portugal and Luso-Brazilians from the coast in large numbers. Suddenly, backlanders, whose lifestyle mixed Indian and European elements and who used Tupí as the lingua franca, faced an alien invasion that threatened their unique culture and contested their claims to the gold they had discovered. Such claims could not be sustained in the face of the massive influx of newcomers, nor in the end could their traditional lifestyle be preserved.

In addition to the battle between backland inhabitants and the new arrivals, a struggle ensued between Portuguese officials and Brazilian miners over taxes. The law required miners to bring their gold to a smelting house to be cast into bars and to pay one-fifth to the Crown—all of which required a difficult, time-consuming journey to a smelter and a degree of honesty sufficient to challenge a saint. In reality, nuggets and gold dust served as immediate currency, and traveling goldsmiths exercised their trade in defiance of the laws and out of sight of Crown agents. In 1701 only thirty-six people paid the fifth. By 1710, 30,000 people worked in the gold fields, but tax collection lagged in the face of widespread tax avoidance. Dispatching tax agents directly to the gold fields stimulated revenues but heightened the level of hostility.

In the latter half of the century, as gold production declined, tax collection provoked anger and open resentment. The Tiradentes Conspiracy of 1788–89, while centered in the gold fields of Minas Gerais, nevertheless drew together the broad socioeconomic tensions

2

that characterized virtually all parts of Brazil in the eighteenth century. In Vila Rica a small group of Brazilians plotted a revolt using as a pretext an expected new head tax. All the conspirators appeared to be in debt. A central role in the planned revolt went to Joaquim José da Silva Xavier, a junior officer in the mounted dragoons and an amateur dentist, a *tiradentes* in Portuguese. The conspiracy broadened to consider a revolt in Rio, then the colonial capital, and attracted Portuguese-born merchants. Economics provided the thread that drew them together, from free trade to tax and debt relief. Clearly, Portugal had alienated diverse constituencies in the southeast. The conspiratorial planners studied various state constitutions from North America as well as the polemical works of the Abbé Raynal. Their overall organizing scheme mixed the workable with fantasy. They believed Brazil, with its resources and potential new industries, could be independent of Portugal and self-sufficient economically. Their current poverty allegedly resulted from the fact that Europe sucked all the substance from Brazil. Portugal devoured all that rightfully belonged to the natives of Brazil.

As information about the conspiracy reached the authorities, they moved successfully to placate the Minas oligarchy, separating their interests from those of the hard-core conspirators. In the end, only the hapless Tiradentes faced the gallows, beheaded, drawn, and quartered. Several others suffered exile in Africa. Nevertheless, officials understood that the disaffected merchants and miners had been only temporarily reconciled. Unless the economic relationship between the mother country and its colony could be rationalized, it became only a question of time before the chasm between their interests reopened with unfortunate political consequences.

Several other events and a resurgence of Portuguese pragmatism provided a temporary conservative solution. The French Revolution of 1789, followed by the successful slave rebellion in Haiti, shook the foundations of slavery. The violence, terror, and economic destruction of the Haitian revolt forced slave owners to assess the possibility of a similar revolt in Brazil. Their fears appeared to be confirmed in 1798 when a plot of lower-class conspirators, including many mulattoes and black artisans, came to light in Bahia. Acting in the name of the "Republican Bahian People," the group issued a manifesto calling for liberty, equality, and fraternity and the breaking of the chains that bound Brazil to Portugal. Bahia at the time had a population of some 40 percent free black and mulatto and another 34 percent slave. The Revolt of the Tailors demonstrated that the radical ideas of the French Revolution had trickled down. Those at the bottom dared to conceive of a different and more favorable socioeconomic reality. In retrospect, although a widespread revolt

3

seemed unlikely, fear led to a harsh and exaggerated response with little mercy shown for the principal conspirators. To the elite, their personal safety appeared to be dependent on the status quo, which meant Portugal. Certainly, few favored any radical change in the colonial relationship—at least for the moment.

Imperial policy following the Tiradentes Conspiracy reinforced the conservative reaction. Rodrigo de Sousa Coutinho, appointed overseas secretary in 1796, attempted to lift the burden on the mining industry, did away with minor irritating taxes, and supported the establishment of iron foundries. He made it known that the Crown stood ready to accommodate Brazilian interests. Sousa Coutinho, related by marriage to a wealthy family in Minas Gerais and a landowner in the captaincy, supported modernization and the creation of colonial industry. There appeared to be little the elite wanted that did not receive a favorable response in Lisbon. Sousa Coutinho and other ministers understood that Portugal had never governed, nor could it rule, by force. At the end of the eighteenth century only 2,000 regular troops scattered along the coast, mostly officered by Brazilians, provided an illusion of strength. The political relationship had always been based on a shared sense of legitimacy, culture, and Portugal's role as an economic representative in Europe with all the attendant responsibilities such as dealing with often dangerous European diplomacy. When the relationship came under significant stress the cause was economic. In the latter part of the century the mother country ran a huge trade surplus with Britain and an equally large deficit with its colony. Former imperial services no longer compensated for a parasitic relationship.

The main task of governing on a day-to-day basis fell to Brazilians. Lisbon could not afford to maintain an extensive colonial bureaucracy in its overseas territories or indeed find sufficient, reasonably competent individuals to staff such positions. A tradition of local authority became ingrained. The upper level of authority also drew upon Brazilians as well as Portuguese. Brazilians on occasion filled positions in Portugal. José Bonifácio de Andrada e Silva, considered the patriarch of Brazilian independence, and his two brothers served in Portugal after graduating from Coimbra University. José Bonifácio, the eldest, remained in Portugal for thirty-five years before returning to Rio on the eve of the political separation.

The ultimate solution, transferring the Crown from Portugal to the New World, had been discussed both in the mother country and its colony at least as far back as the latter part of the eighteenth century. The Marquês de Pombal, who served as secretary of state and virtual prime minister from 1750 to 1776, understood the great potential of Brazil relative to the meager prospects for Portugal, as did many Crown ministers who came after him. Portuguese officials politically and psychologically prepared for the possibility of a transfer of the court to Brazil. The timing of such a move was overtaken by events. Napoleon demanded that Portugal cut its economic and political ties to Britain, which in turn elicited a threat that the British navy would cut off all contact with Brazil if they did so. On the other hand, if the royal family chose to move to Brazil, the British navy would assist and escort them to the New World. Given the economic and military reality, the Portuguese state embarked for Brazil. French troops entered Lisbon just at the moment when the royal convoy cleared the harbor.

The removal went beyond a flight of royal refugees. Some 10,000 individuals, from bureaucrats to clerics, boarded ship along with all the treasure that could be gathered, the royal library, and useful state papers. The government intended to establish a new capital and rule a Portuguese system from its most viable part. A combined Portuguese-British fleet arrived in Bahia in late 1807. In the interim capital of Bahia, D. João, regent for his mentally ill mother, Queen Maria I, dismantled the lingering remnants of the old economic system. The prince regent opened all ports to direct trade with friendly nations, immediately causing a surge of activity. Another decree ended restrictions on manufacturing. Direct trade, rather than attempting to funnel commerce through Portugal, pleased many merchants and producers but also introduced unwelcome competition. Cheap British imports, efficiently produced by the world's then industrial powerhouse, undercut colonial industry.

English merchants, with better accounting procedures, more capital at their disposal, and worldwide networks that spanned several continents, provided stiff competition, particularly now that they could reside legally in Brazil. A series of treaties in 1810 fixed the maximum duty on British imports at 15 percent and that on all other countries at 20 percent except for Portugal, which was set at 16 percent. The Swedish representative grumbled that favorable treatment of Britain made Brazil into an economic dependency of that country. In reality, it changed little. Establishing maximum but not minimum tariffs constituted fiscal symbolism. British manufacturing imports already captured the lion's share of the market, and London's financial markets supplied modernization capital in the nineteenth century. What the British wanted could not be refused. By the 1820s, Brazil had become Britain's third most important foreign market. Perhaps more significant, England's inability to absorb all the country's primary products spared Brazil from total dependency, forcing exporters to search for other markets. Dependency would be spread across a number of different markets, as it remains today. Nevertheless, the 15 percent tariff cap on British imports, renewed in 1827, limited the ability to raise badly needed revenues. Moreover, Britain increasingly favored free trade and lower duties.

The arrival of the Crown resolved, at least for the moment, the political problem but could do little to address the economic and social tensions created by internal contradictions, including slavery, or external factors such as the growing commercial demands as Europe industrialized. The new reality itself contributed to uncertainty—economic winners and losers divided the country into favored, less favored, and backward regions. The one open rebellion against Rio's legitimacy and authority occurred in Pernambuco in 1817. A military revolt, infused with liberal notions and joined by elements upset over the low prices of cotton and sugar, proclaimed the Republic of Pernambuco. The rebellion soon spread to other parts of the northeast to form the Republic of the Northeast. Lack of British support doomed the enterprise. João's troops took two and one-half months to quash the movement. The revolt instilled a destructive suspicion of Brazilians among Crown officials and growing reliance on presumed-to-be-loyal Portuguese in the government and the army.

At a crucial moment in their history, Brazilians psychologically accepted the notion that power radiated out from "imperial" Rio de Janeiro. The established notion of Rio as a center of union partially explains the country's ability to weather the forces of political disintegration that battered the nation in the first half of the century. Had not the monarchy arrived to impose an artificial unity, Portuguese America might well have fragmented into a handful of independent states along the lines of Spanish America after 1810.

Imperial demands transformed Rio de Janeiro into a cultural center, and the presence of the royal family instantly made it into the political capital of the Portuguese empire. The Crown established the General Intendancy of Police of the Court and State to operate the capital as well as ensure public security. Major institutions formerly associated with Lisbon took on a Brazilian character, much to the irritation of those left behind in Portugal. In effect, the old colonial relationship had been turned on its head, with Portugal now a de facto dependency of Brazil and the colonial parts drawn together as a whole.

The imperial capital doubled in size within a decade. A significant foreign population added a European touch. The royal library that had accompanied the court opened to the general public in 1814, creating a cultural core. A French mission invited by the government led to the founding of the Academy of Fine Arts. Courses on medicine and surgery evolved into the Academy of Medicine and Surgery, which eventually became a full-fledged medical school in 1832. Mathematics, physics, chemistry, economics, and engineering along with the latest texts could be studied in a variety of settings. Printing presses provided books, and the first newspaper, the *Gazeta do Rio de Janeiro* (1808), kept the literate population abreast of the latest developments from around the world. Another newspaper, the *Idade d'Ouro do Brasil* (The Golden Age of Brazil), established in the old colonial capital of Bahia in 1811, captured in its name the general sense that Brazil had become a cosmopolitan part of the modern world. A naval academy (1808) and a military academy established two years later suggested a gathering of strength and imperial ambitions.

The reluctance of João, now king with the death of his mother, to return to Portugal after the British had driven out Napoleon's troops drew the attention of the Congress of Vienna in 1814. Talleyrand (Charles Maurice de Talleyrand-Périgord, the Prince of Benevento), who headed the French delegation, insinuated that some sort of tropical perversion held João in thrall to his distant South Atlantic paradise. Anxious to return governing responsibility to João, the British sent warships to escort the Portuguese monarch home. He declined, putting an end to the notion of a king in exile.

The monarch, reacting to criticism and pressure, elevated Brazil to the status of a kingdom in 1815. In theory, the new kingdom became politically equal to all others of the monarchy including Portugal itself, all of which delighted the Brazilians as much as it angered the Portuguese. Making the obvious point that the dynamic future lay with Brazil, troops in 1817 invaded the Spanish territory of the Banda Oriental (Uruguay). Ironically, the conquest of Montevideo relied upon Portuguese troops fresh from the Napoleonic Wars and a Portuguese fleet. In July 1821 the region became the Cisplatine Province of the Kingdom of Brazil. The old dream of expanding to the banks of the Río de la Plata became a reality. Symbolic of the fresh winds of change, Swiss and Germans arrived in 1818. The rise from colony to de facto center of the empire, to coequal status as a kingdom in less than twenty years, seemed meteoric. The country appeared to be Europeanized, modernized, and drawn into a broader international role at a breathtaking pace.

Nevertheless, the colonial relationship had not been dissolved but merely suspended. Eventually, some sort of political resolution had to be worked out acceptable to both the mother country and its colony. Another political option presented itself in 1820 when a liberal revolt in Oporto and Lisbon in favor of a constitutional monarchy seized control of Portugal. A provisional committee drew up a document along the lines of the Spanish Constitution of 1812 to govern the United Kingdom of Portugal and Brazil. The liberals ordered that provisional governing committees be established in the various Brazilian provinces. Representation on the basis of one man for each 30,000 free inhabitants gave Brazil some seventy or so out of a little over 200 deputies. It might have prolonged the political ties a few more years at best. Almost predictably, the Côrtes became hostile to Brazil and sought to reestablish the old colonial subordination, which made even temporary union impossible.

João briefly considered sending Crown Prince Pedro, then in his early twenties, to Portugal. Instead, under increasing pressure from the army and the British, João left his son as regent and departed on a British warship. The Brazilian elite saw Pedro as the key to ending the apparently impossible relationship with Portugal. As crown prince, he possessed legitimacy and public acceptance, both of which could be used to end the impasse without endangering the social stability of a fragile society. After much courting by the elite, Crown Prince Pedro agreed to lead the political separation from the mother country. Portugal, now a constitutional monarchy, sought to lure the crown prince back allegedly to complete his education. Such a transparent ploy evoked some amusement. An irritated Portuguese government decreed the removal of native Brazilians from high positions, and the army dissolved the central government in Rio and ordered each New World province to report to Lisbon directly. With little force at their disposal, the Portuguese unwisely chose to rhetorically bully the Brazilians, who in turn ignored such orders. José Bonifácio de Andrada became a close adviser to the crown prince and supported the independent prerogatives of the Kingdom of Brazil. When it became obvious that independence could not be avoided, he played a key role in transferring royal authority virtually intact to the new emperor of Brazil.

The final step, a declaration of independence, came on September 7, 1822. An ill crown prince, regent of the Kingdom of Brazil, during a stop by the banks of the Ipiranga, ended the union. Incensed by the tone of Lisbon's dispatches as well as undoubtedly by his own physical discomfort, he drew his sword and cried, "Independence or Death, we have separated from Portugal." Under the circumstances one could have expected a less formal, more human declaration. If Pedro, known for his earthy language, made one, it went unrecorded. On December 1, 1822, he accepted the crown as Constitutional Emperor and Perpetual Defender of Brazil.

The immediate problem of forcing out the few remaining Portuguese troops would be accomplished but not without bloodshed. In the north, a yearlong siege of Salvador da Bahia and battles in Piauí and Maranhão resulted in significant casualties. In Uruguay (then the Cisplatine Province of Brazil) it required a major effort to dislodge the Portuguese garrison from Montevideo. The hastily formed Brazilian navy, under the command of Lord Cochrane, the earl of Dundonald, a mercenary and former British Royal Navy officer of some distinction, succeeded in driving out the coastal garrisons that studded the coast as far north as Belém. In the end, resistance proved fruitless, but it played a role in the anti-Portuguese sentiment that plagued the early decades of independence.

A more difficult problem involved the question of determining just who was a Brazilian. A short-term solution made nationality a question of personal declaration. Portuguese merchants, miners, and other residents could declare loyalty to the empire of Brazil or leave the country. The fact that Pedro, himself Portuguese born (he arrived in Brazil as a boy of nine), remained the crown prince of Portugal presented yet another complication. The possibility technically existed that the emperor of Brazil also might become the king of Portugal, thus reestablishing the recently severed ties. In the short term, such worries would be pushed aside.

The First Empire, 1822–1831

Pedro had expressed publicly his willingness to govern with a constitution. Brazilians understood this to mean under a constitution. Indeed, it became evident that they desired a more symbolic monarchy, a legitimate figurehead behind which they could safely engage in the politics of governing the empire. Worries that the emperor had not cut his ties with Portugal in a definitive manner and seemed too eager to safeguard the interests of Portuguese merchants remained only slightly below the surface. Fears of attempts to continue the old relationship in some guise or even of a reinvasion added tension. Many would have preferred to follow the liberal example in Portugal, but without any political connection with Lisbon and with a Brazilian monarch firmly off to the political sidelines. All their worries and fears had some degree of reality. Not surprisingly, the constituent assembly stocked with lawyers and judges decided that the emperor should not have the power to approve or disapprove legislation. They envisioned a parliamentary monarchy. Inevitably, the debates and discussions took on an anti-Portuguese tone; and in the end, rather than crafting a governing structure, they appeared to be caught up in a struggle over status and power. The personal machinations of the Andrada brothers, bitterly angry because of their dismissal as ministers, added to the poisonous debate.[1] An impatient and furious emperor accused the assembly of irresponsible behavior, surrounded it with troops, and disbanded it. Ironically, the liberals' use of force to seize power in Portugal provided the pattern to head off what might have been a liberal structure in Rio de Janeiro.

Taking few chances, Pedro and his close advisers, organized as a council of state, elaborated their own charter, the Constitution of 1824, which served until the end of the empire in 1889. The emperor submitted the constitution to the major municipal councils for their approval, thus drawing in the popular sectors to give it the necessary legitimacy. The document provided for a two-house parliament: a lower chamber of deputies indirectly elected for four years, and a lifetime senate selected by the emperor from a list of three candidates in each province who received the most votes of provincial electors. Property requirements limited the number of eligible individuals for political office as well as voters. Under the charter, Pedro, serving as the regulating power, could disapprove of legislation and dissolve parliament. The ability of the monarch to appoint provincial presidents assured regional control. A council of state and a ministry assisted the emperor. The constitution established four distinct powers—the regulating (moderating power), executive, legislative, and judicial. Centralized power lay with the monarch, who controlled three of the four powers and indirectly the legislative branch. Nevertheless, the Constitution of 1824 provided sufficient room for politics although, given Pedro's personality, criticism carried risks. Concessions to liberal opinion included a provision for local elected justices of the peace. This move challenged the notion of all judicial authority emanating from the monarch. Justices of the peace soon emerged as regional political bosses.

When word of the monarch's actions reached the northeast, scattered riots broke out. Once again, Pernambuco took the political lead with a full-scale rebellion. Other provinces joined in, resulting in the declaration of the Republic of the Confederation of the Equator. Pedro's troops harshly put down the rebellion in six months. The emperor's preference for the use of force over politics had serious and lingering consequences. Instead of winning over provincial oligarchs, he temporarily cowed them. In place of positive support, Pedro settled for acquiescence. In an effort to reinforce what remained of his constituency, he created 104 titles of nobility in 1825–26. The chamber of deputies, particularly the first (1826–1829) and the second (1830–1833) legislatures, along with the establishment of the independent newspaper *Aurora Fluminense*, began the formation of a reasonably unified political elite able to provide a counterbalance to the emperor.

The problem of recognition of the new empire by European powers required acceptance by Portugal of the reality of Brazilian independence. The Holy Alliance would not sanction general recognition of the Empire of Brazil without Portugal's agreement. The United States, not so bound, became the first to recognize Brazil (May 24, 1824), a detail often fussed over at ceremonial occasions today. The key actors in the process of European recognition, the British, had their own interests in mind. The conditions extracted in return for their vital assistance, a new commercial agreement and a treaty to liquidate the slave trade, struck directly at the existing economic structure.

Under British pressure, Portugal negotiated a settlement that opened the way for normal relations with Europe. To Brazilians the excessively cozy agreement appeared to be a family arrangement. More important, Emperor Pedro lost the ability to influence external events to protect perceived Brazilian interests.

War with Argentina, in a fruitless attempt to hold on to the Cisplatine Province, drained the treasury. In the end, the British forced Brazil to relinquish the recently annexed province and created a buffer state between it and Argentina. The introduction of copper money, easy to produce and just as easy to counterfeit, disrupted commercial exchange, which had an impact on modest street vendors and merchants. The subsequent introduction of paper currency constituted only a slight improvement—excessive paper money caused inflation and widespread economic hardship. Poor budgeting practices resulted in unpaid Irish and German mercenary soldiers rioting in the capital over the course of several days. Adding to the emperor's problems, his personal life became the topic of gossip among his opponents. The emperor breached decorum by taking a young woman, unhappily married to an army officer, as his mistress. She appeared to be able to twist the monarch around her finger and made demands that angered the elite. Initially elevated to the position of a lady-in-waiting, she soon became the viscountess of Santos, then marchioness. Subsequently, Pedro recognized her daughter Isabel Maria as his child and gave her the noble title of duchess of Goiás with the right to be addressed as "Royal Highness." His public humiliation and dismissive treatment of the empress, Leopoldina, angered many. Pedro in turn reacted badly to criticism and resented the low-level murmuring and the much louder complaints of his being too Portuguese and meddling too much in his family's dynastic affairs. Given Pedro's volatile personality, he soon tired of the constant struggle for respect, authority, and power.

The First Empire ended messily. In March 1831 the aptly named Noite das Garrafadas (bottle-throwing night) rocked the capital. Street battles between the emperor's partisans and opponents became common events. The creation of a liberal council of state and then its sudden replacement with an old-style pro-Portuguese one incensed what had by now become a mob. Demands for expulsion of the Portuguese, the replacement of Portuguese military officers, and the return of the dismissed council of state suggested the unraveling of authority. In the absence of army or elite support, with mob street violence adding to the tension, only a few options remained. Pedro chose the most dramatic one, shocking the country by abdicating in favor of his five-year-old son, also named Pedro, and taking refuge on European ships in the harbor. The royal entourage sailed for Europe in April 1831.

Abdication did not guarantee the survival of the monarchy or restore its tattered prestige. The young boy went by coach, accompanied by his governess without the usual escort, to the Campo de Santa Ana to wave to the crowd before proceeding to the imperial chapel for a celebratory Mass. To everyone's relief the street crowd greeted him warmly, unhitched the horses, and pulled the coach to the chapel. A supporter carried the royal child into the building. Street demonstrations slowly subsided, soldiers drifted back to the barracks, and life returned to a fragile normalcy. Nevertheless, the physical security of Pedro continued to be a concern for some time.

The Regency: Federated Oligarchies

The popular uprisings that played such a prominent part in the abdication concerned the elite. The reluctance of the army to fire on rioters and the involvement of soldiers in street violence added to the sense of insecurity. To provide a reliable force under their direction, provincial oligarchies established a national guard with units in every province. It served to control disturbances and counterbalance the army, soon to be reduced to a token force of 6,000. A new uniformed police force, the Corpo Municipal de Permanentes, replaced the Royal Guard.[2]

In spite of the role of the lower classes in bringing down the First Empire, only the still ill-defined political elite could pick up the pieces and rearrange them. Regional tendencies dominated crisis politics. While most supported the notion of union, they preferred to allow each province to govern itself with little interference from Rio. The national elite, still in the process of emerging and elaborating a broader outlook, remained weak. The elected three-man regency, provided for by the Constitution of 1824 until the emperor came of age at eighteen, could not exercise regulating power or bestow titles of nobility. Nor could the regency effectively balance the provincial elite.

To complicate matters, a restoration faction pressed for the return of Pedro I. The so-called *caramurus* (named after a pro-Portuguese newspaper) aggressively pressed for restoration. They seized Ouro Prêto, then the capital of the province of Minas Gerais, and held it for several months hoping to force the issue. They had considerable influence in coastal cities particularly among merchants.

Of the three other blocs, two, the nativists and the republicans, favored decentralized provincial authority with the national government relegated to a restricted supporting role. The Coimbra bloc, made up of Coimbra University graduates, favored a strong constitutional monarchy but not the return of Pedro I. Reluctantly they sided with the nativists as a tactical move. In case Pedro I returned, he could be rendered powerless by decentralized authority in the provinces. An amendment (Ato Adicional) in 1834 reduced the number of regents to one elected for a four-year term, abolished the council of state, and authorized the establishment of legislative assemblies in the provinces. The amendment also prohibited entailed estates. Collectively, these actions created a federated monarchy with muted republican overtones. Diogo Antônio Feijó, a nativist, somewhat unwillingly became regent. In office he soon developed traits, including authoritarian pretensions, that made him ineffective.

The death of Pedro I in 1834 after the passing of the Ato Adicional ended the restorationists' destructive agitation and simplified politics. They shifted their support to the young emperor, and the Coimbra bloc now felt free to press for centralism and the restoration of order and respect for authority under a constitutional emperor.

The lower classes also had a role to play in determining the nature of the central government, a role strengthened by the lack of political agreement. The existence of a sizable free black and mixed population outside the institution of slavery, with neither a secure social position nor a defined economic role, constituted an undifferentiated mass both scorned and feared by all sides. They had no way of making their wishes known except to employ the blunt political tools of riots, demonstrations, and the threat of violence. As a group, they preferred Crown paternalism and distrusted the intentions of regional oligarchs who manipulated and sought to control them.

Provincial revolts on the periphery of the empire seemed endless. The War of the Cabanos in the backlands of Alagoas and Pernambuco

13

(1832–1835), the Sabinada in Bahia (1837–38), the Balaiada in Maranhão (1838–1841), the Farroupilha in the southernmost province of Rio Grande do Sul (1835–1845), and the Cabanagem in the northern province of Pará all drew upon the unarticulated discontent of the lower classes.

The most difficult challenges came from the extremes of the north and south. In the north social grievances, including forced labor, heavy-handed recruitment for military service, and general disdain for the lower classes by the provincial elite, created endemic tension. The War of the Cabanos in Pernambuco dragged on for three years. Peasants, small landholders, and some slaves engaged in a backlands guerrilla war. Social grievances mixed with suspicion that they were being stripped of the paternalism of the monarchy by liberal elements partially explained their desperate struggle.

In Pará conflict within the elite and the insensitive actions of an authoritarian governor, Lobo de Souza, supplied the fuse for the smoldering tinder of resentment. The festival of São Tomé, which attracted a large number of rural inhabitants to the city of Belém, provided the ideal moment for an uprising. Initially led by disaffected members of the elite, the rebels eventually came under the leadership of a tenant farmer, Eduardo Angelim Nogueira. In the revolt's first months Lobo de Souza was executed and Belém occupied twice. Black slaves joined them in a broad popular uprising. The arrival of government troops in 1836 followed by brutal suppression, random killings, and eventually famine and disease quashed the rebellion, although small groups continued to function into the 1840s. An estimated 20 percent of the population died and many fled deep into the interior of the Amazon basin. For the provincial elite the Cabanagem proved to be a sobering experience, but one that they believed required more organized force, not reform. For the defeated rebels, the episode was an aborted social revolution that changed little and at great cost.

In Rio Grande do Sul the Revolução Farroupilha (Revolution of the Ragamuffins) resulted in the seizure of Pôrto Alegre, the provincial capital, in September 1835. It developed into a war for independence. Rebels from Rio Grande do Sul spilled into the neighboring province of Santa Catarina and established a short-lived republic. The sense of transnational regionalism of the extreme south made the situation very serious. Uruguayan caudillo Fructuoso Rivera supplied arms, provisions, horses, and financial support in the hope of uniting Uruguay, Rio Grande do Sul, and the Argentine provinces of Entre Ríos and Corrientes. Italian political exiles, including Giuseppe Garibaldi and Luigi Rossetti, added international drama to the struggle of the Republic of Piratim to emerge. A territorial realignment in the Río de la Plata could have been the outcome.

The one-man regency of Feijó appeared helpless, eventually resulting in his resignation. The initiative increasingly fell to the *regressos*. The *regressos* hoped to centralize the government before installing Pedro as emperor, while the nativists, concerned with provincial interests, sought to install the young emperor as soon as possible to preserve at least some of the reforms and perhaps control the government. In 1838 the legislature received a bill to interpret the Ato Adicional in the way the *regressos* had in mind. Once the bill had passed, a second law to exert centralized control over police and judicial authority could be enacted. In the face of the deliberate, relentless strategy of the *regressos*, the nativists formed the Clube da Maioridade, which pressed for the immediate assumption of power by D. Pedro. Both sides engaged in manipulating the emperor and his household as well as parliament to achieve their objectives. *Regresso* maneuvering to delay for two years declaring Pedro of age backfired. Outraged deputies now talked of violently forcing the issue. Meeting in the senate, the dissidents, less than half the chamber of deputies, and an even smaller percentage of senators voted to dispatch a delegation to appeal to the young emperor to save the nation.

The following morning (July 23, 1840) a general assembly voted in favor of Pedro's immediate assumption of authority against the backdrop of an unruly gallery. That afternoon, Pedro took the oath of office. Three days of civic celebration signaled the end of the regency experiment. Pedro II would be ceremonially installed the following year amid all the pomp and circumstance that could be mustered by an anxious nation. The restoration of centralization did not extinguish the strong strain of regionalism that reemerged with the establishment of a federal republic following the end of the empire in 1889.

Imperial Politics

Pedro II gave substance to the politics of the empire as a direct result of the role assigned the monarch under the Constitution of 1824. Through the use of his constitutional regulating power (*poder moderador*) to dismiss the governing party and arrange for a new ministry, he ensured that politics did not march too far in front of what he believed to be acceptable at any particular moment. It also made ministers attentive to his views. To go against the wishes of the emperor forced a resignation or a constitutional change in government. D. Pedro dismissed the governing party eleven times and changed cabinets thirty-six times during his reign. Nevertheless, dismissing a ministry had to be done with care to avoid any suggestion of casual whim. His personality constituted a key political element. Abandoned by his father and stepmother when they returned to Portugal, then indifferently raised by courtiers with their own agendas, he suffered emotionally.[3] The damage to his personality reflected in a childhood fear of strangers, an inability to be trusting and open, an understandable reluctance to become emotionally attached, and timidity occasioned much concern among those who were hoping for signs that he would make an effective ruler. Loneliness undermined his self-esteem and retarded the development of the social skills expected in a young ruler. Eventually he retreated into solitude and books.

When Pedro II assumed his constitutional duties he found himself manipulated by self-interested courtiers who sought to play on his inexperience. Prior to 1850 various elite factions ran the empire with little regard for the young emperor. Not surprisingly, his level of maturity lagged far behind his years, leading some to wonder whether he had inherited the mental failings of the Hapsburgs. A high-pitched voice added to the perception of immaturity, although it remained unchanged in adulthood. He developed an inordinate appetite for the comforts of sweets and sugar, resulting in a slightly unbecoming pudginess that appeared to emphasize his inherited protruding jaw. Those who saw a weak man in the boy and political factionalism as a result fortunately proved to be wrong.

As Pedro II emerged from adolescence his personality changed. A combination of factors, not the least a calculated attempt to overcome negative traits, remade him into an effective person. While never able to completely erase the emotional trauma of his childhood, he sought to mask its impact just as he grew a beard to disguise his jaw and to project a considered maturity. The emperor developed effective social graces. A polite, unpretentious, and considerate manner that contrasted with his regal rank never failed to charm those who came in contact with him. He redirected his unease with idle conversation into learned curiosity, seeming to want to know everything. For similar reasons he threw himself into his burdensome constitutional duties. He seldom lost his temper and tended to keep negative opinions to himself. Marriage to D. Teresa Cristina and the birth of children provided the previously missing emotional anchor.[4]

The lack of contact with European monarchs deprived him of a sense of the importance of ceremony as well as a strong belief in the monarchist system. Moreover, his self-esteem could not be repaired completely. He preferred to live and dress as a nineteenth-century businessman—even as a modest music professor. Dining with the emperor, while an honor, revealed more than Pedro intended. Those so honored endured a dreadful evening of poor food and nondescript wines served by slovenly attendants. All was consumed in twenty minutes. Scarcely guarded, his royal palaces failed to match the opulence of the houses of many of his subjects. When the French

Petrópolis created as D. Pedro's summer residence with the imperial palace in the background. By 1845 some 400 immigrant families, mostly Germans from the Rhineland, had transformed a former plantation into a European village. Note the gingerbread trim on the houses. D. Pedro's body lies in the cathedral. *Courtesy of the Latin American Library, Tulane University*

actress Sarah Bernhardt, who knew most of Europe's princes and crowned heads intimately, played in Rio, she disdainfully described him arriving at the theater in a simple carriage drawn by mules. Much like his American contemporary Abraham Lincoln, he substituted republican decorum for the trappings of royalty. During D. Pedro's European trip in 1877, Queen Victoria expressed indignation that he appeared at a ball in a black frock coat.

PEDRO II IN NEW ORLEANS

The arrival of the emperor of Brazil in New Orleans caused a sensation. To the city's inhabitants, Brazil seemed an exotic country yet one linked to the South through the emigration of unreconciled Confederates—some 2,500 to 4,000—who, between 1867 and 1868, had gone to Brazil, home to a slave-based plantation history and curiously a place that still clung to slavery. The emperor's tour of the United States included opening the Centennial Exposition in Philadelphia along with President Ulysses S. Grant. Few seemed to be troubled by the presence of the only monarch in the Western Hemisphere at a decidedly republican celebration. It may have been because by 1870 the United States had become Brazil's most important market, absorbing over half its coffee and latex as well as a good proportion of its cacao production. Before the formal event, D. Pedro traveled across the country to San Francisco on the transcontinental railway, less than a decade old, and then back to Philadelphia. After his official duties in Philadelphia he went to St. Louis and embarked on the steamboat *Grand Republic* to travel downriver to New Orleans, arriving in the city six days later. Local newspapers reported his progress down the Mississippi and published information on Brazil and its commerce, trade, and resources.

The emperor immediately impressed the citizens with his command of French and, to the delight of the population, English. While the imperial party stayed at the Hotel St. Charles, the most luxurious in the city, he insisted on being treated without ceremony. The *New Orleans Republican* approved and referred to him as Mr. D. Pedro. One French-language newspaper, perhaps longing for a touch of regal elegance, could not resist claiming that the emperor of Brazil outdid the czar of Russia as well as the emperors of both Germany and Austria. A more down-to-earth observer noted that "this is the type of king I like; he comes to a republican country dressed as a republican." Others described him as a steamboat captain or a portly gentleman of the old school. His simplicity and humility endeared him to all who came in contact with him. Nevertheless, when he appeared before a crowd, doffing his hat in salute, people responded with cries of "Long Live the Emperor!" In his four days in New Orleans, Pedro continually moved around the city, talking to a wide range of people and visiting all the local attractions. His curiosity and quest for information amazed citizens, newspaper editors, and municipal officials. Not one building of any distinction was missed in his desire to get a sense of New Orleans. Privately, he thought that the city appeared run down and noted the grass that grew in the streets but politely kept his thoughts to himself.

A subject of great interest to Pedro was how the American South had adjusted to the end of slavery. One newspaper advised him in a somewhat muted manner to consider the idea that "emancipated labor" is more productive than labor under "the former system of bondage." D. Pedro reported that the planters he had talked to assured him that former slaves worked well as free laborers. Looking to the future, city visionaries speculated about the possibility of a direct steamship connection between New Orleans and Rio de Janeiro. D. Pedro left the city for Washington, DC, on May 28, 1876, but not before making a generous donation to the Drama Club of Louisiana. The citizens of New Orleans agreed that they could not have welcomed a more gracious visitor.

Factionalism in parliament after the formation of political parties made the emperor's power to regulate necessary in order to break stalemates as well as psychologically to clear the air. The Conservative Party emerged out of the Coimbra-*regresso* bloc, while the Liberals represented provincial aspirations. It made it easier to have two parties with proclaimed differences when the moment came to change ministries. In general, the differences between the Conservatives and the Liberals could be bridged with a minimum of public rancor in spite of occasional political squabbling. Measures initially proposed by one side often became law under the other. The two parties shared values that moderated their political behavior. In the absence of sharply divisive interests, switching parties could be accepted.

A high point in elite cooperation came with the *conciliação* ministry of the Marquês de Paraná (1853–1859), in modern terms a national unity government. The turmoil associated with parties seemed an unnecessary diversion that hindered the movement to modernize. With prosperity seemingly threatened by the definitive end of the slave trade and a sense that Brazil had missed a turn on the road to progress, it appeared to be the time to pull together. The Marquês de Paraná failed to anticipate that the progress he hoped for— railways, modern ports, and educational reforms—could not be achieved quickly or easily. Moreover, emerging interest groups could be best served by a party system. When the marquês died, so did the experiment.

Growing economic differentiation in the latter half of the century made politics more difficult for the emperor to handle. His insistence on keeping a tight grip on events frustrated those who understood that a small inner circle could not deal with the complexities of the country's problems. Only a much freer, more flexible political arena could accommodate the stresses engendered by the liquidation of slavery and the transition to free labor and economic demands. The Constitution of 1824, designed for that moment in history, could not change rapidly enough. Adjustments in the number of representatives did not keep pace with economic and demographic change. For example, Minas Gerais had more representation than the much more important São Paulo. At the end of the empire, São Paulo, Pará, and Rio Grande do Sul suffered from a political imbalance that had little connection to their economic contributions. Other provinces defended their positions, making adjustments difficult. Consequently, senators and members of the council of state often came from provinces no longer central. Politicians increasingly resented the emperor's use of the regulating power. Dismissal of a government resulted in change at the provincial level, including the presidency of a province. Provinces seemed at the mercy of events in distant Rio. Calls for reform and more autonomy grew ever more strident.

The need to liquidate slavery could not be addressed because of the war with Paraguay. The war required all the energy the country could muster. With its army at the front, the country could not ignore the danger of a revolt by slaveholders or anything else that might encourage popular turmoil. In 1866 the government assured the French Committee on the Abolition of Slavery that the empire would move toward ending servile labor. D. Pedro cautiously referred to the issue in his Speech from the Throne to the chamber of deputies in May 1867, noting that action should be taken at the appropriate time while respecting property rights and the needs of agriculture upon which the economy rested. The conservatives preferred to leave such a potentially divisive issue off to the sidelines as long as possible. With the end of the war in 1870 the emperor pressed for more measures, particularly the Law of Free Birth, eventually signed by D. Isabel as regent in September 1871. Meanwhile, Pedro embarked on a trip to Europe so that he could not be used to derail the national debate. The emperor's gradualism unintentionally complimented the delaying tactics of slaveholders. Nevertheless, his support for the Law of Free Birth alienated slaveholders. Paradoxically, he became associated negatively with both the delay and the end of slavery.

The emergence of a formal Republican Party in 1870 and the growing popularity of positivism represented a natural reaction to the frustration engendered by an outdated political system. Republicans called for a more decentralized government. The emperor and his constitutional powers appeared to be the major obstacle to reform. Pedro himself did not see the continuation of imperial rule as important. The early death of two sons perhaps played a role in his lack of effort to pass on the throne. His eldest daughter, Isabel, as a woman could not play the patriarchal political game, nor could she rely on a strong royal mystique to overwhelm the elite of what in reality constituted a bourgeois kingdom. Moreover, Isabel did not enjoy exercising her authority as regent during her father's absences, finding it an almost unbearable burden.

D. Pedro had been overtaken not by events as much as by their impact. The sand shifted under his feet in ways both obvious and imperceptible. Railways, submarine cables, improved transatlantic shipping, immigrants, war, and free labor all had transformative influences that in turn started a new chain. Coffee wealth created a privileged young elite detached from their traditional roots. Travel and residence abroad, frequently in Paris, altered their perceptions of what it meant to be modern. Fluent in French, and perhaps German or English, and avid followers of what seemed to be the new trends, their mental construct changed. Adopted and modified European attitudes altered the perceived nature of the family and one's responsibilities toward parents, relatives, and eventually the monarchy. A new generation with little historical memory could be only lukewarm supporters at best. The openly disrespectful attitude toward the emperor in the chamber of deputies after 1870 reflected the younger generation's impatience.

An important yet barely noticed social shift occurred in the status of women. Muted changes in family structure and expectations began a subtle sociopolitical process. Pedro's patriarchal notions could not easily accommodate the shift. Isabel, heir to the throne, remained subordinate to male direction. When she married, Pedro took some satisfaction in passing the "burden" to her husband, "abdicating to him my power as a father."[5] Pedro did not believe in universal suffrage or in extending the vote to women. As he made clear verbally and by his actions, he distrusted change. A little over a half-century later, literate women had the right to vote.

The emperor and the imperial political structure became archaic far in advance of the creation of the republic. In a wide variety of ways, social changes caused a disjunctive gap between reality and the type of society needed to support a monarchy. Pedro's age and his diabetes deprived him of energy, but in the end change took away his throne. Nevertheless, for crucial decades he presided over a functioning state and succeeded in creating a sense of legitimacy that preserved an acceptable degree of order and facilitated modernization.

Developing Brazil

The relatively passive unfolding of agriculture, commerce, and nascent industrialization that characterized much of the colonial period changed in the second half of the eighteenth and in the early nineteenth centuries. When the royal family arrived in Brazil, the transplanted regime distributed coffee saplings and land to accelerate what officials believed correctly to be the next agricultural boom. By independence, coffee had become the third most important crop after sugar and cotton, and a little over a decade later it surpassed both to become the principal export. Coffee had weak export competition while demand grew exponentially, as Europeans and Americans developed a taste for the beverage. By midcentury, Brazil became

Mule train loaded with ore ready to make the difficult trek to a coastal smelter around 1880. *Courtesy of the Latin American Library, Tulane University.*

the world's largest coffee producer. To meet demand the coffee frontier moved beyond the province of Rio into São Paulo and Minas Gerais. The southeast—particularly the province of Rio de Janeiro and to a lesser extent Minas Gerais and São Paulo, beginning to feel the promise of prosperity—pressed for more influence. The Constitution of 1824, weighted in favor of the northern provinces, ignored the growing economic strength of the southeast.

Public revenues severely constrained by the treaty of 1827, which set the maximum tariff of 15 percent on British goods, could be increased when that treaty expired in 1844. It then became possible to devise an industrial strategy using protective tariffs. On the eve of the expiration of the 1827 treaty, a tariff commission recommended increases, with the highest duties levied on articles that could be produced in the country. They also advised that textile machinery should be exempt. Actual tariff increases, while modest, nevertheless raised revenues substantially and provided a welcome degree of stability for the government. When the limitation imposed by the treaty ended, protective tariffs could be carefully and selectively used. Domestically, agricultural interests wanted reasonably priced supplies and understood that in order to export, a country had to import or risk some form of retaliation. Coffee exports created a reasonable tax base and a welcome degree of fiscal stability despite occasional external financial crises that periodically rocked world markets.

The need for infrastructure to service exports and finance the technology to overcome distance and transportation costs became pressing as the coffee industry expanded. Agricultural investments, including slaves, consumed much of the country's capital with the remaining profit underwriting imports. The creation of a free working class to replace slave labor required a massive perceptual shift and a reallocation of resources not easily or quickly accomplished. The shift away from slavery appeared to demand technologies that would make wage labor more productive and thus affordable. Britain provided the modernization model in the nineteenth century as well as ideas. Nevertheless, progressives had to mesh their enthusiasm with reality. The compromises and adaptations required often made for slow progress.

Effective use of credit as well as the productive use of capital depended on a banking system. Private moneylenders and family networks could not provide adequate resources. Up until 1845 only one bank, the Commercial Bank of Rio de Janeiro, served the economy. The Commercial Bank of Bahia, founded in 1845, set off a flurry of new establishments around the empire. In 1862 the first foreign bank, the Bank of London and Brazil, opened for business in the capital, and within two years it had branches in other important cities. The introduction of the telegraph and submarine cable connection to Europe, noted below, made it possible to quickly discount receivables and speed up the circulation of capital.

In the pre–Paraguayan war era the most notable modernizer functioned as an entrepreneur, avid proponent of new schemes, and imperial politician. Irineu Evangelista de Sousa (1813–1889), later baron and subsequently Viscount Mauá, mirrored the trajectory of development in his own life. At the age of thirteen he began working for a large British importing firm. Within seven years he became a partner and eventually manager. A visit to England in the 1840s convinced him that industrialization and banking were the keys to mobilize the capital needed to finance his industrial vision. The government even lent public funds to Mauá and others to encourage their activities. A protective tariff also helped. By 1850, Mauá's ironworks produced pipes to drain the swamps around Rio, built ships, and employed 300 workers, many brought in from England and Scotland. In 1854 the first railway in Brazil, only 14 kilometers long, served as a demonstration model as Mauá intended. Subsequently, he had a hand in most other railway projects and even proposed a railway spanning the country from Paraná across Mato Grosso to the international border with the idea of opening the interior to development. Mauá became an ardent believer in free labor and an early abolitionist. In his view, free labor, capital, and industrialization would transform Brazil along the lines of Britain in an earlier century.

He pushed his country forward, but unfortunately, he was ahead of his time. Mauá's interest in finance resulted in a series of banks, some more successful than others. The Bank of Mauá, MacGregor, and Company had offices across Brazil and in Montevideo and Buenos Aires. Financial mistakes and involvement in Uruguayan politics encouraged by the imperial government resulted in bankruptcy. He struggled until his death to pay off his debts. In spite of bad luck, mistakes, and, perhaps most important, an incomplete commercial code, Mauá advanced the modernization of Brazil. The Rebouças brothers, André (1838–1898) and Antônio (1839–1874), and others steeped in economic liberalism thought in similar terms. Significantly, they understood that slavery and industrialization could not mix. André Rebouças declared freedom to be the mother and guardian angel of industry—a lesson the imperial government also learned.

The transformation of Brazil proceeded at a pace and in a manner that seemed beyond human comprehension. Communication, previously dependent on messengers carrying dispatches, suddenly became eerily impersonal with the introduction of the telegraph in 1852. A submarine cable in 1875 provided instant contact with Europe. An excited emperor composed the first message. With the outbreak of the war with Paraguay in 1865, it required only six months to string telegraph lines that tied the south to the capital and followed the advance of Brazilian troops into enemy territory. By 1885, 6,560 miles of telegraph lines carried over 600,000 messages. Telegraph lines soon reached every major region.

The difficulties and the promise of industrialization became evident in the imperial government's shipyards. Organized navy yards (*arsenais de marinha*) began with the founding of the first yard in Rio de Janeiro in 1763 by the Marquês de Pombal. The sea remained the most important means of long-distance transportation well into the twentieth century. Steam magically revolutionized shipping. The first steamboat went into service in Bahia in 1819. Coastal shipping dependent on sail only slowly adopted steam. A steamship line connected the north with the capital in 1839. European service began in 1851 with the Royal English Mail Line. The exploits of the steamship *Guapiassú*, which in 1843 proceeded up the Amazon from Belém to Manaus and returned within fifteen days, left the country gasping with astonishment. Previously, it had required three to four months to make the trip by sail. In 1852, Mauá went on to form a steamship company to serve the Amazonian economy. The navy also took an intense interest in the new technology and purchased steamships.

During the course of the nineteenth century, technology overtook the skills of the craftsmen of the past. Iron and steam required new, more advanced skills not easily learned on the job and dangerous to shipyard workers and sailors. A mixed labor force of slaves and free workers directed by highly paid foreign technicians proved to be an expensive stopgap measure. Each new technical development demanded the hiring of ever more expensive experts. The solution—to upgrade the skills and status of shipbuilders and sailors—could be delayed no longer. The creation of the Apprentice Sailor School in 1840, filled with orphans and street children, represented a major step in modernizing labor. Eventually, eleven such schools trained sailors to handle the new technology on board the imperial fleet. In addition, the government needed a new generation of technical workers. The Companhia de Aprendizes Menores, established in 1857 in Rio, recruited lower-class youths and gave them a solid technical education. In time, graduates of these schools replaced most of the foreign technicians. Along with professional skills came increased status as well as better wages and working conditions. After the War of the Triple Alliance, technically trained individuals left government service for the private sector, drawn by higher wages, improved working conditions, and more respect. By this time, most thoughtful people understood that constantly changing and increasingly sophisticated technology required advanced education along with more equitable compensation and improved status for workers. Slavery and modern methods of production could not be reconciled.

In agriculture the concern for the long-range viability of slave workers appeared to be secondary to the need for an adequate supply of labor. Nevertheless, in the end the lesson would be the same as that learned in the imperial government's navy yards—the demands of the nineteenth century required free labor with a corresponding change in status. Moreover, antislavery pressure could not be ignored. Agricultural producers—of mainly coffee, sugar, and cotton—understood international trends thanks to their close ties to coffee factors. As agents, the factors stored the crop, sold the harvest to exporters at the best price, collected the money, arranged credit as required, and purchased supplies, even the latest imported luxury goods, for planters. Factors dealt directly with the export houses. The largest exporting firms—all foreign owned, including British firms and the American company Maxwell—purchased and exported

Coffee plantation with the main house, drying terraces, and slave quarters, c. 1882. *Courtesy of the Latin American Library, Tulane University*

80 percent of Brazil's coffee production. Factors married into *fazendeiro* families in effect creating a semivertical industry. Inevitably, they became planters as well as factors. Antônio Clemente Pinto (1795–1869), one of the most successful, arrived in Brazil from Portugal with only the clothes on his back. He went from slave trader to factor to moneylender to the largest landholder in Rio. Along the way he became the baron of Novo Friburgo. His mansion in Rio later became Catete Palace, for many years home to Brazil's presidents. Upon his death he left fourteen coffee plantations, investments in railways, an export firm, and some 2,000 slaves as well as several houses and 1,500 bottles of fine wine—in all an estate worth at the time a staggering $3.5 million. Pinto functioned on an international level. Most factors operated in a much more modest fashion, but they all understood the economic and political drawbacks of the ag-

ricultural labor system and the uncertainty and dangers posed by changing international attitudes.

The Rivers of Slavery Run Dry

The economic, political, social, and moral underpinnings of the African slave trade came under attack in the second half of the eighteenth century, and by the first quarter of the next century it became obvious that the trade and slavery had become archaic. Britain had long profited from both the trade itself and slave labor in its own sugar colonies. Bristol, Glasgow, and other port cities flourished on the African slave trade. Nevertheless, new economic thinking suggested that free labor both produced more and consumed more. Increasingly, industrialized Britain needed to expand its markets and the number of consumers for its products. Political objectives closely tailored to perceived economic needs supported the creation of free societies and open commerce. Self-interest opened the way for an outpouring of moral objections to all aspects of slavery. The combination of economics, politics, and moral principles created an antislavery juggernaut carried into the South Atlantic by the Royal Navy.

England's antislave tactics involved ending the slave trade and then pressing for the gradual elimination of the institution itself. A series of preliminary steps included the treaty of 1815, which ended the slave trade north of the equator. The emperor of Brazil would be pressured into signing a treaty (1828) to end the slave trade in 1831. Brazil's elite, while somewhat ambivalent about slavery as an institution, believed that the country had no economic alternative. Incorporating the growing number of free blacks and mulattoes into a structured agricultural wage labor system appeared beyond their ability, so they continued to cling to slave labor as the core of their labor force. The expansion and profitability of coffee as well as the production of sugar and cotton, which depended on cheap labor using intensive methods, seemed threatened. Moreover, nonwage labor appeared to compensate for high transatlantic shipping costs. Not surprisingly, an illegal trade flourished much to the frustration of the British. Patrolling the slave ship routes in the South Atlantic proved only marginally effective. Nevertheless, the combination of antislavery rhetoric, growing moral revulsion, economic theory, escalating prices for slaves, and seizure of slavers on the high seas doomed the institution. In 1850, British warships entered Brazilian waters and ports in pursuit of slave ships. The violation of Brazil's sovereignty could not be tolerated, nor could it be resisted by a weak regime. There was only one option—end the trade. The end of the transatlantic trade led to an internal movement of slave labor from the north to the south. Newly developed coffee districts in the south-center counted on a sustained flow of slaves from the north until 1865, when the market tightened. Slavery became a regional issue. Many parts of the country, already drained of their slave population, moved toward the formal end of the institution.

Typical of an institution in decline, slavery had fragmented into several subtypes. *Fazendeiros* (planters) fell into three major groups—traditional, hard-core, and progressive. The traditional group had roots several generations deep in slaveholding and functioned within a plantation society. Many of them lived in the sugar regions of the northeast, particularly Pernambuco and Bahia. To them the patriarchal, paternalistic, and social aspects of the slave system, not just economics, made life worthwhile. In decline, slaveholders created a community with themselves at the center. They served as a bridge group between the enforced poverty of slavery and that of marginal free labor. They relied on slaves but also on free labor willing to work alongside slaves at low wages—in effect, slavery and its quasi-equivalent.

The second group, the hard-core slaveholders, saw no alternative to slavery. Many resided in sugar and cotton regions as well as the coffee districts of central São Paulo. A high concentration of hard-core planters occupied land in the Paraíba River Valley extending from northeastern São Paulo, southern Minas Gerais, and a part of what is now the state of Rio de Janeiro. The "River of Slavery" produced the most intransigent defenders of the institution. This region experienced boom times in the nineteenth century that drained slaves from other parts of Brazil. By 1850 they were the richest coffee barons. Nevertheless, soil exhaustion, dependence on inefficient slave labor, and outmoded agricultural techniques plunged them into debt and decline by the 1880s. Despite reality, they clung to slavery as they sank into poverty.

The third group, the progressive planters, resided mainly in the sugar area of Campos in Rio de Janeiro, in central and western São Paulo, and in Recife in the northern province of Pernambuco. The progressive planters shared an urban, not rural, mentality. Many also engaged in other businesses. They tended to have small farmer roots and approached the plantation as a business, not a way of life. They invested heavily in labor-saving machinery, banks, railroads, and other activities after the end of the slave trade in 1850. New machinery to hull and clean coffee beans along with up-to-date agricultural methods made their enterprises profitable. Nevertheless, they also depended on a core force of slave labor. They feared that abolition would disrupt their prosperity. Economics, not social or moral considerations, conditioned their attitude. They held on to slavery almost to the end even though they had made ample use of European immigrant workers and in fact recovered from the loss of slave property within three years of emancipation in 1888.

Urban economic development from the 1870s increasingly developed its own momentum. Rio, the imperial capital, boomed as the population surged. New businesses, railroads, and expanding exports created a different economic and sociopolitical outlook. Railroads penetrating the interior led to the growth of secondary cities. The war with Paraguay stimulated industrial growth and, along with expansion, a sense of modernity. Not surprisingly, abolitionists had a city face. Urban inhabitants saw themselves as creatures of liberal economics and thus endorsed a principal tenet of liberalism—the idea that free labor produced and consumed more. Urban professional schools—medicine, law, engineering, military, and mining—along with writers and journalists provided much of the leadership. Businessmen, both exporters and importers, saw the continued existence of slavery as a worldwide embarrassment. Tapping into an emerging nationalism, antislavery proponents argued that the elimination of slavery constituted a fundamental modernizing step. With forced labor, Brazil could not gain the respect or approach the socio-economic level of the much-admired European countries or the rapidly industrializing United States.

From the 1880s abolitionist clubs formed, following the lead of the Anti-Slavery Society established in November 7, 1880. Abolitionists took advantage of the rapid expansion of newspapers following the introduction of inexpensive printing machinery. Some antislave groups founded their own newspapers. The *Gazette da Tarde* (1880) became a major antislavery paper under the editorship of José Patrocinos, a mulatto. Joaquim Nabuco, a member of an important family, represented elite antislavery leadership. A firm supporter of liberal economics, Nabuco believed slavery had corrupted and degraded society. A reading of Harriet Beecher Stowe's *Uncle Tom's Cabin* provided emotional fuel. Nevertheless, Nabuco emphasized legal avenues and the importance of debate, hoping to avoid mass violence. Rui Barbosa, a brilliant intellectual, shared Nabuco's desire for an orderly end to the institution.

The John Brown of the Brazilian abolitionist movement had other ideas. Antônio Bento, a lawyer, pharmacist, and one-time public prosecutor, visited fire and brimstone on slave owners. A man deeply obsessed by religion and antiauthoritarian by nature, Bento embraced the abolitionist's sword. A cold intense hatred motivated him to direct action—to smite the evil and liberate the innocent. Bento had little patience with the legislative process. Striding around in a long black cape and tall black hat, his face drawn and his eyes burning, he struck fear in his enemies and inspired the righteous. Over the years, he collected torture instruments allegedly used on slaves. His touring exhibits enraged slaveholders. He directed an efficient Underground Railroad to assist runaway slaves to escape to various havens around the country. Bento may have been the most bizarre individual involved in direct action, but not the only one.

Abolitionists realized that slave owners used the legal, and especially the legislative, process to delay abolition as much as possible. The Rio Branco Law, sometimes referred to as the Law of Free Birth (1871), bought time for slaveholders. It proclaimed that all children of slave parents, while born free, must remain in the custody of those who held their parents until they reached the age of twenty-one or the owner would receive compensation. The law's extreme gradualism theoretically prolonged slavery, at least until the first decade of the twentieth century. The repellent cynicism of the gradualists angered even moderate abolitionists, thus beginning the process of radicalization. In order to quell antislavery agitation, the gradualists tried again in 1885. This time the law would be so confusing and complex that public opinion could not determine whether the state sincerely intended to end slavery as soon as possible or sought to prolong it. In reality, the Saraiva-Cotegipe Law of 1885 represented yet another delaying tactic.

Under the law of 1885, a slave then sixty years of age would be freed in three years, and all would be freed at sixty-five. The law required a new accounting and registration of slaves and the determination of their value based on age. An emancipation pool funded by taxes and other means provided money to purchase and free them. The law also included fines for aiding fugitives, supposedly to ensure an orderly process. Supporters of the legislation claimed that slavery would end in about seventeen years, or around 1902–03. The most expensive slaves, those in their prime working years, could be expected to be the last bought by the emancipation fund while the very young or old, valued at much less, would be purchased. The law outraged abolitionists, who believed that it compensated slaveholders and at the same time relieved them of any responsibility for caring for elderly ex-slaves and the very young. The freeing of the young and old, always a social problem, became even more frequent as slave owners realized that they would be unable to recover their costs. Nevertheless, the extremely complex legislation appeared to place the state in support of ending the institution using tax revenues, among other strategies. Its partically convincing approach temporarily calmed public agitation. Slave owners prematurely congratulated themselves—three years later slavery ended without compensation and with violence just barely averted.

The State and Popular Religion under Pressure

The Constitution of 1824 established Catholicism as the official religion but also declared freedom of religion.[6] In practice this meant ignoring religious sects that sprang up in various forms throughout the country, while exercising control over the formally dominant religious body—the Catholic Church. The reasons for doing so rested on a historic relationship as well as the reality that the Church functioned abroad as a sovereign international power and within Brazil as an arm of the state. The Church reluctantly permitted the state to exercise the Portuguese Crown's *padroado real* (royal patronage), which dated back to the fifteenth century. The royal patronage allowed the Crown to nominate clerics for positions and decide whether to prohibit or permit the circulation of papal pronouncements, among other administrative functions. A combination of privileges made the Church an arm of the state, with a particular national flavor.

The historical circumstances that led to the dispersal of Church powers changed by the eighteenth century, thus setting the stage for the attempt by the Church to regain control of its clerics and to escape from the secular authority of the government. At the same time the Crown tightened its control and attempted to bring the regular orders under the state, which led to the expulsion of the Jesuits and increased friction between Rome and Lisbon.

In colonial Brazil, under frontier conditions clerics became ever more lax, a tradition that carried over into the empire. Clerical celibacy remained an ideal but a highly theoretical one. The vicar general of the Holy See of Rio de Janeiro, for example, joyously and notoriously ignored his vows of celibacy. His example inspired others to follow in his footsteps. Imaginative and unauthorized modification of Catholic ritual occasioned little notice. A folk Catholicism emerged unimpeded by dogma. In a celebrated case a priest-showman conducted a Mass in honor of his mother's soul and that of his mistress's mother. In the excitement of the moment his mistress, who took part in the ceremony, declared she could see her mother in front of the tabernacle, at which point her priest-lover ordered the congregation to sing hymns of praise. Less flamboyant clerics lived more privately with their mistresses and children. Generally, Rome overlooked clerical transgressions. On occasion, when things got out of hand, the Vatican protested. In 1834, for example, when the regency government nominated as bishop of the capital Antonio Maria de Moura, well known for his call for an end to clerical celibacy and other unacceptable positions, Rome refused to proceed. When he withdrew his nomination, matters returned to normal.

Clerics functioned as part of the political system, trading favors and receiving them. The government paid them, and politicians treated the Church as part of the official structure. A comfortable position depended upon a political appointment. An ambitious individual needed a network of friends willing to push him forward. Drinking, gambling, and whoring in the company of local officials established bonds of mutual obligation. Contacts and the exchange of favors provided for material advancement. Individual priests who decided not to play the political and social game could expect to be stuck in a modest parish. An attractive personality counted for more than priestly virtues. Consequently, the Church hierarchy and major benefices fell into the hands of agreeable clerical politicians. Most of the public accepted this reality without comment.

D. Pedro, while not a religious person, had a strong sense of decorum. He felt a degree of personal embarrassment because of his constitutional position as head of the state and its Church. Aware that Brazil had a reputation as a dissolute tropical land given to moral degeneration, the emperor hoped to demonstrate to his European counterparts that his imperial administration could enforce high standards of priestly conduct. As a result, he used his influence to favor clerics deemed virtuous. The emperor had no intention of interfering in matters of doctrine or religious practice but believed a reformed Church would make a more effective and useful governing instrument.

Pedro's reformist tendencies complimented trends in the Church, but with conflicting objectives. The Ultramontanists, those trained in strict obedience to the pope, intended to purify clerical and lay practices worldwide. They believed that political interference by various states had corrupted the clergy and Catholic traditions. All agreed that the inadequate training of priests needed attention. Rather than establish new reformed seminaries, D. Pedro preferred to send carefully selected young men to Europe for training. On their return, he placed them in influential positions and ignored their theoretical rejection of state control of the Church.

The issue that provoked confrontation between the new clerics and the emperor involved an eighteenth-century creation—the Masonic Order. Pope Pius IX's anti-Masonic campaign became increasingly contentious after 1864. The Church had long regarded the Masonic Order, its rituals, and beliefs as dangerous heresy designed to replace Catholic beliefs with a cosmopolitan universalism that accepted the validity of all religions. The position of Pope Pius represented a reactionary attack on the Enlightenment and the liberalization of Church practices influenced by it. The campaign reached a climax with the assertion in 1870 of papal infallibility. The issue split the Church into the Old Catholics, who rejected the notion, and the Ultramontanists, who succeeded in gaining control.[7]

The anti-Masonic movement arrived unexpectedly in 1872. A priest chosen to celebrate Mass at the Grand Masonic Lodge to commemorate the Law of Free Birth was ordered by his bishop to forswear Masonry or be suspended. The recalcitrant priest ignored his bishop and celebrated the Mass. The bishop's heavy-handed action set off a barrage of criticism in the press. The next move, instigated by Bishop Vital Maria Gonçalves de Oliveira in Pernambuco, took the form of a blanket prohibition of any clerical involvement with the Masonic Order. Moreover, Bishop Vital, trained in France, denounced the exercise of the royal patronage. Broadening his attack, he ordered all lay religious brotherhoods to expel members who had Masonic affiliations. The Brotherhood of the Santíssimo Sacramento, singled out because of its open rejection of the bishop's order, found itself suspended and its chapel under an interdict, all of which caused a furor and street demonstrations.

The controversy ballooned beyond control. Emperor Pedro, the Church, and the general public failed to comprehend each other's position. The emperor, involved in the activities of the Grand Lodge in Rio but not a member of the Masonic Order, did not see any contradiction between Catholicism and the Masons. He repeatedly made the point that the order in Brazil had very little to do with religion. Rome, however, approached the Masonic Order as if it functioned in the same way worldwide, without adaptations to regional cultures.

An uncomprehending population, whose routines revolved around such organizations as lay religious brotherhoods, Masonic groups, and the various festivals that filled their daily and yearly calendar, believed that something had gone terribly wrong. In their view the Church had turned against the cultural foundations of the people, and the government appeared unable to defend them from the inexplicable assault. Bishop Vital, along with the Bishop of Pará, Antônio de Macedo Costa, also trained in France, could not be restrained in their zeal to follow the papal pronouncement in an inflexible Ultramontane manner. Unable to persuade them to be reasonable, the government in the end had to uphold the law. Both bishops, charged with violation of the Constitution of 1824, were transported to Rio aboard warships, tried, and banished to hard labor, a sentence that was immediately commuted to simple imprisonment.

33

The constitutional judicial process and its swift conclusion disrupted the behind-the-scenes negotiations with the Vatican. Rome had been on the verge of agreeing to a face-saving solution when news of the sentence dashed the compromise. By the time the dust settled a series of embarrassing disclosures made all involved look ridiculous. An angry D. Pedro pardoned the bishops, Bishop Vital went off to Europe, and the matter ended.

The spat alienated many clerics who resented the attacks mounted by the pro-Masonic elements and blamed the state for overreacting and dragging the bishops in front of a constitutional tribunal. The Masons believed the controversy had damaged their image, and the lay religious brotherhoods complained that the state had not protected them from unauthorized clerical meddling. A hapless D. Pedro received much of the blame. Prudently, every subsequent constitution separated Church and state—a political measure that benefited politicians more than clerics.

The Church's insistence on clerical control and the purity of Catholic practices ignored the reality that it could not provide sufficient priests to guide believers. Popular religion emerged out of a mixture of Indian, African, and peasant beliefs and coexisted with the more formal Catholic practices. The nineteenth-century reform movement rejected the religious tradition that sustained the lower classes. While the rural and urban lower classes continued to borrow Catholic forms and adapt them as needed, the Church, without the ability to suppress such practices, withheld approval.[8] As a consequence, the Church eventually lost the loyalty of much of the population. The Ultramontane purified version of Catholicism appealed to the upper classes, which saw it as a way to disassociate themselves from the masses. The Church's identification with the rich, powerful, and well-off eventually made it vulnerable to competing religious systems that met the spiritual needs of those at the bottom of the social structure.

The Rise of the Military

The Río de la Plata long constituted a politically volatile region. Two large countries, Argentina and Brazil, hoped to dominate politically, if not territorially, the smaller republics of Bolivia, Uruguay, and Paraguay, which, during Spanish times, had been part of the Viceroyalty of La Plata with its capital in Buenos Aires. Brazil incorporated Uruguay briefly as one of its provinces, until the British forced the establishment of an independent buffer state between the two larger contenders. Rivalry between Brazil and Argentina, held in check by a delicate balance of power, made for constant tension. Meddling in the politics of the smaller countries by one or the other became customary. Border violence offered innumerable pretexts for intervention. Paraguay, ruled by a series of suspicious, at times paranoid presidents, worried that eventually the two large powers would devour their smaller prey. Thus, Paraguay believed it had to maintain the delicate balance in the region at all costs. Fear, well-justified, led to the creation of a large, well-equipped Paraguayan army. A lethal combination of factors made serious conflict only a question of time.

Brazilian troops entered Uruguay in 1852 in support of a presidential contender who, along with several rebellious Argentine provinces, had attacked Juan Manuel de Rosas, the Argentine president. A defeated Rosas fled to Europe. Again, in 1863, Brazil protested alleged border incursions from the Uruguayan side. The following year Rio delivered an ultimatum—Uruguay must pay damages and punish the guilty or the army would force it to do so. Uruguay turned to Paraguay for help as the Brazilian navy mounted a blockade and troops poured across the border. The Uruguayan regime soon collapsed, to be replaced by one that would meet Brazil's demands. Paraguay, fearing larger designs, closed the Paraguay River, seized a riverboat carrying the new provincial president of Mato Grosso, and broke off diplomatic relations. Paraguayan army units entered Brazilian territory hoping to unite with allies in Uruguay. When Argentina refused permission to cross its territory, Paraguay declared war and attacked that country. Paraguay had managed to force an alliance between the two normally antagonistic larger powers. The War of the Triple Alliance—Brazil, Argentina, and the puppet regime of Uruguay against Paraguay—soon became a bloody war attracting observers from around the world.

A key victory, the naval Battle of Riachuelo on June 11, 1865, wiped out the Paraguayan riverboat fleet, thereby opening the river network to the allies. A major battle involved a siege of the fortress of Humaita, which blocked the Paraguay River and protected the capital of Asunción. Both Brazil and Argentina expected a quick victory. Unexpectedly, the war dragged on as the Paraguayans fought to the bitter end. Commanders seldom surrendered even when their position had become untenable.

Plunged unexpectedly into an all-out war, Brazil mobilized its resources, modernized its army, and created a large professional military institution. In the end, the war cost over $300 million, required the mobilization of 200,000 men over the course of the conflict, caused inflation, and left the country in debt. An insatiable demand for manpower—some 50,000 men died or were wounded on the Brazilian side—placed major strains on the social structure and slave system. Unfounded rumors that the government planned to expropriate 10,000 slaves to fight in Paraguay seemed plausible under the circumstances. Few parts of the empire remained untouched by wartime demands. The war jeopardized the stability of the monarchy, consuming emotional and physical resources. D. Pedro's insistence on total victory made a diplomatic resolution impossible; as a result it became his war rather than one of all the people.

In the early days, when all believed Brazilian arms would sweep the field and the war seemed to be an exciting adventure, volunteers rushed to the colors. Few realized that the nature of war had changed. The industrial revolution in the 1860s produced weapons that made for extremely bloody encounters, unlike the earlier conflicts in the region when irregular mounted units opposed each other. As the fighting took its toll in blood, war fever subsided and criticism became widespread both in the streets and in parliament. National guard units did their utmost to avoid active service. As a result, the organization all but faded away, eclipsed by the army. The military reacted to criticism by angrily denouncing politicians who, far from the battlefield, second-guessed commanders and overlooked their hard-won victories. While politicians demonstrated little respect for the army, the officer corps felt betrayed by civilians who appeared not to understand the meaning of military honor.

Finally, Asunción fell on January 5, 1869. A jubilant Brazil celebrated the end of the war only to learn that President Francisco Solano López continued to wage a guerrilla campaign from his mountain redoubt. A little over a year after the fall of the Paraguayan capital, army units defeated an enemy force, killing López in the process. At last the fighting ended.

A new political generation, which viewed the war as partially a consequence of an imperial political structure, turned away from the monarchy. Emperor Pedro II, no longer seen as the country's savior, appeared to many to be an anachronism. The war drained the country's institutions, including the Crown, while providing an opening for new groups intent on building institutional structures that reflected their needs.

Notes

1. All three Andrada brothers had difficult, self-centered personalities.
2. The force is often referred to as the forerunner of the present-day Policia Militar (PM); however, it prefers to date its formation back to 1808 and the organization that was established to administer and secure the capital with the arrival of the monarchy. The PM's smartly painted kiosks along Avenida Atlântico (Copacabana) note the year 1808, and for good measure use the Crown symbol.

3. The departing emperor selected José Bonifácio de Andrada as the young Pedro's guardian—a poor choice. In 1833 the more suitable Marquês de Itanhaem became his guardian.
4. The importance of spouse and children to Pedro did not preclude a series of affairs. D. Teresa Cristina, an arranged marriage partner, did not have beauty or intellectual interests. To the emperor she would be a spouse, not a mate. Nevertheless, in spite of his disappointment, he treated her with affection.
5. Quoted in Roderick J. Barman, *Citizen Emperor: Pedro II and the Making of Brazil, 1825–1891* (Stanford, 1999), 262.
6. Article 5, Title I, stated: *All other religions will be permitted to worship in buildings designated for this purpose without any exterior indication of their use.* Nevertheless, the state recognized only Catholic marriages and only the Church's control of cemeteries.
7. Ultramontane clerics reacted against liberalization and to what some believed to be the growing Protestant influence on the Church. It constituted a rejection of pluralism and individuality as well as of modern trends. Practices had to be judged by the extent to which they conformed to Catholic teachings—a notion referred to as integralism. For a concise discussion, see Thomas Nipperdey, *Germany from Napoleon to Bismarck, 1800–1866* (Princeton, 1996), 359–73.
8. The Second Vatican Council, meeting from 1962 through 1965, altered the stance toward the modern world, including events from the Renaissance through the Enlightenment, industrialization, and urbanization, to one of sympathy that ruled out rigidity, reversing some of the attitudes of the Ultramontane clergy. Mass celebrated in the vernacular with the active participation of the laity, often accompanied by contemporary music, attempted to dispel the elitism of the nineteenth century. The outdoor Day of the Dead "Showmissa" of Father Marcelo Rossi in 2002 in São Paulo, for example, included actors and pop singers. Father Marcelo performed songs from his own CDs while helicopters dropped rose petals on the crowd of 150,000.

CHAPTER TWO

Ascendant Republic

The Collapse of Slavery and Its Aftermath

The steady trickle of runaways that characterized the institution of slavery from its earliest beginnings eventually became a torrent. By 1885–86 emboldened slaves left the plantations in droves. Radical abolitionists urged them to flee and even armed them, while the owners stood by helplessly, unable to stop what seemed an unplanned and disorderly collapse of the institution. The army and the police refused to uphold the laws and regulations that favored slaveholders. While the army refused to be used as slave catchers, they wanted to avoid a violent collapse of order. The solution, rapid abolition before it became too late, appealed to virtually the entire officer corps.

In the process, Brazil became a series of slave archipelagos dotted with urban islands of freedom. Abolitionists controlled the cities of Fortaleza and Recife in the north and Ouro Prêto, Campos, Rio de Janeiro, São Paulo, and Santos in the south. Santos, the principal coffee-exporting port, offered employment opportunities and relative safety. Even in the slave archipelago, plantation owners, short of labor, often hired runaways with few questions asked. Fleeing slaves, however, viewed the city and urban life as true liberation. By late 1886, Santos had some 10,000 runaways who lived in the hills around the city. Jabaquara, constructed out of mud and straw in the African style on the outskirts of Santos under the leadership of Quintino Lacerda, had its own government and self-defense force in case of a police attack. Mass abandonment became common on the plantations. Angry slave owners organized gangs to raid small towns in search of fugitives and to punish those who aided them. As slaves confronted slaveholders directly, the struggle became one of blacks against whites. A newspaper, with a touch of hysteria, warned that the army would not allow the smashing of blacks by whites but also would protect whites against blacks. Many planters by 1886 concluded that the institution had become unworkable, troublesome, and more expensive than hiring immigrants. By the time the Golden Law of May 13, 1888, ended slavery, few serious proponents of the institution remained. The establishment of the republic the following year psychologically separated the slave past from what appeared to be a new beginning. While former slaveholders applauded the republic, their freed slaves distrusted the change.

The aftermath of slavery, the bitter fruits of forced labor, proved difficult for ex-slaves. To many, freedom meant the absence of work and little else. As they drifted back to the plantations, they found a mixed, even hostile reception. In the rich coffee-producing area of São Paulo, 92,086 European immigrants had taken their place. Sharecropping and tenant farming on eroded, exhausted coffee lands offered only a marginal existence. In the cities, Italians, Germans, and others pushed black artisans out of the market. Former slaves and the black population in general found themselves shackled to the past—a history many hoped to forget. To the political and economic elite, European immigrants represented a new and brighter future. Brazilians turned the page, so they thought, on slavery as well as its victims.

The Immigrant Experience

Brazil went through several immigrant stages. In the early nineteenth century the imperial government envisioned importing a European peasantry, settling them on land in the southern part of the country where the climate appeared to mirror that of Europe, and helping them become independent small farmers—productive, industrious, and a model for all to follow. The romantic view of peasants collapsed in the face of reality. Brazil needed plantation workers.

In 1845 the imperial government, influenced by Nicolau Vergueiro, a prominent planter, made money available to provincial governments to make interest-free loans to recruit European labor. Only Vergueiro took advantage of the scheme. He proposed to transport 1,000 immigrants for labor in the coffee industry. The first group arrived in 1847 consisting of 432 men, women, and children in sixty-four families. Vergueiro offered recruits an indentured contract that made them independently responsible for a mature grove of coffee trees, picking berries, transporting them to the drying terraces, and contributing labor to process the harvest. Payment consisted of shares amounting to 50 percent of the sale after expenses and taxes. Immigrant families could farm a small plot for their own use although any surplus had to be shared with the planter. Vergueiro withheld 50 percent of the workers' share until the transportation costs had been repaid. Although he received an interest-free loan from the provincial government, Vergueiro charged his indebted workers 6 percent interest. The entire family remained responsible for the debt in case of the death of a worker.

The journey itself proved an unforgettable experience. After an almost two-month voyage in miserable conditions, the recruits arrived in Santos, rested briefly, then walked cross-country for two weeks to arrive at the plantation. Their lodgings—one-room huts with straw roofs, dirt floors, and mud and stick walls— could scarcely be distinguished from slave huts. In spite of primitive conditions, the *colonos* improved their accommodations and recreated a tiny bit of Germany in their new environment. Vergueiro's experiment eventually led to sixty colonies in the western part of the province.

How to treat free immigrant labor posed another problem. Planters attempting to control immigrants in a fashion similar to slaves applied the harsh terms of the Employment Law of 1837. Under this law, a worker fired for cause had to pay his entire debt immediately or be assigned to public works or jail. Quitting without notice required the debtor to pay twice the amount owed. A worker who completed the terms of his indenture received a certificate similar to that of an emancipated slave. Anyone who hired a foreigner without such a certificate suffered severe penalties. As the indenture contract evolved, a worker could be transferred to another planter—that is, an individual followed his debt. It is clear that most planters, while not taking open advantage of their indentured workers, settled any dispute over methods of calculating cost and profits in their own favor. Workers could not leave without authorization, nor could guests set foot on the plantation without permission. Planters also punished drunkenness, laziness, and other minor infractions by imposing fines and on occasion corporal punishment. On some plantations mail was censored to minimize negative information that might discourage others from immigrating. Vergueiro faced a worker rebellion. Various countries eventually conducted investigations leading to prohibition and active discouragement of immigration to Brazil.

As late as 1878, planters demonstrated their inability to deal with free immigrant labor. Paulista delegates to the Agricultural Congress of that year advocated the importation of Chinese coolies. While they viewed them as vice ridden and racially inferior as well as diseased, they favored them because they worked for low wages and allegedly accepted a slave-like regime. As slaveholders, planters lived in a two-tiered reality—one of status, privilege, and money, and the other of degradation, imposed control, and punishment.[1] It mattered little whether those at the bottom were African or Chinese. The planters proposed that the Employment Law be extended to include preventive imprisonment and summary trials with jail terms for agitators. While such radical proposals would not be politically or socially acceptable, a new revised law relied upon coercion in worker-employer relations.

Planters believed that any expenses they incurred with immigrant labor entitled them to exercise quasi-property rights over them. Only a full-fare subsidy could break that psychological connection. Finally, the province of São Paulo voted a full-fare subsidy in early 1884 and increased it in 1887 when slavery hovered on the verge of collapse. The first subsidy resulted in the arrival of 33,163 immigrants and another 52,964 at the end of the year. Aggressive recruitment efforts maintained a steady stream. The central government's unlimited guarantee to all who wished to work in Brazil remained in effect until 1895. Immigrants understood that slavery had all but collapsed and entire plantations had switched to free labor. Hopeful European immigrants believed that with a free labor system, Brazil's patriarchal structure would disappear and thus enable them to move up the social and economic ladder. Competition for immigrant workers led to sharply improved planter attitudes and better conditions for workers. Discrimination against native workers, particularly blacks, rested on the presumption that immigrants made better and more productive laborers. Newer groves tended to hire Europeans, while declining coffee plantations hired much cheaper native-born workers, which reinforced the myth of superior immigrant productivity.

From independence in 1822 to 1880 some 400,000 immigrants entered the country. Slightly more than 40 percent were Portuguese, followed by Italians and Germans and others at much lower percentages. Most settled in Rio de Janeiro and in southern Brazil, particularly Rio Grande do Sul. São Paulo received only 4.6 percent during this period. The much more important second immigrant flow from 1881 to 1903 explains the stabilization of the coffee economy in spite of the end of slavery. In 1881 the then-province of São Paulo organized an Immigration Service. In the following twenty-two-year period 1.8 million immigrants arrived, with São Paulo receiving 58.5 percent of the flow. Italians made up close to 60 percent.

Immigrants appeared to have saved coffee. Five years before the end of slavery in 1888, few new groves were planted. In the 1890s growers planted some 350 million new coffee trees. Many now portrayed themselves as forward-looking modernizers. Successful transition to free wage labor in such plentiful supply had its downside. By 1896 the industry faced the problem of overproduction. Surplus immigrants moved into towns and cities to engage in crafts and provide services, leading to a surge in urban economic activity and pros-

perity for the lucky ones.[2] Small-scale manufacturing, shoe factories, brick works, foundries, breweries, even pasta and sausages,
among a wide variety of enterprises, depended on immigrants as
entrepreneurs as well as customers. Italian- and German-language
schools proliferated across the southeast. Coffee's problems resulted
in the dispersal of immigrants across the economy.

The Military Question

Military discontent arose from a complex series of factors and events.
The prolonged Paraguayan War, bloodied by enemies in front and
from politicians behind, and then the anticlimatic victory followed
by a disinterested reception when the army returned home masked
less obvious but more important factors. The army, numbering a bare
17,000 in 1864, swelled to 100,000 by 1870. After the war the drop in
promotions dimmed the career aspirations of junior officers. Both
status and pay fell during peacetime. The victorious veterans, suppliers who provisioned the army, industrialists who manufactured
instruments of war, and others who associated it with nationalism
as distinct from the Crown itself, created a new political and social
element. Alienated from the monarchy and confident that they represented the future, they could not be integrated into the traditional
patriarchal structure of the empire.

The officer corps had been transformed by the war. The number
of officers ballooned from 1,500 to 10,000 as the war progressed. With
their technical training, professionalism, and officer status, they became the most important element of a still tiny middle class. Unlike
petty professionals, lawyers, journalists, administrators, and bureaucrats, they possessed a unifying corporate self-interest. The military's
organizational clarity made it into a powerful and dynamic element
within the middle class. The notions of virtue and merit, not family
connections or background, lay at the heart of middle-class aspirations and of the military ethos. A military career offered status and
employment in a society with few possibilities. As a result, officers
favored philosophical notions that promised expanded opportunities. The positivism of Auguste Comte suggested that a republican
political structure facilitated change. Officers and civilian members
of the middle class, particularly journalists, found much to admire
in positivism.

Comte, born in France in the year of the outbreak of the Revolution
of 1789 and raised in its chaotic aftermath, desired a society where
order could be meshed with individual aspirations and virtue and
merit. A society based on scientific principles would eliminate social

stresses and hence disorder. Without order, progress could not be achieved. In many ways Comtian notions appeared to offer an ideal middle-class society. Positivism stressed evolution, not revolution. It envisioned a technocratic society under a benevolent director who regulated rather than governed. As with any popular philosophy, the finer points of the system escaped the attention of its adherents, who nevertheless embraced the positivist spirit as they interpreted it. Comte appeared to oppose monarchies for all the right reasons and supported the creation of virtuous republics. Here indeed was a scheme to replace the empire and all its patriarchal props, modernize the country, and create a technologically based society. Predictably, the young cadets and their professors at the military academy felt a sense of excitement and pressure to move toward the Comtian ideal.

Lieutenant Colonel Benjamin Constant (Botelho de Magalhães), a highly popular instructor, effectively combined Comtian and republican agitation to stir his student audience at the academy and subsequently discontented officers at the military club. Meanwhile, the relationship between the empire and its soldiers continued to deteriorate. Officers went from grumbling, to opposition to official policies, to hostility, and in the end to disloyalty.

Exciting events in Europe, the overthrow in 1870 of Napoleon III and the establishment of the French Republic, seized the imagination of the young officers. The Republican Party (founded in 1870) and an alienated military formed a dangerous, soon to be fatal, anti-government alliance that potentially combined armed force with an alternative political system. Comtian positivism drew them all together with the lure of national development once the empire had been swept into history.

The army first appealed to public opinion over the head of the government in 1879. To the officer corps, the issue—reduction in the size of the military—appeared to be one of survival. They ignored regulations against criticizing political authorities in the press to accuse the government of bad faith and ingratitude. Opposition successfully killed the proposed reduction in force. Four years later the strategy worked again over another issue. An angry government reprimanded and punished some military critics. Marshal Deodoro da Fonseca, a respected and popular senior officer, defended his colleagues in a partisan fashion regardless of the issue. Military honor justified all opposition to the state. In 1887 officers established the Clube Militar as an organized army lobby. It served as the political arm of the officer corps, often taking positions in opposition to the government. Marshal da Fonseca served as its first president. At the time the military club served as the personal platform for its president.

By the 1880s, most officers accepted the notion that only a vigorous republic could assure future greatness. The empire, an empty shell with little real support, awaited the inevitable coup de grâce. In a last-minute effort to shore up support the government eased banking laws and pumped money into the system. A speculative fever attracted foreign and domestic capital into new risky ventures that drove up the stock market to unsustainable levels. While it came too late, the financial bubble carried over into the republic with predictable results.

To lessen the level of political intrigue the government transferred Marshal da Fonseca to a command in distant Mato Grosso. He returned to the capital in September 1889, intent on reestablishing his dominance. Meanwhile, the Republican Party found itself excluded from the election of that year, which led it to advocate seizure of the government by force. The government appointed active military men to head the Ministry of War and the Navy hoping that they could hold the military in check. Plans to revitalize the national guard, barely functioning at the time, came too late. Before an effective counterbalance could build up, the army toppled the monarchy on November 15, 1889. Marshal da Fonseca informed the nation—few bothered to contest the decision. The army quickly reassured the provincial authorities that order would be maintained, a critical guarantee considering the fall of the empire followed the end of slavery by only one year.

The place of the black population in republican politics posed its own uncertainties. Ex-slaves saw the connection between the two events as retaliation against the imperial government for the liquidation of slavery. The public debate among slave owners over the issue of compensation added substance to this view. Indeed, the planters of São Paulo had become alienated from the monarchy in the 1870s and 1880s. The Paulista elite had conspired with the army in the capital, the only nonmilitary group to have a part in the overthrow. They claimed a role in what followed. Many former slave owners became republicans.

In the city of São Paulo blacks, many born free and often with some limited schooling, supported the republic with the hope that it would institute a more open society and broaden access to education. Their social aspirations initially blinded them to the possibility that the ex-slaves had correctly assessed the new system. They lost the perceived paternalism of the empire and gained much less than they hoped. Black abolitionists expressed their own reservations about the republic. André Rebouças had earlier linked calls for abolition with demands for land reform and some sort of political place for freed slaves. He attacked feudal barons, landlords, and what he called the landocracy—all the elements that the planter elite held near and dear, although they hardly classified them in the same fashion as Rebouças. José Patrocinos, an early supporter of the Republican Party, switched sides and organized the monarchist paramilitary Black Guard in Rio. A São Paulo newspaper observed that it came down to the fact that whites sided with the republic and blacks with the monarchy. As late as 1930 Afro-Brazilian newspapers carried reports about black monarchist organizations, and the Vai Vai Samba School in São Paulo, today one of the most important, placed a crown on its flag in honor of the empire.[3]

The Military Republic

During the closing decades of the empire, the Republican Party skillfully allied itself with the army. Both agreed on the need for a republican form of government. The party assumed that it would be a civilian republic. Bitterly, they realized that the transition would not be easy. While Marshal Deodoro da Fonseca had been a somewhat reluctant traitor to the emperor, he now became a firm republican—perhaps too firm. He became provisional president, then the first president under the Constitution of 1891. Unfortunately, he lacked political skills, often acting in what to others seemed an arbitrary fashion. His cabinet ministers, equally inexperienced, rushed to prove the superiority of the new republic over the now defunct empire. Rui Barbosa, who became finance minister, believed Brazil could duplicate the experience of the United States and could do so in short order. He pressed for continuation of the liberal credit and favorable business regulations introduced during the last months of the empire. The promise of rapid development led to wild financial manipulations, inflation, and economic distortions. A protective tariff, designed to stimulate industrialization, increased the cost of imported goods, while industry only slowly expanded and found itself unable to meet demand. In the end, the movement collapsed as spectacularly as it had flourished. The era would be labeled the Encilhamento (saddle your horse), a racing term. It discredited and tarred entrepreneurs as charlatans and made the government appear irresponsible. The rush to transform the country set off a counterreaction that strengthened the agri-export oligarchy's bid to return to power in 1894.

A Constituent Assembly studied several constitutions, including that of the United States, made a number of modifications, and borrowed many of the workable aspects of the old imperial document.

Yet the document contained important sections that changed the political balance between the elite and the middle class, while excluding the lower class. It dropped property qualifications, although illiterates and women remained ineligible to vote. An attempt to reconfigure the states to avoid the dominance of the larger entities and their powerful bosses failed. The constitution strengthened the elite by permitting states to elect governors and their own legislatures, directly contract foreign loans, and establish their own militias. Power shifted from those states that had dominated the empire to the coffee states, creating a new regional imbalance. Since 1891, Brazilian states have exercised much more power and authority than, for example, the various states of the United States. The more powerful state oligarchies eventually dominated the republic. The military, however, posed the immediate obstacle to the return of the oligarchs, now sporting their newfound republicanism.

Provisional President da Fonseca disillusioned many with his arbitrary manner to the point that some contemplated denying him the presidency under the Constitution of 1891. Marshal Floriano Peixoto, the adjutant general of the army, reluctantly endorsed the candidacy of Fonseca and became vice president—a position he used to plot against the president. The legislative body spent most of its time opposing the president. Eventually, an angry Fonseca dissolved the congress (November 3, 1891) and ruled by decree. Disenchanted elements of the army and navy threatened a civil war and the navy announced it would bombard Rio. Fortunately, they fired only one shot, which toppled the dome of Candelaria church. Even though most of the army still backed Fonseca, the angry, depressed president resigned and turned the government over to the vice president. Marshal da Fonseca died the following year, buried, as he instructed, in civilian clothes without military honors.

The second military president, a man without the slightest hint of humor or apparent generosity, the former vice president, Marshal Peixoto, had all the makings of a dictator. Cunning, intelligent, embittered, and resentful, the Sphinx talked with an economy of expression that made others uncomfortable. His reputation as a ruthless individual sprang in part from his reluctance to waste time convincing others. A man with a limited education, from a poverty-stricken family in a marginal state (Alagoas), he could not shake off the psychological and social damage inflicted by his background. He disliked the elite and distrusted everyone else. While he posed as a defender of the constitution, he resorted to a technicality to avoid calling a new election as constitutionally specified. Peixoto dealt harshly with his critics, demoting military officers and stripping some of their commissions, made life difficult for journalists, and intimidated congressmen. While Fonseca stepped aside to avoid civil war, the new president intended to crush any and all opposition. The Sphinx turned into the Iron Marshal. Yet for all his failings he understood that decentralization favored the oligarchy, not the new, still weak middle-class nationalists, urban professionals, and the army. In spite of political ineptness, Peixoto represented the wave of the future. He understood the social potential of a republic.

The decisive challenge to Peixoto's type of republicanism came sooner than he expected. Rio Grande do Sul, the southernmost state, opposed the governor supported by the president. The issue, control over state government, challenged Peixoto's desire to direct state administrations in spite of the constitution. Rio Grande do Sul's resort to violence in support of state control represented the beginning of the resurgence of oligarchic authority. A naval revolt on September 6, 1893, in Rio's harbor, supposedly led by officers intent on restoring the monarchy, turned the struggle into a debate over the form of government, obscuring the revolt of the oligarchy. Federalists and the navy proposed a plebiscite to choose between a monarchy and a republic, which further clouded the issue of oligarchic control. The naval revolt sputtered to a conclusion when 500 sailors, given refuge on a Portuguese ship, sailed out of the harbor and went ashore in Montevideo and Buenos Aires. Rio Grande do Sul's revolt against the president relied upon dissident army elements—but by itself the state could not hold out against Peixoto. Everything depended on whether other states joined the movement, setting off a civil war with all the negative consequences involved.

The Paulista elite, justifiably concerned about the military government's economic mismanagement but also anxious to avoid disorder, devised an ingenious plan to regain control of the national government. This group understood that it held the balance of power. São Paulo had a well-organized Republican Party with more than adequate financial resources. The Paulistas made it plain to President Peixoto that they would support the federal government but expected scheduled elections to be held even before the revolt ended. The state of São Paulo reorganized police and firemen into battalions armed with modern weapons, including machine guns. Their "state army" of some 3,000, well trained, equipped, and commanded, could tip the situation as they decided. President Peixoto reluctantly agreed to what amounted to polite blackmail. The Paulistas even had a presidential candidate ready to go. Prudente de Morais had served as a republican deputy in the former imperial parliament and as president of the constituent assembly that drafted the Constitution of 1891. During the first presidential election under the new constitution, Prudente had run against the military candidates, much to their annoyance. Nevertheless, his experience and republican credentials could not be questioned. Even after the election of Morais, it remained uncertain whether Peixoto would step down. With the revolt under control, the president had tremendous support in the army. Reportedly, Peixoto contemplated extending his mandate in defiance of the Paulista elite—particularly because of his personal distaste for the president-elect. Nevertheless, Brazil's first civilian republican president assumed office on November 15, 1894, without a major incident, although Peixoto avoided the public formalities of the constitutional transfer of authority. The "Republic of the Sword" ended along with the immediate promise of an open and inclusive republic.

President Prudente de Morais faced several immediate challenges. He had to gently press the military back into its traditional role and out of politics, finish the pacification of Rio Grande do Sul, firmly establish civilian authority over the state, and, perhaps most vexing, unite political factions. Fortunately, a student revolt at the military academy against an unpopular commandant allowed the government to demonstrate its support of military discipline and underscored the dangers of politics in the ranks. The government elaborated a table of organization for the army that specified the number of officers and the levels of command. While ignored in practice, the table of organization at least succeeded in reducing the number of soldiers and placed the government in the position of a semi-indulgent patron of the officer corps.

In Rio Grande do Sul an armistice on July 1, 1895, followed several months later by a general amnesty, ended the revolt. In all respects it had been a useful one for the Paulistas. The third objective, establishing civilian control over politics, proved much trickier and long term. Morais's cautious approach effectively assured but did not guarantee civilian control. Last, the problem of the nature of the republic still remained up for grabs by one faction or another. Peixoto envisioned a middle-class republic rather than an elite one. His now disappointed supporters fully appreciated that Prudente represented the oligarchy. The conservatives had engineered a return to elite control, but they declared victory far too early. Radical republicans (Jacobins) believed that the urban and broader political values of the republic had been betrayed. Vice President Manuel Vitorino, a radical, took advantage of the president's illness to attempt to push the country back to the broader republican path. Only the recovery and return of Prudente foiled the plan.

Revolt from Below: Canudos

Change, reaction, and counterreaction touched all social levels. The oligarchy, determined to regain political control in order to preserve its socioeconomic position, saw threats virtually everywhere. The middle class, entranced with Comtian notions, envisioned rapid progress. The army, an important subset of the middle class and the perceived father of the republic as well as its ever vigilant defender, had a grander vision. All saw the inhabitants of the backlands, the *sertanejos*, as obstacles to achieving their differing visions and as endangering order. They represented objects to be brushed aside or remolded as the country moved toward its radiant future. Their explanation of Brazil and their vision of what it could be, indeed should be, assumed that the rural peasantry had no reasonable explanation of their condition and culture.

Slaves harvesting coffee, c. 1882. *Courtesy of the Latin American Library, Tulane University*

Politically and socially inarticulate, and usually illiterate, backlanders functioned within their own reality, one largely unknown to the more favored groups. Popular culture, and particularly folk religion, provided the parameters of their world and molded their ideas of the future. The rural lower class functioned within its own mental construct without effective verbal and written bridges to the upper and middle elements. In reality, Brazil existed differently in the minds of each class. When peasants engaged in violence, such incidents appeared to the rest of the country to come out of the blue.

Uncomprehending and frightened, the government tended to over-react.

Reactionary revolts and peasant rebellions occurred from the co-lonial era into the empire. Nevertheless, they became more desper-ate as the pace of change exceeded the ability of the lower classes to adjust and thus to survive. The empire coped with peasant violence in 1874–75 in the interior of the northeast. The Quebra-Quilo Revolt (break the kilos), provoked by an attempt to introduce the metric system, swept through the backlands. The suspicion was that the proposal actually had more to do with taxes and land titles. Wide-spread violence frightened the imperial government, as rampaging peasants burned records and archives and assaulted notaries. The refusal to pay taxes and the attacks on revenue collectors eventually forced the government to retreat. State authorities talked about the forces of barbarism when in fact the issue constituted a question of survival.

Changing land laws, the growth of plantation agriculture, the ability of the state to extend its power into the backlands and to ex-pand its taxing authority far beyond coastal urban areas, different values deemed progressive, and diminished respect for religion cre-ated an almost incomprehensible world. The previously isolated, uneducated peasantry saw major props of their all-important imagi-nary world under attack. For generations their existence depended on their own initiative, and they experienced limited and generally unsatisfactory contact with constituted authority. To backlanders, land titles had little significance. They hacked out small plots from virgin land or ran a few cattle and goats on the open range. Their lives revolved around a largely self-fabricated religious system that combined elements of African and Indian beliefs within a loose Catholic framework. *Sertanejos* placed more trust in *beatos* or *beatas* (holy men or women) than in civil authorities. To them, the state at all levels appeared to be yet another predator, imposing taxes, laws, regulations, and on occasion military service, all of which made an already precarious existence even more difficult.

The Canudos incident in a similar manner resulted from state in-trusion into the backlands provoking a desperate response. A series of totally unexpected, even improbable, events turned the Canudos conflict into a government nightmare. Before the episode ended, the foundations of the not yet fully established republican-oligarchic system shook. The peasant reality of Canudos disappeared amid the political paranoia of the republic.

Antônio Conselheiro (Antônio Vicente Mendes Maciel), the cen-tral figure in the drama, took religious refuge from a failed life. A man of many brief careers, he drifted around the interior of Bahia.

His religious passion and disdain for material goods, two highly respected virtues among the impoverished inhabitants of the backlands, attracted a dedicated group of disciples. His New Jerusalem, the interior settlement of Canudos some 200 miles north of Salvador in the state of Bahia, functioned as a spiritual haven protected from external change. Its inhabitants lived by an intense, self-sacrificing order alien to the urban coast. They led a strict moral existence in the expectation of a much better next life. The inhabitants of Canudos rejected state-defined modernity and progress, two of the republic's grand illusions. They viewed the republic as essentially godless. To them the paternalism of the Kingdom of Heaven had no reflection in a republic. The still insecure republic in turn believed that Antônio Conselheiro and his followers constituted a dangerous assortment of fanatical monarchists—a tragic misreading of a backland popular religious movement. Fanatical republicans suspected that it represented a much broader elite plot to restore the monarchy.

The backlands disciples' disdain for temporal authority irritated officials. Even more disturbing, Canudos attracted so many followers that a labor shortage developed. Landholders bitterly complained to the authorities in the state capital and to the federal government in Rio. Eventually, the state government dispatched a small police detachment to demonstrate its authority over Canudos. To their surprise, they encountered hostility and violent resistance, which forced them to withdraw. A prudent governor might have left well enough alone. Unfortunately, another group composed of some 500 men, including federal and state personnel, set out to teach them a lesson only to be sent reeling back to civilization. Yet another expedition of 1,000 men, including cavalry and artillery, fared no better; its commander was killed in the assault. When news of the humiliating defeat reached Rio de Janeiro, radical republicans chose to interpret the affair as a monarchist counterrevolution in the making. Crowds surged through the streets attacking individuals and institutions they believed to be in league with monarchists. A mob dragged the owners of two monarchist newspapers into the streets and brutally murdered them. Other potential victims fled.

The government now had no option but to treat the resistance at Canudos as a serious attack on the republic. The state had to crush Canudos or risk the mob turning on political leaders. The defenders of Canudos, well equipped with captured weapons, now faced an army of 6,000 under the command of General Artur Oscar. To the country's utter astonishment, the army went down to defeat. General Oscar barely escaped with his life after losing almost all of his supplies. The embarrassed general claimed that the defenders of Canudos had received arms and other assistance from European

monarchists. In reality, by this time the defenders had more captured arms than they could use.

An increasingly frantic federal government dispatched fresh
troops under a well-respected veteran of Paraguay, Marshal Machado
Bittencourt. Command had gone from a modest police captain to an
army soldier of the highest rank. Fortunately for the government,
Marshal Bittencourt proved a competent leader. Nevertheless, in spite
of being pounded by field artillery, it took wave after wave of at-
tackers and finally house-to-house fighting to seize the settlement.
Suddenly there was a horrible silence—not one defender remained
alive in the smoking ruins. Antônio Conselheiro had already per-
ished. Prisoners taken earlier had their throats cut, and troops dug
up the decaying corpse of their leader, cutting off his head to display as the centerpiece of a gruesome military parade. The republic
had been saved from a self-manufactured threat. The observations
on the three-year saga by Euclides da Cunha, a former army officer
turned reporter for the newspaper *O Estado do São Paulo*, subsequently resulted in a classic work, *Os Sertões* (1902), translated and
published in English as *Rebellion in the Backlands*. Da Cunha's description of army incompetence led to loud denunciations of the
book, all of which added to its lasting fame.

The whole affair created a lingering crisis of confidence in the
government and the nation. A closure of sorts followed a nearly successful assassination attempt on the president that instead took the
life of Marshal Bittencourt. Both Antônio Conselheiro and the marshal unwillingly became martyrs to republican insecurity—joined
in death as they had been in battle. In fact, a small group of republicans who favored a broader, more socially open structure planned
the assassination. The president used the incident as a pretext to
destroy their influence. He took full advantage of the opportunity
to strengthen the oligarchy's grip on the republic. A state of siege
and the temporary closing of the Clube Militar, a Jacobin strong-
hold, ended the challenge

Regional Oligarchies

As a political consequence of the new republican structure, quasi-
independent state oligarchies emerged. The republic, partly in reaction to the centralism of the empire, embraced federalism almost in
the extreme. The second civilian president, Campos Sales, made it
understood that he would not interfere in the internal politics of the
various states. The need to develop workable monetary and fiscal
policies to bring down inflation led Sales to deal directly with state

governors. The "Politics of the Governors" provided a useful network. In turn the president pledged to address only those issues that had a direct bearing on the federal union. The states conceded that the president represented the country as a whole in matters of foreign relations, defense, external tariff policies, and border issues, and at times when the country had to speak with one voice. They also recognized, with reluctance, that the powerful states of the southeast—São Paulo and Minas Gerais in particular—dominated the federal government. The weaker states accepted the reality but expected that they would be permitted to run matters as they preferred within their own borders. In the north impoverished states fell into unequal alliances and formed an internal political bloc within the larger nation. State flags flew over capitals of what seemed like independent countries.

The largely tacit arrangement represented the federal government's recognition of many Brazils. Congress became an expression of state camarilla politics. Once the pattern had been set, subsequent presidents found it too useful to be tampered with. Congress acted more as an assembly of states than a national legislative body but nevertheless provided an effective arena in which to adjust relationships between the various state oligarchies. For the powerful states of the southeast, the structure also offered an escape from what they viewed as the dangerous primitivism of the backward areas of the country. Canudos demonstrated the destructive potential. Better to allow those who understood the backlands to deal with what to the civilized southeast seemed the lingering barbarism of the seventeenth century.

An example of a skillful accommodation between the oligarchy of the northern state of Ceará and the peasants of the backlands revolved around Padre Cícero Romão Batista. At the same time Canudos rocked the republic, a miracle in the Cariri backlands led to the rise of a powerful political priest in the northeast. In 1889 and again in 1891, the year of Canudos's bloody end, Padre Cícero became legendary after a Communion wafer purportedly turned to blood in the mouth of one of the faithful. The small, impoverished village of Joaseiro became a pilgrimage center and Padre Cícero the focal point of a religious cult. The Church reluctantly tolerated both the priest and the cult, while the priest's followers viewed him as a saint who could protect them and ease their entrance into Heaven. Peasant believers constituted a powerful political constituency and, unlike Antônio Conselheiro, Padre Cícero understood how to use them to negotiate with Ceará's oligarchy in the state capital of Fortaleza. Controlled violence, along with the implied threat of barbarism, made him a powerful force until his death in 1934. The authorities had little choice but to accommodate him. He could be reasonable and understood the needs of other political actors, but an arrangement had to be made. In one incident his followers marched on Fortaleza to bring an end to an inflexible state government. Padre Cícero maintained indirect contact with the federal government in Rio. While he was a primitive leader, politicians could work with him, even if reluctantly.

In the backlands of the northeast, the bandit Lampião (1897–1938) and his companion Maria Bonita established a semiorganized regime (*cangaço*) that combined banditry and a type of political control that spanned the region. Lampião carefully cultivated the press to create useful political capital. Protected by local politicians, and at one point by a state governor, he resisted all force sent against him until he was surprised and killed by the police. He lives on in folklore and myth. Death, the final political arbitrator, served in place of workable politics.

Ironically, the southeast, by ignoring its own backlands areas, failed to develop a suitable political mechanism to deal with the social and political disconnect between "its civilization" and the backlands. When João Maria, the Monk (1912–1915), and his fanatical followers emerged in the Contestado (a disputed strip between the states of Paraná and Santa Catarina), an army of 6,000 had to be dispatched to eliminate the threat. The issue, a railway that crossed the backlands and opened the region to outsiders, again seemed a matter of peasant survival.

The politics of the oligarchic republic encouraged violence and assassination. A horizontal political system across oligarchies left little room for others to influence the state or national government. Without political recourse, frustrations personalized politics and led to attempts to remove a particular individual and create a random opportunity for change. Violence served in the absence of effective politics and as a reaction to the established order as determined by the powerful. Such violence often involved complex motives combining regional politics, honor, vengeance, and access to resources through banditry or force.

Political murders and attempted assassinations were visited upon the higher levels of the old republic. As previously noted, President Prudente de Morais barely escaped death at the hands of a young soldier. Marshal Machado Bittencourt, minister of war, died attempting to disarm the young man. Pinheiro Machado, a powerful politician from Rio Grande do Sul, died of stab wounds suffered as he entered a fashionable hotel.

The assassination of Governor João Pessôa of Paraíba had an unintended national impact. As Getúlio Vargas's vice presidential running mate, in what at the time seemed a futile attempt to break the hold of the Paulistas on the presidency, he died, shot at close range, in a Recife ice cream parlor. The assassin had been victimized by Pessôa's thugs and considered the killing an affair of honor. Revenge came quickly. The governor's henchmen slaughtered the assassin's entire family. Vargas and others painted Pessôa's violent death as a political killing intended to destroy the Liberal Alliance. It mattered little that Pessôa had traveled to Recife, supposedly to talk with Pernambuco's governor but rather, as many knew, to meet his mistress, a singer on her way up from Rio. Nor did anyone consider the likelihood that the late governor's brutality invited revenge.

The capital of Paraíba, hastily renamed João Pessôa, remains a geopolitical monument to an invented reality. When Pessôa's body, covered with the national flag, arrived in Rio for burial, a huge crowd gathered to hear him eulogized as the "corpse of the nation" and "this Christ of patriotism." The crowd responded to overblown rhetoric with an emotion that transcended reason, willing to be assured that this "man died for you." At that moment, Rio and the backlands of the northeast briefly became one.

Gasping for Air

Pressure to modernize had been relentless for over a hundred years beginning with the establishment of the empire. The need to create a secure position in the worldwide economic system dominated by industrial powers, while retaining control in the hands of an agricultural-export elite, made the task difficult. Moreover, it seemed urgent to rationalize the country's borders in order to protect natural resources and carve out a respectable share of influence in South America. In retrospect, the challenge appeared overwhelming, both socially and politically. It included making a transition to free labor, attracting European immigrants, upgrading urban centers to international standards, and attending to the quality of life, including sanitation and disease control, all of which required almost nonstop adjustments. The need for connections with the outside world became more immediate. Telegraph lines tied major regions together, and submarine cables reached Europe and from there other parts of the world. Such pressures resulted in a major war, abolition of slavery, collapse of the empire, economic opportunities and dislocations, and social disruptions. Adjusting to ongoing and seemly accelerating change required a massive collective and individual effort.

Collectively, Brazilians felt a disjunctive gap between what they had become and how they presented themselves to the world. In their existing state they were unsure that they merited the world's respect. Modernizing at least the capital of Rio de Janeiro to present an up-to-date façade became a major objective. At the time, Rio had little to recommend it to foreign visitors. Crowded, dirty, disease-ridden, with few buildings of any architectural distinction, the city appeared to be a backward capital of a backward nation. Rather than oriented toward the sea, with its refreshing breezes and lovely vistas, Rio, like many colonial creations, had been turned protectively in on itself. The shanty settlements (favelas) in the hills overlooking the capital and the *cortiços* (dilapidated buildings used for cheap rentals) that marred older sections of town needed attention. Demolition appeared to be the answer. Mayor Candido Barata Ribeiro in 1893 assembled a team of workers and soldiers to swoop down on the infamous Cabeça de Porco (pig's head), a group of shacks sheltering some 4,000, and destroy the settlement under cover of darkness.

Beginning in 1903, city officials began the process of opening up the old colonial heart of Rio, pushing streets through embarrassingly poor areas and reducing the population density that made sanitation such a problem This time, confident planners expected more permanent results. Public health became the excuse to remove the poor from the city's core and shove them to the outskirts, where they could not be seen and where primitive living conditions caused little embarrassment. Mandatory smallpox vaccinations pressed on a suspicious poor and laboring class set off rioting that almost toppled the government. Unpaved streets, lack of potable water, and poor sanitation became part of the cost of modernization borne by the displaced poor. Long-promised replacement housing failed to materialize.

Officials, along with most of the Western World, turned to Paris as the model of what a modern city should be. The French capital, as redesigned by Baron Georges-Eugène Haussmann with inspired details added by Napoleon III, dazzled the entire world. Physically, Rio would be transformed into the Cidade Maravilhosa (marvelous city). Avenida Central (subsequently, Avenida Rio Branco) became Brazil's Champs-Elysées. Graced by the National Library, Municipal Theater, Museum of Fine Arts, and the imposing Senate building, among other architectural extravaganzas, the ceremonial avenue projected a cosmopolitan look. Italian opera companies presented the latest productions only months after their European debuts, and the Brazilian Academy of Letters provided what passed for intellectual ferment. The government subsidized the publication of books in French and English to change Brazil's image abroad as well as to stimulate foreign trade. These efforts worked almost immediately. In 1906 the Third International Conference of American States met in Rio. Elihu Root made the first trip abroad by any U.S. secretary of state. Two years later, the National Exposition, well attended by foreigners, created a favorable impression. The United States, Britain, France, and the Vatican raised their diplomatic representatives to the rank of ambassador.

Copacabana, a small isolated fishing village until the opening of the Real Grandeza tunnel in 1892. Its subsequent transformation into Copacabana Beach created one of the world's most spectacular landscapes. *Courtesy of the Latin American Library, Tulane University*

To the elite and the progressive middle class, the altered city symbolized what they had become, or would become in the future. The natural beauty of Guanabara Bay, the interesting mountains that touched the sea, and miles of open beaches combined to make Rio into a pleasant place—a temple of civilization worshipped by the forward-looking elements of a modern country. To them, the transformed city crowned the civilization process and, once modernized and cleaned up, would remain that way. Barbarism and primitive violence, features of rural areas and the backlands, were beyond their urban conception. Eventually, they believed the city would conquer and civilize the countryside as its influence radiated out. Rio's inhabitants began to see themselves as distinct, using the term "carioca" to set themselves apart from those who lived on the outskirts of such beauty.[4] Nevertheless, the physical transformation, disappointingly, did not bring about a social one. The poor could not be made to vanish. Moreover, they constituted an important pool of labor and provided services without which the city could not function. The rural population, soon to become the urban poor, limited the ability of urban planners to create ceremonial cities.

COPACABANA BEACH

Copacabana Beach is perhaps the most famous beach in the world. It is synonymous with the city of Rio de Janeiro, remarkable as much for its beauty as for its devoted sun worshippers wearing the barest of fashionable swimwear. It was not always so. Indeed, sunbathing and a dip in the sea held no attraction for the well to do. While the poor might cleanse themselves at the shore or toss offerings to Iemanjá, the goddess of the sea, few entered the water or ventured beyond the surf. Most did not know how to swim, nor did they have much interest in doing so. The beach remained separated from the city until regular and relatively rapid tram service began after the opening of the Real Grandeza tunnel in 1892.

Rio's approach to the sun and surf began to change with the arrival of the renowned French actress Sarah Bernhardt in 1886 to star in *Frou-Frou* and *The Lady of the Camellias* at the São Pedro Theater. She soon shocked society with her daring swimsuit and alarmed the city's inhabitants by entering the water. The actress spent hours in the sun enjoying the breeze and the magnificent vista of Copacabana Beach.

At the time, Brazilians believed a quick dip in the sea had some medical efficacy, but only around dawn before the sun became too strong and only if prescribed by a doctor. The elite cultivated their whiteness to set themselves apart from the darker-skinned lower classes. To actually sit in the sun was considered déclassé and a serious breach of social decorum.

In 1917 the city established strict regulations to govern seaside conduct. Bathing in the sea was allowed only from five to eight in the morning and from five to seven in the evening. As a special concession to those eager for weekend fun, the law permitted an extra hour on Sundays and holidays. Beachgoers had to wear appropriate clothing and conduct themselves properly. Noise and shouting on the beach, or bathing during prohibited hours, brought a stiff fine or five days in jail.

Foreign visitors' appreciation of the ocean and the beauty of the beach slowly but eventually convinced Brazilians to abandon themselves to its pleasures. The transformation of attitudes toward sunbathing appears closely connected with the Copacabana Palace Hotel. In 1923 the now legendary hotelier Octavo Guinle built this truly first-class hotel, which became a favorite destination for distinguished travelers from Europe and the United States. Designed by the French architect Joseph Gire along the lines of the great hotels of France's Côte d'Azur, it assured Copacabana's fame as one of the world's finest beaches.

Factories and urban beauty proved hard to reconcile. Industrialization required infrastructure that only an urban center provided. It needed labor of all sorts and places for these people to live. Industrial development, long associated with a modern nation, brought with it negative and positive social changes. Auguste Comte emphasized the usefulness of industrialization, particularly its ability to create jobs for a technocratic middle class. President Peixoto, steeped in positivism and intent on assuring a broad-based inclusive republicanism, attempted to shift priority from agriculture to industry. The president designed a protective tariff to shield fragile industries and to encourage others.

The return of the oligarchy to power put agriculture back in its traditional place but did not necessarily stop industrialization. Coffee's reliance on railways to open up new areas to cultivation as well as to transport the beans to ports inevitably opened the door to industrial enterprises linked to railways—engine repair facilities, metal working, and the like. Industry developed slowly but relentlessly expanded in concentric circles with railway repair shops at the initial core. Capital, directly or indirectly, came from commercial agriculture. As a result, agricultural interests also had a stake in industry.

Prudent growers invested surplus profits, often in light manufacturing, and then withdrew their money when necessary to transfer operations to a new plantation. Predictable expenses and a profitable cash flow encouraged a useful investment pattern nominally tied to an agricultural cycle. Over time, São Paulo moved far beyond a railway repair center to become the modern industrial heartland. Textiles, beer, food processing (mainly flour milling), and furniture manufacture followed in due time, all linked back to the railway repair facilities. Electrification, capital-intensive and requiring a high degree of technology, attracted foreign firms. Canadian investors underwrote the Light and Power Company, which supplied electricity to consumers in São Paulo and in Rio. Electric power created its own ripple effect that led to other enterprises and yet another cycle of industrial development.

A commercial street in turn-of-the-century Rio de Janeiro. Urbanization and reliance upon animal power for transportation of all types made poor sanitation a growing menace to public health. *Courtesy of the Latin American Library, Tulane University.*

Industrialization had strong links to the immigrant community. Foreign workers, believed to have better technical skills and usually able to read and write at a functional level, accounted for a large percentage of industrial labor. In spite of self-sustaining momentum, industrial workers still made up a small portion of the entire work force. Agriculture and services employed the vast majority of workers. Factories, including those in São Paulo, employed some 136,000 workers in 1907. By 1920 the number of industrial workers had doubled. Though the number was still small, the direction of urban change had been set.

Boom, Bust, and Decline

Coffee underpinned Brazil's economy from the Second Empire to 1889. World demand expanded almost magically in tandem with production. Each coffee harvest sold within months. Inevitably, success enticed others into the coffee industry in Latin America, the Caribbean, and Africa. Eventually, surplus brought with it price competition. At the same time, railways opened up new land for coffee cultivation in the interior. A hollow frontier emerged of abandoned, exhausted, and eroded land. Producers shrugged off the warning signs as the coffee frontier pushed farther west—after all, Brazil still controlled 75 percent of the world market in 1900, amounting to 66 percent of total exports. By 1906 a combination of good weather and new plantings produced a record harvest of twenty-two million sacks—60 percent more than the market could absorb, resulting in a sharp price decline. The three principal coffee states—Rio de Janeiro, São Paulo, and Minas Gerais—agreed to support prices by holding back the surplus. The Taubaté Convention appeared absolutely necessary. The plan involved setting a minimum price, storing surplus production, and taxing each bag exported, payable in gold. The federal government resisted the scheme fearing that coffee price supports would drain the Treasury. São Paulo almost went bankrupt in an attempt to prop up prices. To avert disaster, the Treasury stepped in to guarantee loans to the state in 1907. Subsequently, federal authorities floated a loan of £15 million to finance the manipulation of prices. In 1913 and 1914 two new loans of £7.5 and £4.2 million supported the industry. Fortunately, coffee prosperity returned with a rush in August 1914, as demand surged with the outbreak of World War I. Coffee interests came to view the government as a tool to undergird their economic position, if necessary, as it did again in 1917, 1921, and subsequently in the 1930s. Meanwhile, Brazil's share of the world coffee market continued to decline.

Rubber briefly promised to take up the slack as coffee exports drifted lower. The rubber industry had more in common with mining than with plantation agriculture. It relied upon natural resources, rather than creating resources. In many respects, it provided an unexpected source of profit. The waterproof qualities of latex were well known, but its sticky instability made it more of a novelty item than a commercially useful product. Technology transformed latex into an industrial commodity in great demand. Beginning with impregnating textiles in 1823, vulcanization in 1840 to make the substance stable, then a virtual flood of uses from industrial belts to water proofing and, most important, balloon tires for bicycles, rubber soon became a valuable commodity. The automobile craze created even more demand for natural latex.

While latex can be extracted from a wide variety of plants, trees are the most productive and Brazil contained the largest concentrations of rubber trees in the world. By the first decade of the twentieth century, raw rubber made up one-third of the country's exports. New uses created a boom with seemingly no end in sight. The rubber industry depended on collecting sap from trees scattered throughout the Amazon basin. Highly susceptible to disease, the trees grew in small groves and often at some distance from each other—a common rain forest defense against the spread of disease. Attempts to create rubber tree plantations inevitably failed. A primitive collecting industry with little ability to expand production supported a growing high technology market. Every new demand for raw rubber pushed the price higher. Rubber became the black gold (a reference to raw rubber balls blackened over a fire by collectors) of the Amazon. During the boom, Manaus, in the heart of the Amazon, became a modern city with a $10 million opera house prefabricated in Italy, modern dock facilities, arc street lighting, and many municipal innovations. Direct steamship connections with Europe brought in imported food and wine. Manaus at the time consumed more French wine than New York City. Rubber barons sent their laundry to Portugal, purchased grand pianos (which deteriorated quickly in the high humidity), and in general squandered vast amounts of money. Brothels staffed by alleged European countesses occupied some 60 percent of all the mansions in Manaus. The excesses of the rubber barons rivaled those of gold miners while the laborers who actually gathered the latex in the forest received only a minor share of the wealth. Unfortunately, the boom did not last.

Industrial users of raw rubber understood that steadily rising prices threatened them. Obviously, rubber prices had to be brought under control by increasing production. Disease-resistant trees became the objective. Seeds gathered in the Amazon and nurtured in the greenhouses of Kew Gardens in London eventually matured into a disease-free tree. Finding the right location for plantations proved easy enough, despite a few miscalculations. The far-flung British empire had a number of colonies on the equator that mirrored Amazonian conditions. British Malaya soon had productive rubber plantations using labor imported from South India. Plantation rubber quickly drove down prices and ended the Brazilian monopoly. The boom became a bust.

Rallying the Workers

The power balance between owners and workers inevitably changed based on the needs and complexity of production. The shift from slave labor to hired workers represented a major step. As skills became more important, worker pressure to change the socioeconomic balance became more intense. The adjustment tended to be slow and often met violence resistance. An important step in forcing a change in the employer-employee relationship came in 1891 with the encyclical of Pope Leo XIII, *Rerum Novarum*. Rome moved beyond the notion of Christian charity to insist that workers had a right to respect, fair wages, and reasonable working conditions. *Rerum Novarum* provided a moral basis for worker demands—the very element missing from economic liberalism. While some attempted to dismiss the Church's position as "white communism," it lent social legitimacy to labor organizations and social demands.

Employers steeped in economic liberalism drew a rigid line between property rights and worker rights. They believed that employers and workers should be free to do as they pleased. The employer set the conditions of work and the workers could accept them or find another job. The notion that workers could demand certain conditions and terms of employment made little sense to business owners and managers. Nineteenth-century liberalism rejected compulsory moral obligations—none of which ruled out fair and paternalistic treatment of labor—but employees could not demand such treatment. Workers reacted in a variety of ways, forming mutual self-help and burial societies and otherwise attempting to improve their lot.

Radical political ideas arrived with European immigrants. Italian and Spanish anarchists and socialists proposed different approaches. Immigrant newspapers thundered about inadequate wages and poor working conditions with little effect. Considering the obstacles to organizing workers, it seems quite incredible that some preliminary organization occurred at all. The First Socialist Congress briefly convened in 1892. The second conference, in 1902, formally established the Socialist Party, issued a manifesto, and then promptly disappeared. The manifesto demanded an eight-hour workday, obligatory education, and compulsory labor arbitration. The socialists also supported divorce, equal pay for women, suppression of the army, free electricity, and women's suffrage. The first observance of May Day occurred in Santos in 1895, with only a handful of celebrants.

Anarchism enjoyed greater popularity in São Paulo, while socialists had more success in Rio de Janeiro. The Brazilian Labor Confederation (1908) grew out of a workers' congress held several years earlier in Rio. Its organizers established branches in all the major states and published a newspaper, *The Voice of the Workers*, which reached some 4,000 subscribers.

Calling a strike often resulted in a collapse of the union as fearful workers refused the call or employers fired employees. Congress recognized labor unions in 1907 although it viewed strikes as dangerous to society and the state. Brazil's first major strike, in 1907, testified to the level of labor frustration. Beginning in São Paulo the movement soon spread across several states. The objectives of better wages and reduced work hours had to be conceded, at least in part. Approximately 10,000 agricultural workers struck in 1913, deserting the fields until force broke the strike. In general, employers considered labor disputes a matter for the police to handle.

The connection between unions and immigrant radicalism proved useful to employers who preferred to dismiss all demands as agitation. Many foreign radicals, anarchists, and socialists spent time in South America, often moving between Argentina, Uruguay, and Brazil one step ahead of the police. Oreste Ristori, a classic outside agitator, reputedly could talk a king into becoming an anarchist if he had the opportunity. On being deported from Argentina, as the story goes, he jumped into a small boat and broke both legs; the doctor called to attend Ristori became an anarchist before he had applied the last bandage. Capping a long and fantastic life, Ristori returned to Italy in the 1940s and died fighting the Nazis. Antilabor elements claimed that such dedicated radicalism had no roots in Brazilian culture or society and represented a pernicious foreign import. For their part, many immigrants, disdainful of illiterate, mixed-blood, or black native workers, missed the opportunity to create a broader movement by including them. Nevertheless, union organizing established a foundation for the future under difficult circumstances.

Immigration and Race

Just as Europe provided the model civilization, it also suggested the type of people best able to advance a country's progress. To the elite, whitening of the population seemed essential to progress, and the more rapidly the better. It appeared that Argentina, Chile, and Uruguay might become Europeanized through immigration faster than

Brazil, a situation that threatened Brazil's future prospects in South America. Justification for such fears could be drawn from the influential theories of so-called scientific racism, including the pseudo-scientific writings of Joseph Arthur de Gobineau and Gustave LeBon. Such works classified people into superior and inferior races. LeBon refurbished the centuries-old notion that racial mixture brought out the worst characteristics of both parents. Miscegenation, of course, had created the Brazilian people. The French anthropologist Georges Vacher de La Pouge described Brazil as "an enormous Negro state on its way back to barbarism." Brazilian writers indulged in self-castigation and acceptance of national racial inferiority. In their minds, only European blood could wipe away the stain. At the First Universal Race Congress held in London in 1911, Brazilian anthropologist João Batista de Lacerda predicted that within a century mixed bloods and blacks would disappear.

In order to avoid any slippage in the ongoing genetic process, an 1890 decree prohibited Africans and Asians from entering Brazil without congressional permission. In reality, at that time few Africans and Asians desired to do so. The decree served more as a statement than a functional barrier, and five years after its promulgation the government signed the Treaty of Friendship, Commerce, and Navigation with Japan (1895). Official Japanese immigration began in 1908 when a group of 799 individuals arrived, and it gained a boost when the United States restricted Japanese immigration to Hawaii and the American mainland in 1924. In reaction the Tokyo government offered free passage to Brazil. The experience of Japanese immigrants differed from that of Europeans. Cultural acceptance facilitated integration of Europeans in spite of political radicalism. The Japanese, however, encountered a culture totally alien to their own. As a result they tended to form long-lasting enclaves. Most had been farmers in their homeland and were better educated than earlier immigrants and native workers. Cultivating small plots of land, they soon introduced fresh produce in abundance. Many eventually moved to the cities, particularly São Paulo and Rio, to open small shops and restaurants. In all, some 300,000 Japanese went to Brazil in the twentieth century.

It soon became evident that any racial transformation—were it to ever occur—would take generations. This realization led in the meantime to efforts to strengthen European cultural dominance. It implied tacit acceptance of a brown Brazil—a unique population of Indian, African, and European roots, but within a Europeanized cultural structure. The desire to whiten the population, while incorporating attractive aspects of other racial groups, represented a compromise. The creation of Umbanda in the 1920s, largely by middle-class whites, offers a good example. Attracted by African spiritualism but repelled by its close identification with race, its founders chose to purify and de-Africanize it. While many of its rituals came from then-current Afro-Brazilian practices, Umbanda added a strong Catholic element and drew also upon the writings of Allan Kardec and the spiritual movement known as Kardecismo. Umbanda allegedly sought to restore ancient practices and rituals by cleansing spiritualism of fetishism or African practices such as animal sac-

Street vendors in their finery complete with necklaces of worked silver, rings, and amulets about 1895. Such women, respected and often prosperous, dominated street markets in Bahia well into the twentieth century. *Courtesy of the Latin American Library, Tulane University*

rifice. Believed to have roots in ancient Egypt and India, the name Umbanda allegedly had Sanskrit origins.[5] Umbanda sought to incorporate all races. While clearly assimilationist, yet with a white bias, Umbanda federations linked people across class and color. In the 1920s, late 1930s, and early 1940s, influenced by the modernist movement and by the writings of Gilberto Freyre, particularly his *Casa grande e senzala* (1933), translated into English as the *The Masters and the Slaves*, Umbanda dropped its fabricated roots. The new Umbanda adopted a version of cultural nationalism that recognized yet submerged African influences within a unique culture. As a racial bridge religion, it attracted many away from traditional beliefs and in part supported the myth of racial democracy.

Public Health, Science, and Social Responsibility

Following a typical process, science developed out of medicine and in the context of public health concerns. Epidemic disease understandably engaged the attention of the government. The Medical Society, founded in 1829 by Brazilian and foreign physicians, advised the authorities in times of public health emergencies. When epidemics broke out in the capital the Society dispatched medical students and investigators who treated the sick and recorded the circumstances. Medical journals with readerships in Brazil and Europe published the latest findings and research advances. While few in number, medical doctors enjoyed high status.

The public health movement in the United States and Europe, stimulated by rampant cholera that overcame one country and region after another in the 1830s, contributed to a sharper understanding of how diseases spread. The obvious connection between poor sanitary practices and epidemic illness led to the establishment of boards of public health to regulate sanitation in the streets and impose quarantines as necessary. Nevertheless, urban health conditions deteriorated in the first half of the nineteenth century as methods more appropriate for a dispersed rural population failed in towns and cities. Government concern with the extent of the public health problem led to active interest at the imperial level after 1850. A centralized approach conflicted with the traditional colonial structure then still in place, which assigned responsibility for sanitation to municipal officials. Local, state, and national jurisdictional barriers remain to this day. Before the middle of the century, Brazil did not experience major epidemics in spite of generally deteriorating health conditions. In 1849, however, yellow fever arrived with a vengeance. Cholera epidemics swept the country in 1855–56, and yellow fever returned in 1874 and 1886 and accompanied the collapse of the empire in 1889.

While the theory of disease remained incomplete and sketchy, the connection between unsanitary conditions and the spread of disease was understood. The well to do instructed their servants to carry refuse and excrement some distance away, but the lower class simply used the streets as a garbage dump. The urban poor often occupied unsanitary dwellings. That they often lived in large numbers packed into a small space simply compounded the problem. Garbage piled up uncollected—home for rats and flies. Stagnant pools of foul-smelling water and dirty water poured into the streets by washerwomen attracted mosquitoes, carriers of infectious disease. Horse- and mule-drawn transportation added its inevitable contribution. Wind and rain carried refuse throughout the city.

Poor nourishment, untreated disease, and unsanitary conditions made the *cortiços* (tenements) centers of contagion. An estimated one-third of Rio's population lived in such buildings in the 1870s. The filth they dealt with on a daily basis touched everybody from shop-keepers to the wealthy. It made its way into the most intimate spaces along with the servants who attended the well to do. Domestic servants lived in some of the poorest sections of the city. Even live-in servants, whether slave or free, spent considerable time in the streets buying food and tending to other tasks. With the end of slavery, living out became more common. Washerwomen went from door to door in the course of their day. Widespread hiring of wet nurses who lived under similar conditions may have had a direct impact on infant mortality. Efforts to deal with the public health problem could not touch the root causes. Poverty and all that accompanied it remained beyond the ability of society to remedy and indeed appeared to be a natural situation. As a result, the poor, long associated with ignorance and slavery, had now become objects of contagion in the minds of the more favored classes.

In 1857 the imperial government contracted with a British firm to lay sewage and water pipes in the capital. While an improvement, the system did not serve the entire population. Regulations attempted to set standards but had little immediate success. Municipal authorities prohibited washerwomen from mixing clothing of different clients in the same batch of laundry or from using the communal tubs of the *cortiços*. Officials discussed ways to regulate the conduct and behavior of wet nurses. The president of the Central Board of Hygiene declared that wet nurses and the absence of sewers constituted the empire's two major public health problems.

Unrealistic regulations and behavioral expectations moved a large part of the blame for disease onto the lower classes and emphasized their failure to be sanitary and modern. They served as public health scapegoats in much the same fashion as they had become identified with crime. According to constant complaints, the *cortiços* gave birth to epidemics and nourished them until they ran their course.

The state of São Paulo in the first years of the republic created a public health system supported by modern research laboratories that applied the latest scientific knowledge. From 1897 to 1918 the Sanitary Service of São Paulo, under the direction of Dr. Emilio Ribas, established a reputation for adopting the very latest European procedures. More important, the service moved away from strictly epidemic control to begin to address endemic diseases. Perhaps as an indication of the growing sophistication of the city and state of São Paulo, newspapers played a major role in shaping public health science. The latest scientific advances in Europe and the United States received extensive coverage. Journalists reported pointedly on what needed to be done and used public awareness to pressure political authorities to take action. The authorities increasingly demonstrated a willingness to impose approved procedures on the population in case of epidemics. Meanwhile, in rural areas and small towns, lax sanitary enforcement provided the fuel for epidemics.

The development of bacteriology identified new enemies—microbes and vectors—and suggested that science hovered on the verge of a new era. Between 1880 and 1900 the causes of twenty different diseases had been determined. The revolution in bacteriology is generally considered the dividing line between early public health science and the modern period. Advances in serum therapy and immunization along with the discovery of the vectors for yellow fever (1900) and malaria (1894) made it possible to envision overcoming subtropical and tropical diseases. Significantly, the Sanitary Service of São Paulo was the first group in South America to repeat successfully the Cuban yellow fever experiment. Unfortunately, by that time Brazil was already reputed to be one of the world's most unhealthy places in which to live. Foreigners in particular seemed susceptible to epidemic disease and only with trepidation chose to live in the capital. Medical science held out the promise that the flight of the well to do from the city to salubrious summer resorts, which caused an annual economic slowdown, would take place as a matter of comfort, not fear. Even seemingly small scientific advances had important consequences. Adolfo Lutz, director of São Paulo's Bacteriological Institute, identified in 1894 the so-called Paulista fevers, which the population had long complained about, as typhoid. Once correctly understood, the illness could be dealt with effectively.

The arrival of the plague in Brazil in 1899–1900 made the connection between economic survival and science absolutely clear. The pandemic started in the Far East in 1894. One hundred thousand people died in Hong Kong alone, and the disease killed over a million people in India. Brazil faced a human and economic disaster at a time when the coffee industry had moved to free labor following the end of slavery in 1888. Medical confirmation of the plague in Santos, the main port for coffee exports as well as the port of entry for immigrant workers from Europe, caused near panic. It could not be contained in the port city. Fleas carried in shipments from Santos spread the plague to São Paulo and beyond. Fortunately, advances in understanding the causes led to the development of a vaccine in 1896 and antiplague serums two years later. The theory that the disease was transmitted from rats to fleas to humans, while correct, could not be confirmed until 1914. Nevertheless, the rapid response of public health officials checked the plague relatively easily. What did not happen constituted a victory. To ensure ready supplies of plague and diphtheria vaccines the state of São Paulo created the Butantan Institute. A similar laboratory in Rio produced inexpensive plague serums and vaccines.

A medical doctor recently returned from Paris after studying at the Pasteur Institute accepted the post of chief bacteriologist in 1903 in the federal capital. Dr. Oswaldo Cruz, still in his twenties, eventually became Brazil's best-known medical scientist. He hoped to transform his organization into another Pasteur Institute. His appointment as director of the Federal Department of Public Health allowed him to divert resources to the institute. The immediate assignment, to eliminate yellow fever, smallpox, and the plague, required mosquito control and an aggressive campaign to eliminate Rio's vast rat population in order to break the cycle of transmission. Smallpox appeared to require mandatory vaccination. Dr. Cruz, working in the capital, had a major influence on federal public health policy, although in some respects he followed the lead of Dr. Ribas in São Paulo.

The sanitation effort had the support of the government, but not the people. The still very influential positivists objected to mandatory vaccination saying that the procedure violated freedom of choice. Businessmen opposed the widening of streets and the cleanup campaign because such projects interrupted their daily activities. Others merely wanted to embarrass the government. People of all social levels resented the intrusion of sanitary inspectors into their homes. Substandard dwellings could be condemned on health grounds. The lower classes correctly associated urban redevelopment with the destruction of affordable housing, with public health programs used as the excuse for demolition. Street rioting against mandatory vaccination followed by a short-lived revolt of the cadets of the military academy over compulsory vaccination forced the state to abandon its smallpox plan. Dr. Cruz underestimated the need for political and public relations skills.[6] As if in revenge, Rio in 1908 experienced its worst outbreak of smallpox, in which 9,000 people died.

Brazil, the only Latin American country invited to attend the 12th International Conference of Hygiene in Berlin in 1907, received gold medals for experimental work conducted under the direction of Dr. Cruz, already a national hero over the success of the yellow fever campaign. When he returned from Berlin, admirers almost mobbed him. The government subsequently renamed the institute in his honor. The Oswaldo Cruz Institute in Rio, along with the laboratories in São Paulo, could now attract and train Brazilian investigators secure in the knowledge that the country recognized the importance of scientific research. One of the most brilliant scientists, Carlos Chagas, played a major role in controlling malaria. In 1909, Chagas identified the carrier of what would be called Chagas' disease, a beetle that infested the walls of mud huts and killed or blinded its impoverished victims. Experimentation by that time had advanced beyond random procedures, such as attempting to cure leprosy by subjecting hapless patients to deadly snakebites.

The victory of public health officials over epidemic disease eventually led to a broadening of concerns, first to endemic disease such as trachoma, then to the matter of social assistance, as many people began to understand, if somewhat dimly, the relationship between health and the social structure. A convergence of factors, from positivism's glorification of science in spite of ambivalence about excessive state intervention, to the papal pronouncement (*Rerum Novarum*) of 1891, to the desire to emulate European bureaucracies, provided some political incentive. Public health successes and a better understanding of nutrition and the role of living conditions added another scientific dimension. The still manageable urban population contributed to socio-scientific optimism. Newspapers reported on French school programs that required the study of hygiene. The reorganization of São Paulo's Sanitary Service in 1911 created an Infant Protection Agency. Ending the old administrative limitations of the era of epidemics, the agency's duties included school hygiene. Dr. Ribas later campaigned for better social treatment of lepers including allowing contact with their families. Nevertheless, the social and religious stigmas attached to the ancient disease remained.

In spite of major successes, results lagged behind changing definitions of public health. Rural agricultural interests discouraged programs that appeared to interfere with the production of their work force. Appealing to their self-interest by pointing out that healthy workers free of malaria and other debilitating illnesses produced more seldom proved effective. Landholders were more concerned about maintaining their control over labor than with abstract health issues. Resistance in urban centers revolved around expansion of public health to include areas perceived to be nontraditional or political such as public well-being. São Paulo state deputy Cazemiro da Rocha represented those who envisioned a comprehensive approach. During the debate on the 1917 Sanitary Code he cited Herbert Spencer and his belief that industrial superiority belonged to those countries with the best-nourished workers. Moreover, he declared that "world supremacy" would fall to the people who "best follow the precepts of hygiene." Efforts to reduce infant mortality, which stood at 155 deaths per thousand in 1916, or to inspect the health of wet nurses fared poorly. Nevertheless, constant debate inevitably changed the definition of public health and the state's obligations to people of all classes.

All sides of the debate supported the basic public health mission as a result of events such as the 1918 flu pandemic. São Paulo moved rapidly to increase the number of hospital beds and opened sixty-four pharmacies with controlled low prices while distributing free medicine to the poor. As a result, the city lost 6,361 to the flu, while in Rio some 14,504 people died. Growing out of the era of epidemics, medicine laid the foundation for scientific research in Brazil. It linked politics and health and in a negative sense demonstrated the socially unifying, although grim, impact of disease.

The Army and the People Together

While maneuvered out of power, the army still retained its philosophical and psychological connections with the modernizing middle class. The links to a large extent depended on Comtian positivism and a shared, if still somewhat fuzzy, notion of how the country should develop. The army wanted a concrete bond with the middle class. Officers sought a type of social and political legitimacy based on the merging of aspirations. The new professional military establishment aimed to nurture ties with civilians and to position itself as a respected and necessary part of civil society. The army's initial bumbling efforts after the Paraguayan War, noted earlier, made it look self-serving and even greedy. The Constitution of 1891 included language suggesting that the people and the army acted together as allies in republican progress to dethrone the emperor. Rhetorical statements, while of some value, were not enough. A more promising approach—the French notion of a nation in arms, the citizen as soldier and the soldier as citizen—seized the imagination of the army but could not be sold to the rest of the population.

In a similar fashion, nation-building activities—constructing roads and stringing telegraph wires—burnished the army's image. Such projects made the army popular in local areas impacted by its efforts, but its stature still fell short of what the officer corps wanted. The founding of shooting clubs provided a firmer connection. The first such club, established in Rio Grande do Sul by a pharmacist, set the pattern for others. The clubs attracted middle-class members who shared the military's attachment to target practice. They came together to form the Brazilian Federation of Shooting Clubs, which became the army's first organized reserve. An emotional, even touching, scene took place as the club members, drawn up in formation and dressed in khaki uniforms topped with a bush hat with an impressive plume, received the colors from a proud old veteran of the Paraguayan War. The flag carried down the ranks lightly touched their hats as a military band played the national anthem. Scarcely a dry eye could be observed among the assembled patriots. For all their social and political usefulness, shooting clubs still involved only a small number of people. Nevertheless, they represented an early manifestation of what remains a firm underlying desire of the military—to have a strong bond with the people. The consequences have been both good and bad.

The army found its broader and enduring unifying theme in the notion of active economic development, an idea that fused Comte and development with patriotism to become economic nationalism. The writings of Alberto Tôrres (1865–1917), a man bitterly disillusioned with the republic, provided the rational and philosophical base. His book *O Problema Nacional Brasileiro* (1914) declared that a people could not be truly free unless they controlled their own resources. Tôrres believed that the oligarchy, with its roots in agriculture, had allied itself with foreigners. In Tôrres's view, Brazil existed as a nation without a nationality—a creature of external forces that differed little from a colony. His views aggressively mixed insight, truth, and hostility.

Notes

1. C. G. Jung noted the insidious influence: "surrounded by slaves . . . every Roman became inwardly, and of course unwittingly a slave. . . . Neither the pride of the patrician, nor the thickest walls of the imperial palace availed to keep out the slave infection." *Contributions to Analytical Psychology* (London, 1928), 173–74. In the Brazilian context a French woman in the 1850s noted the drastic personality change that overtook an otherwise genial *fazendeiro* when he returned from the city to the plantation and the slaves. Adele Toussaint-Samson, *A Parisian in Brazil* (Wilmington, DE, 2001), 83–87.
2. Some Portuguese on returning to their native land built mansions with green and gold bricks to acknowledge their success.
3. As used in this work, Afro-Brazilian and black are interchangeable. For more on the actual racial complexity, see Afro-Brazilian in the Glossary.
4. Carioca is the name of a river that once flowed freely through Rio. It is now highly polluted and channeled underground.
5. The similarity with the invented roots of the Masonic movement in the early eighteenth century is striking.
6. President Getúlio Vargas in the 1930s launched an eradication program to control the mosquito vector of yellow fever. Rather than relying on voluntary compliance he authorized the use of force if necessary.

CHAPTER THREE

Republican Complexity

The Republic in Decline

The civilian architects of the old republic failed to understand that modernization and increasing economic and social complexity had created new groups, interests, and objectives that could not be restrained by narrow elite politics. In many respects, the military republic maneuvered out of power represented the wave of the future. The lack of experience by the still small middle class, including army officers, made it easy for the elite to retain power. Oligarchic politics, however, could not control ongoing changes. Nor did the elite realize the extent to which abolition and modern economic demands, including coffee price volatility, had splintered elite interests.

World War I marked a major turning point. The rush to export to war-torn Europe at attractive prices squeezed the domestic market. Overseas demand raised prices at home and caused some acute shortages and lower class hardships as well as general complaints. Nevertheless, a booming wartime export economy increased the middle class and expanded employment opportunities at all levels. Brazil came out of World War I with a handsome trade surplus. A postwar boom, further strengthened by higher prices for exports, enabled industry to double expenditures in capital goods. Rapid industrial growth in the 1920s created jobs for technicians, managers, and workers. Perhaps equally important, the war and the Paris peace conference altered the nation's perception of the modern world. As the only Latin American nation to declare war on the Central Powers, Brazil inserted itself in a minor way into European politics. The elite, middle class, and workers shared the uneasy sensation that somehow everything had changed. The Brazil of 1914, now firmly in the past, had given way to a new era of uncertain prospects.

In Russia the October Revolution of 1917, the collapse of the czarist regime, and the frantic pace of ideological change suddenly made radicalism into an operational system—it could work. The entire left spectrum from anarchism, to socialism, to communism could no longer be ignored as the wild rantings of a few deranged individuals. Liberal capitalism, with its dismissal of workers' rights and presumptive privilege of governing, seemed less secure. The lower classes, once seen as the dangerous classes, had become the masses. A challenge from below in Brazil no longer seemed unthinkable. The founding of the Brazilian Communist Party (PCB) in 1922 supplied some substance to the fear. Many anarchists, anarcho-syndicalists, and socialists accepted communism's leading role in the revolutionary struggle.

Deep divisions within the country caused a sense of unease. The southeast, with coffee and an industrial base, had little in common with the north and northeast. Politics became increasingly dysfunctional and narrow. The southeast still dominated the federal government, manipulating it in its own interests, particularly to prop up coffee prices, but broke the agreement to allow the oligarchies of the weaker states to run matters as they pleased. Their economic and political strength encouraged São Paulo, Minas Gerais, Rio de Janeiro, and Rio Grande do Sul to engage in a type of internal colonialism greatly resented by their unwilling subjects. The political elite of the state of São Paulo at the time numbered less than 300 individuals tied together by kinship and marriage. States created their own armed forces whose combined strength outnumbered the federal army. São Paulo contracted a French military mission from 1906 to 1924 to train its Força Pública, which included a cavalry brigade and airplanes. The Constitution of 1891 allowed states to establish internal tariff barriers, control exports, and contract foreign debts. Already favored states used these tools to advance far beyond the backward states. Unequal modernization created a regional hierarchy based on resources, economic standing, and political influence. Those who lived in the southeast viewed it as the national core and hence the real and effective Brazil. While they sneered at northern states as empty boxcars being pulled along for a free ride and laughed at the rustic provincialism of others from backward regions, they assumed that such elements would support them as they directed the federal government in their interests. They were wrong. Acceptance of the legitimacy of the old republic decayed.

The Advertising Age

Modernization is linked to economic demands and the elaboration of structures to meet them. A large part of modernization revolves around consumption of products deemed to convey a person's status and attachment to items associated with an approved lifestyle.

The broadening of consumption and development go in tandem. At a certain point, products formerly associated with a small elite are in demand by other groups, and the market generally results in satisfying demand through such devices as smuggling or adjusting quality to meet resources. England, the first to experience the full impact of the Industrial Revolution, quickly understood the utility of meeting the demands of all classes. Other Europeans and the rapidly industrializing United States would not be far behind. Early advertising indicated yet another stage of development in creating needs to stimulate consumption and further production.

The establishment of the *Gazeta do Rio de Janeiro* provided a vehicle for advertising, usually of property, including slaves, rather than individual consumer items. Nevertheless, it set the process in motion. Around 1860 the first wall posters appeared in the capital and inexpensive printed pamphlets circulated, often touting amazing medical potions. New manufactured devices from abroad generally required advertising. In 1858, Singer Sewing Machine began to create a Brazilian market. Two newspapers, the *Mequetrefe* and the *Mosquito*, in 1875 printed illustrated ads. In the last decade of the century the *Mercurio* set a new standard with illustrations by noted graphic artists and the use of two colors. Around 1900 the Art Nouveau style enlivened advertisements with a modern French touch and blurred the line between high and popular culture.

By the turn of the century, advertisers became more concerned with establishing brand loyalty than with mere product availability. Antarctica, Brahma, and Paraense, three of the largest industries in 1907, produced beer distinctively labeled and marketed by brand. Hat manufacturers produced 1.5 million hats in 1905, promoted as the crowning touch of elegance for both men and women. Magazines provided another venue for advertisers interested in certain types of consumers. The *Revista da Semana* in 1900 offered guidance on modern conduct, high society gossip, food, and fashions as well as pictures of pretty girls. Historical figures, previously only used as patriotic symbols, now endorsed consumption. *Fon-Fon*, a slick modern magazine, presented the baron of Rio Branco, one of the great men of the empire, who advised readers to buy Manah brand tonic, which also offered an attractive prize. A high point in modern consumption came with the branding of coffee, previously a mundane everyday bulk product. The need to coordinate a growing volume of print advertising led to the founding of advertising agencies. Just prior to World War I the first advertising agency, the Eclética (1914), opened in São Paulo and by the end of the war four more agencies offered professional designs and ad placement. A generation gap separated the new mass consumers from those who clung to the modest prewar pattern. For the younger generation, the flapper in both her positive and negative excesses became the symbol of post–World War I change.

Sometime in the 1920s, the first free-standing billboard, then called the "Reclame Yankee," went up in Rio de Janeiro urging people to buy Bromil cough syrup. In the 1920s foreign companies such as Swiss Nestlé, the American pen manufacturer Parker, and Colgate toothpaste entered the market. Tobacco products underwent a transformation with the opening of a cigarette factory in Rio de Janeiro in 1903. Before then, loose tobacco, cigars, pipes, snuff, and chewing tobacco dominated the market. The cigarette, a cleanly wrapped cylinder that could be smoked in minutes, became associated with a modern lifestyle. Both men and women smoked the "cigarro chic," La Reine. A sheer woman's stocking—the Mousseline Super Extra Fina—was marketed not just to aristocrats but to women in rural towns and villages as well.

American and European automobiles developed a market in the 1920s and 1930s. Ford Motor Company established a Brazilian subsidiary in 1919. At the 1924 Automobile Exhibition held in São Paulo's Palace of Industry (later the city hall), Ford introduced a Model T assembled in Brazil. The following year at a Rio exhibition, the company constructed a working assembly line to the amazement and delight of all. By 1925, Ford had sold 24,000 cars. To demonstrate that the Model T could handle even the suggestion of a road, the company sponsored endurance events. Colonel Candido Mariano da Silva Rondon, head of Brazil's Indian Protective Service (SPI), drove from São Paulo to what is now the state of Rondônia. Using primitive trails widened as necessary, he erected telegraph poles along the way. Earlier, in 1912, Rondon had explored Mato Grosso in a Ford. Always the intrepid explorer, he gained international recognition when he accompanied former American president Teddy Roosevelt in 1913–14 to find the Amazonian headwaters of the Rio Duvida, now the Rio Roosevelt.

General Motors (GM) arrived a little later, in 1925, and by 1928 had sold 50,000 cars. GM introduced widely copied marketing techniques. Sending follow-up letters to showroom visitors created a new sense of respect for middle-class consumers previously absent from Brazilian sales ploys. Undeterred by extremely poor roads and virtually nonexistent interregional highways, GM loaded trains with cars and toured the country by rail. An inspired advertising event occurred in 1938 when the zeppelin *Hindenburg* flew directly from Germany to Rio carrying a four-cylinder Opel manufactured by GM's German subsidiary. A frenzied crowd greeted its arrival. The car remained a popular local attraction for several months.

The American advertising agency, J. Walter Thompson (JWT), pressed by General Motors, one of its major clients, opened an office in São Paulo in 1929 and later another in Rio. Not content to coordinate placement of ads, JWT developed marketing strategies and designed copy. Initially, JWT concentrated on servicing General Motors and related automobile products. McCann Erickson and N. W. Ayers soon followed JWT to Brazil. American advertising methods quickly spread throughout the industry.

In the 1930s, Americans familiar with radio advertising arrived. The most influential, Richard Penn, directed Colgate-Palmolive's campaign. Penn copied methods proven successful in the United States, making adjustments for the Brazilian market. He introduced the now seemingly ubiquitous *novela* (soap opera). In 1914, Penn arranged for a direct translation of the Cuban *novela, In Search of Happiness*, which aired on Rádio Nacional. A proof of purchase scheme offering photos of soap opera stars reportedly caused a widespread toothpaste shortage.

Ad agencies soon attracted some of the brightest young minds in the country. Individuals who might well have made an intellectual contribution chose advertising because of its apparently close connection with psychology. People talked about the science of advertising. It took some time to come down to earth and realize that for all the skill, insight, and imagination involved, it functioned more as an important adjunct of modern business than as a science. Nevertheless, with undeniable social impact, advertising brought new products to the attention of consumers, who associated technology and consumption with progress toward modernity. In the process, consumers altered their perceptions of what constituted a modern life. Advertising suggested that social mobility had a direct connection with one's purchases.

A State of Cultural Rebellion: Modern Art Week

The discontent of the artistic and intellectual community with the pace of change under the republic crystallized around modernism. Modernism as an art form rejected tradition in favor of an authentic representation of reality. It first emerged in Europe, quickly becoming a generation issue immediately after the horror and carnage of World War I. Brazilian writers, playwrights, artists—those considered avant-garde—flocked to Europe to study or applaud modernism. They saw themselves as taking on the past and rejecting the sterile present. Previous critics of the republic, in its social and political manifestations, long neglected and even ignored, suddenly became important to modernists as they gathered in fashionable cafés to discuss their complaints. Much of what they found objectionable antedated the republic. Nevertheless, this was their time and they wanted reinvigorating, sweeping changes. The traditional dismissal of the country's African and Indian roots in favor of the European contribution symbolized the problem—a denial of reality, a rejection of the country's uniqueness.

Literary critic Silvio Romero in the 1880s struggled to deal positively with history and concluded that Afro-Brazilians had played an important civilizing role. Raimundo Nina Rodrigues, an early anthropologist considered a founder of Afro-Brazilian studies, approached the African presence from a negative standpoint but asserted the importance of studying black culture. Others who followed his example rejected his racist theories. A few novelists cast blacks as heroic figures. At the time their notions, while controversial, did not inspire an intellectual movement, but this changed after World War I. A group of disgruntled intellectuals, including Paulo Prado, who later enthusiastically supported Modern Art Week, established the *Revista do Brasil* to examine critically the country's situation.[1]

To many intellectuals such an approach represented the fresh air of reality. Significantly, tying it all together fell to Alberto Tôrres, whose economic nationalism had earlier impressed the young officers. One of the very earliest republicans, a former minister of justice, a former governor of Rio de Janeiro state, and a former member of the Supreme Court, Tôrres wrote with authority. In a series of newspaper columns he criticized the way the republic worked, its lack of ideas, and its willingness to uncritically follow foreign models that did not fit the Brazilian reality. In many ways a conservative reactionary, he believed that Brazil should give up any pretense of being a liberal democracy. Tôrres appeared to support a Comtian director. The modernists selectively focused on his insistence on Brazilian solutions to national problems—in short, uniqueness. He rejected racism as a cynical manipulative tool used to subordinate Brazil to foreigners. Acceptance of racial inferiority made the country vulnerable to self-proclaimed superiors. Tôrres's ideas, no matter how convoluted, fused modernist discontents with those of the military and the middle class.

The arts developed their own modernist heroine in the person of Anita Malfatti. Returning from Europe in 1914, she introduced German expressionism and three years later cubism to an ambivalent audience. Her paintings puzzled buyers, but until a newspaper art critic dismissed her work, they willingly purchased what they believed Europeans found fashionable. After the unrestrained attack on her art many demanded refunds. Anita Malfatti never quite recovered her confidence; nevertheless, she served as a rallying symbol for the outraged café society modernists of São Paulo.

The moment to strike back came in 1922, the centennial of independence. With the moral and financial support of Marinette Prado, who came from a wealthy and influential family, the modernists planned a three-day extravaganza. Dona Marinette suggested that they combine the same cultural mix of art, performance, and music along the lines of Deauville, a fashionable resort on the French coast. Mario de Andrade, an exceptional mulatto artist, and others viewed the occasion as a chance to present, even parade, the new artistic movement in front of its enemies. São Paulo's Municipal Theater, itself a symbol of an earlier modernizing impulse, became the scene of a cultural battle on February 11–15, 1922. Modernist painting, prose, poetry, music, and sculpture went on the attack. Defenders of the status quo rallied to force them back. An outraged man attacked a painting with his cane, others threw ripe vegetables and fruit at the performers, and another inspired detractor leapt up to crow like a rooster and flap his arms—in short, the exhibit was a great success.

The modernist participants spanned the arts and humanities. Author Graça Aranha, a distinguished member of the conservative Brazilian Academy of Letters, opened the program proclaiming intellectuals to be in a state of cultural rebellion. His younger colleagues included Heitor Villa-Lobos, who conducted his own music drawn from folklore and played on indigenous instruments; poet Paulo Menotti del Picchia; author Oswaldo de Andrade; pianist Guiomar Novais; and Plínio Salgado, who subsequently embraced fascism. Virtually all of the participants went on to national and, in the case of Novais and Villa-Lobos, international fame. After the success of Modern Art Week, the excitement swept across the country. Every major city and many minor ones sponsored lectures, poetry readings, and modernist exhibits. Just as Graça Aranha had declared, a revolt was under way against the sterility of the old republic.

Modern Art Week began the process of the psychological draining away of the intellectual and cultural support of the old republic. In a manner too subtle to be countered, the modernists began to erode the existing cultural base. Sarcastic attacks in newspapers merely confirmed the impending victory of modernism. Oswaldo de Andrade typified the process of unbalancing the old cultural order. Two years after the defining event he wrote the *Manifesto de Poesia Pau-Brasil* (Manifesto of Brazilwood Poetry), followed four years later in 1928 by the *Manifesto Antropófago* (Cannibal Manifesto). Both emphasized the Indian roots of national identity. Modernists appropriated indigenous and black images and symbols as their tools in the struggle for a different identity. Nevertheless, they preferred the mythical and exotic to the actual Indian and Afro-Brazilian.

The Evolving Status of Women

In the nineteenth century, values and social attitudes that excluded women from certain activities and professions slowly gave way. In 1827, girls were allowed to attend gender-segregated primary schools. By the latter decades of the century, private secondary schools offered a young woman of modest means but exceptional talent a chance to go into the professions. A growing number of women's Catholic and Protestant secondary schools, including the American School (now the Colegio MacKenzie), mixed domestic instruction with academic subjects. As a result, teaching became an acceptable profession for women. By 1872 women made up one-third of the capital's teachers, soon to become the majority early in the next century. Higher education opened classes to women in 1879. A stiff entrance examination presumed that prospective students had an excellent secondary education—a requirement that many women secondary graduates could not meet. Advanced education remained largely a prerogative of elite women, who did not necessarily have to work for a living. The first Brazilian-trained female medical doctor graduated in 1887. A growing number of women's magazines urged society to make use of female talents, not for economically productive purposes but rather to provide more suitable companions for educated males. It is clear that editors slyly hoped to pry open a cultural back door to allow access to the professions.

In 1882 the notion of a public secondary school system for women was considered, but the idea never advanced beyond discussion. The economic and technical demands of the empire had not reached the point where the need for educated female labor could overcome cultural obstacles. Resistance to educating women, other than those able to afford private schools, the exceptionally gifted, or the lucky ones, condemned most to illiteracy or semi-illiteracy.

During the elaboration of the republican Constitution of 1891, delegates responded to pleas for female suffrage and debated the issue at length before rejecting the notion. Most opposed extending political rights to women based on patriarchal grounds.[2] Nevertheless, a few radicals introduced some new ideas at least on the debating floor. The number of newspaper and magazine articles and public addresses on the subject indicated that the issue would not go away.

An accomplished woman, Bertha Lutz (1894–1976), began the first sustained effort to promote women's suffrage. Her father, Adolfo Lutz, a Swiss-Brazilian public health pioneer, and her English mother, who had worked among lepers in Hawaii, endowed Bertha with an independent spirit. Not surprisingly, given her scientific background, she became a botanist and continued to publish into her old age. Educated in Brazil and in Paris, she graduated from the Sorbonne in 1918. In 1920 she founded a women's rights organization. She redoubled her efforts upon her return from the First Pan American Conference of Women held in 1922 in Baltimore, Maryland. Inspired by the spirited discussion, Bertha Lutz established the Brazilian Federation for the Advancement of Women, which in turn sponsored the Brazilian Female Suffrage Alliance. Wives of prominent politicians made up the leadership group. Bertha Lutz believed that only political rights could guarantee economic and educational advancement. The right to vote and hold public office seemed crucial. Internationally, the women's rights movement appeared to be making rapid progress. Its elite nature provided critics with plenty of satirical material. Novelist Alfonso Henriques de Lima Barreto, dark-skinned and indifferently recognized, with some truth called it the League for the Manumission of White Women. Bertha Lutz drew upon a tradition of persistent, usually polite, pressure.

In the 1920s the image of women underwent what at the time seemed a radical change. In the age of the flapper it became fashionable to flout old conventions. Short skirts, wild dance steps, smoking cigarettes, and drinking in public suggested a cultural revolt of the younger generation. American movies made it all seem modern—could anything be denied such a generation? Among the trendy, advocating women's suffrage became commonplace. The first major break came in 1927 when Rio Grande do Norte extended the vote to women. A small, backward, and politically insignificant state, it represented the initial crumbling of resistance. Five years later the federal electoral code of February 1932 granted working women, excluding illiterates, the vote on the same conditions as men.[3]

The Army and Its Malcontents

The independence centennial in 1922 occasioned an assessment of the country's progress by the officer corps. An amorphous sense of dissatisfaction dwelled on the real and imagined deficiencies of the republic. Its roots are easily identified. The failure of the military to reestablish its political influence during the administration of Marshal Hermes da Fonseca still grated, and the attacks on the marshal during his presidential campaign made it plain that civilian politicians harbored well-founded doubts about the army's integrity.

Hermes da Fonseca's election to the presidency (1910–1914) resulted from the untimely death of the sitting president, Afonso Pena. Subsequently, in 1910, the designated candidate of the Republican Party also died. The unexpected deaths left a political vacuum and made an open race possible. Young army officers suggested that the marshal run for president. The other candidate, Rui Barbosa, toured the country attacking the lack of representative government and elite control and warned of militarism. Given the small electorate, Barbosa's failure could have been predicted. The people he attacked controlled the vote.

The marshal's vision for the country appeared narrow. He emphasized strengthening the military to defend the nation's sovereignty. An incident earlier in 1905, when German sailors from the warship *Panther* went ashore in Santa Catarina to arrest a German immigrant, aroused a good deal of anger. Public concern that the armed forces could not protect the country embarrassed the army. A reorganization of both the army and navy and the purchase of new equipment and ships followed. While the kaiser remained unimpressed, the refurbishing alarmed Argentina and set off a small-scale arms race.

The election of a military man seemed an opportunity to restore the army's image and self-confidence. Moreover, many hoped that he would construct a more inclusive republic. Hermes da Fonseca, however, proved an ineffective leader. Much of his time appeared to be spent dealing with sailors revolting against the harsh treatment inflicted by their officers. He also meddled in state politics, overturning state governments and bullying them with federal troops. The oligarchy resented his failure to follow their rules of the game. When he left office army prestige remained low, which allowed his civilian successors to ignore the military's complaints.

Another source of discontent stemmed from Brazil's paper involvement in World War I. The war to end all wars had been an embarrassment for both the army and the navy. Brazil declared war on the Central Powers but never actively engaged the enemy. At the peace conference few paid serious attention to such a minor player. To make matters worse, President Pessôa (1919–1922) vetoed a military pay increase and broke tradition by putting civilians in charge of the Ministry of War and the Navy. In spite of his lackluster presidency, Hermes da Fonseca, returning from six years in Europe in 1921, became a military rallying point as elected president of the Clube Militar. Fonseca pointedly commented, "political situations change, but the army remains," a remark that resulted in Fonseca's house arrest as well as closure of the military club. A frustrated, disgruntled officer corps, suspicious of politicians and disdainful of the political structure, provided dangerous tinder. Two major violent incidents involving army dissidents rocked the republic in the 1920s.

The first event involved junior officers impatient with the reluctance of the senior ranks to force change. Young lieutenants stationed at the Copacabana Beach fort revolted on July 5, 1922. The pretext, the house arrest of Hermes da Fonseca, masked a much deeper alienation. They found themselves isolated. Senior officers, who supported the government, put down a movement among the cadets at the military academy to join them. While most of the rebellious officers surrendered, eighteen diehards spilled out onto the beach, weapons in hand, to be sacrificed. Fortunately, not all died in the sand, but few escaped unscathed. First Lieutenant Eduardo Gomes, among those wounded, went on to be the first commander of the air force (established in 1942) and an unsuccessful presidential candidate. The incident and its tragic end shocked the army. But for illness, Luís Carlos Prestes, destined to play a major role in the revolt of 1924 and its aftermath, would have been among them.

Young lieutenants again revolted on July 5, 1924, exactly two years and on the same day as the Copacabana revolt, but this time in São Paulo, the emerging industrial heartland. They intended to drain the blood of the old republic rather than spill their own. Captain Luís Carlos Prestes, commanding an engineering unit in Rio Grande do Sul, moved north to join the São Paulo revolt. The rebels bitterly criticized the government and called for broad reforms. After twenty-two days, surrounded by forces loyal to the government, the rebels slipped away and began a three-year trek throughout the backlands under the command of Prestes. Small-scale copycat rebellions broke out on the periphery of the country. Several months later, a mutiny aboard the warship *São Paulo* resulted in seizure of the ship. By now the pattern of revolts seemed almost traditional. What became known as the Prestes Column went north into the state of Maranhão, skirted along the periphery, then moved south. Finally, after 14,000 miles the group disbanded in Bolivia. Prestes's long march became an out-of-sight but powerful antigovernment demonstration, followed eagerly by the press and its urban middle-class readership. Alleged sightings of the Column suggested magical powers—spotted in one place, only to be reported 1,000 miles away, then again in yet another improbable location. The middle class dubbed Prestes the Knight of Hope and savored his challenge to the government.

The young lieutenants, the *tenentes,* formed a quasi-political group with a broad program short on details but with recognized objectives they claimed would resolve the country's major problems. Their list of complaints included economic and financial uncertainty, widespread corruption, high taxes, vote fixing, disrespect for state autonomy, heavy-handed intimidation of the press, lack of social programs, and other government malfeasance. Their plan appeared reactionary and contained only the barest outlines of a positive program. Nevertheless, their vague solutions spoke directly to the middle class. All resented the influence and what they believed to be the greed of the coffee interests, who thought nothing of raiding the national treasury to add to their profits. Propping up coffee prices required expensive borrowing in international capital markets. The foreign debt, not entirely the result of price supports, in 1930 required servicing of $200 million.

The Collapse of the Oligarchic Republic

The worldwide wave of nationalism that followed World War I had its strongest influence on the middle class and its allies in the army. The officer corps viewed the nation as a unified concept, regardless of the level of development or the contribution of individual states to the national economy. They deplored the creation of satraps by the powerful states. Nationalism countered self-interested regionalism and strengthened the idea of unity. The existing political arrangement appeared to be an affront to all they professed. Eight of the republic's civilian presidents came from the state of São Paulo and three from Minas Gerais; Epitácio Pessôa, of Paraíba, assumed the office as the result of a political fluke. The arrangement between the two states, referred to as *café com leite*—coffee (São Paulo) with milk (Minas Gerais)—proved profitable for them. The southeast dominated not only the executive but also the bureaucracy. How to break its hold baffled and frustrated those who viewed the country and themselves as victims.

It took the economic collapse of 1929, followed by the worldwide Great Depression, as well as a political miscalculation to end the situation. President Washington Luís selected another Paulista, Júlio Prestes, as his successor. Ironically, Prestes, a young talented politician, would have made an excellent president. Nevertheless, Minas Gerais resented losing its turn. Many older politicians could not accept being pushed aside for the younger Prestes. The rift between the two most powerful states presented a political opportunity for the others to negotiate a deal. The creation of the Liberal Alliance led by Minas Gerais with Rio Grande do Sul and Paraíba, but dependent on a broad coalition including urban interests and young military officers (the *tenentes*), challenged the Paulistas. The Liberal Alliance nominated Getúlio Vargas, the governor of Rio Grande do Sul as well as a former federal finance minister, for president and João Pessôa of Paraíba for vice president. They called for an amnesty for all participants in the various military revolts, economic development with a focus on industrialization, and reforms of the electoral, educational, and judicial systems. Muted indications of incipient populism could be detected.

Vargas did not expect to win but seized the opportunity to cut a deal. He promised the Paulistas he would not campaign outside of Rio Grande do Sul if they in turn would not support the state's internal opposition to the Liberal Alliance and would seat any Liberal Alliance congressmen elected by Rio Grande do Sul. Candidate Vargas sought to control his own state machine, modestly cut himself in at the federal level, and used what he viewed as a quixotic challenge to the Paulistas to achieve it. Júlio Prestes won, as expected.

To the disaffected group, achieving change at the national level appeared impossible. The arrogance of the victors, who refused to seat some opposition deputies, added to their frustration. Then came the assassination of João Pessôa on July 25, 1930, in Recife. The public viewed the killing as a brutal political act linked to the Paulistas. Vargas and his supporters took full advantage of the public's misperceptions. The Liberal Alliance had its political martyr—the time for action, not politics, had arrived. Juarez Távora, a *tenente*, captured Recife and then Bahia. Rebels from Rio Grande do Sul threatened São Paulo, while forces from Minas Gerais poured into Espírito Santo and Rio de Janeiro. Army units joined in across Brazil. Senior officers in the capital toppled the president and created a military junta. They toyed with the idea of establishing a military government, but Vargas's popularity convinced them to allow him to assume power. The old republic, born of a military coup, ended the same way.

The reluctant campaigner became the people's hero as his journey from Rio Grande do Sul took on triumphal aspects. In fact, the young lieutenants and João Pessôa's timely martyrdom propelled Vargas into the presidency. He had become the leader of the Revolution of 1930, but those responsible for his ascendancy expected to have a powerful voice in how the new regime functioned. Young officers viewed politics as a form of treason against the grandeur of Brazil. Their anger and disappointment with the old republic reflected their belief that the promise of the republican ideal had been betrayed. Thus, they established the October Third Club and later the October Legion. Both groups advocated a cleansing dictatorship —perhaps the Comtian ideal would now be realized. Factionalism undercut their influence, much to the relief of Vargas.

The politics of the republic necessarily would have been adjusted in the 1930s with or without Vargas. Still a coastal and mainly rural nation in the 1930s, but with thirty-five million people living in urban centers on the fringe of a vast underpopulated interior, the country appeared ready for change. The north remained almost in colonial isolation, accessible only by airplane or coastal shipping. Some 76,000 miles of mostly unpaved road served the economy along with 21,000 miles of railway track. Radio had just begun to knit the nation together. The domination of the coffee elite, already undermined by their inability to limit overproduction and their constant appeals for price supports, could not have continued indefinitely. Moreover, the dynamics of the world economy, particularly after the shock of World War I, propelled Brazil toward a more diversified economic structure with multiplying interest groups and required broader political coalitions beyond the ability of an oligarchy to concede. Once again, in a manner similar to the empire, the political system did not, nor could it, make the adjustments necessary to remain viable without relinquishing power.

Taking Charge: Coffee, Industrialization, and Politics

The world economic contraction that followed the crash of 1929 justified emergency measures. The crisis tightly fused politics and economics and made it possible for Vargas to perform the hat trick of pulling industrialization out of coffee's semi-collapse. An immediate and drastic drop in coffee exports, made worse by overproduction and rock-bottom prices, threatened Brazil itself. Foreign debt restructuring in 1931 provided some room to maneuver. Financial markets, bank loans, investment capital—virtually every aspect of the country's economy was directly or indirectly linked to the coffee industry. To abandon growers would set off a chain of falling dominoes, throwing rural workers into poverty, followed inevitably by urban desperation. Coffee and social stability went together. The coffee elite faced hard times, while the working class faced disaster. The new regime had to act quickly. Emergency measures ended the immediate danger, and in 1933 Vargas established the National Coffee Council (CNC) to regulate the industry and provide price supports. Diversification, the long-range solution, depended upon holding the existing economy together at least in the short term. A relieved government found that some agricultural products, such as cotton, still enjoyed a healthy demand.

Reducing coffee dependency, eliminating surpluses, and controlling new plantings could not be easily or quickly achieved. The number of coffee trees, almost 2 billion in 1920, ballooned to 3 billion by 1934, slowly declining to 2.3 billion by 1942. In more of a symbolic gesture than a solution, the government burned coffee and even dumped it at sea. Various barter arrangements with now semi-impoverished trading partners helped, but often what they offered in return was only marginally useful. The country's GDP declined rapidly, by 4 percent in 1930 and by another 5 percent the following year. Meanwhile, coffee, when it could be sold, fell to below 10 cents per pound, less than half the price in 1929, and then to around 7.5 cents before demand and prices increased sharply with the onset of World War II. External buying power, dependent on exports, fell by 50 percent and income levels declined by 25 to 30 percent, all of which caused a 60 percent drop in imports.

The problem, as virtually everyone knew, was that agricultural prices fell more than the cost of manufactured goods. Therefore, the country had to sell double its primary products to keep imports at the precollapse level. The solution, import substitution, appeared obvious. Government policy had long supported industrialization, and indeed the country had a reasonable manufacturing base from which to expand to meet demands for products no longer purchased abroad. Industrial production fell 10 percent at the start of the depression, but by 1932 production surged by 60 percent over 1929 levels. The money used to prop up traditional interests provided some of the capital for industrial expansion, while coffee and other agricultural sectors slowly retrenched. Between 1933 and 1939 annual industrial growth averaged 11.2 percent. The post–World War I consumer, hardened by wartime shortages, ignored the often shoddy goods of protected industries. A new edition (1933) of *O Problema Nacional Brasileiro* suggested the direction of the government.

Strict control over foreign exchange and imports, protective tariffs, and other devices safeguarded the new industries. Nevertheless, manufacturing dependent on imported raw material suffered, which explains the ambivalence of some industrialists. High tariffs on raw materials used in manufacturing encouraged the substitution of Brazilian materials. Quality considerations, in the absence of price competition, could be laid aside. Nevertheless, Vargas could not choke off imports completely. In response to complaints, Vargas eased import restrictions only to cause another economic problem in 1937 when excessive imports coincided with an unexpected drop in coffee prices. That mistake, along with other considerations, played a part in the decision to establish the Estado Novo authoritarian regime in 1937. For all the difficulties and missteps, the depression had a positive influence on the economic mix. Brazil's remarkable economic recovery occurred in 1933, well before the United States and Europe regrouped. The problems of import substitution, not appreciated in the 1930s, would be left to another time and president.

The need to gather ever more capital to industrialize and expand related sectors could only be met by increasing exports. Food products and raw materials offered the best opportunity, but greater variety was required in order to avoid dependency on a handful of commodities. The slow slide into world war posed real danger, but also opportunity. Italy's ambitions in Africa, Japan's in Asia, and Germany's in Europe created demand for what Brazil had to offer. Britain, France, the United States, and other countries in turn would draw in exports. When Japan approached trade officials in 1935, they made it clear that they would be more than willing to discuss their needs. Buyers would not be turned away on matters of abstract moral principle. The objective, as the army chief of staff noted in 1939, would be to forge strong and profitable commercial ties with Europe while avoiding political alliances or compromising relationships. Such pragmatic opportunism, while difficult in practice, complemented the commercial predators who set the tone of the 1930s.

Civil Aviation

Almost in tandem with the development of radio, civil aviation came of age in the 1930s. Earlier initiatives to take to the air included an 1882 scheme to use balloons and a premature attempt to create an airplane service in the Amazon in 1912. A French aircraft maker in Toulouse sent a mission consisting of three biplanes to Brazil in 1924 to study the feasibility of extending its West African service to South America. The primary goal was to establish a link with Argentina, then the richest, most advanced, and most promising country in the southern hemisphere. An experimental flight early the next year from Rio de Janeiro to Buenos Aires required five stops and thirty-six hours. A trip north from Rio to Recife completed the proposed mail route. The biplanes landed on convenient beaches at low tide. It now remained to cross the South Atlantic.

In Germany the Condor Syndikat formed in 1924 with the notion of selling planes in Latin America. Entrance into the Brazilian market unexpectedly resulted from the imagination of a second-generation German-Brazilian. Otto Ernest Meyer, a textile manager for a company with factories scattered around the country, understood the potential of air transport in the absence of an effective road and rail network. Ship travel, while reasonably comfortable, consumed time. Meyer moved to Rio Grande do Sul and began to interest the large German community in the project. In 1926 he traveled to Hamburg to confer with the Condor Syndikat. His proposed company, S.A. Empresa de Viação Aérea Rio Grandense (VARIG), struck a deal with Condor for the flying boat *Atlântico* along with technical support in exchange for a 21 percent share in the company. For the next fifteen years, VARIG operated only within Rio Grande do Sul, finally becoming an international carrier when it added a flight to Montevideo, Uruguay, in August 1942.

A resident French industrialist in 1926 bought out the Compagnie Générale d'Entreprises Aéronautiques (CGEA), renamed it Compagnie Générale Aéropostale (CGA), and began subsidized postal service from its base in Rio north to Natal. A Buenos Aires to Paris service, via Natal, began in 1928. The leg from Natal across the South Atlantic to Dakar depended on a fleet of obsolete destroyers leased from the French government. Eventually, specially constructed vessels cut the time to thirty-six hours. Mail from Argentina arrived in Paris eight to nine days later. A momentous indication of things to come was the seaplane flight of Jean Mermoz between St. Louis, Senegal, and Natal in less than twenty-four hours. Air France would absorb the CGA in a shady political deal in 1933.

Not to be outdone, the Germans Brazilianized the now Syndicato Condor and combined air and sea mail by transferring mail off the coast to fast passenger ships, cutting two days off the French record. Even more promising, the *Graf Zeppelin* touched down in Recife before continuing on to Rio. The dirigible had a virtually unlimited range. By 1932 the *Graf Zeppelin* began regular flights between Germany and Recife, the first air passenger service to cross the Atlantic. Passengers from Germany could be in Rio in 108 hours by airship and connecting airplane.

The founding of the New York, Rio, and Buenos Aires Line (NYRBA) by Ralph O'Neill, a World War I flying ace, provided a connection with the United States in 1929. He had scouted out Brazil the year before as a representative of Boeing Aircraft Company, attempting to sell the F2B fighter to the army.[4] O'Neill's failure to get a U.S. mail contract resulted in a takeover by Pan American, favored by the U.S. postmaster general. NYRBA do Brasil became a Pan American subsidiary, Panair do Brasil.

The Flying Brazilian: High Technology
in the Belle Époque

Alberto Santos-Dumont became the darling of Paris and the pride of Brazil. At a time when Brazilians confronted modernization and wondered whether they could match the genius of Europe, he provided reassurance. The inventor as national hero marked a departure from the days when Brazilians clasped military and political figures to their bosoms. Such was their pride that one of them could advance the frontiers of technology that they hailed him as the Father of Aviation.

An unlikely figure, weighing 110 pounds as an adult and barely five feet tall, Santos-Dumont compensated with elevated shoes and a striped suit and dashingly topped it all with a red scarf and Panama hat. He could not be missed, especially when he dropped from the sky into the streets of Paris.

Born on a coffee plantation in the state of São Paulo in 1873, Santos-Dumont went to France with his father. His perceptive parent advised him to study mechanics—the wave of the future. He needed little urging. Nor did he lack imagination, having devoured the novels of Jules Verne. Ballooning became his passion. Lighter than air technology, in the early stage of development, prompted the Aero Club of France to offer a prize to the first person to fly a dirigible around the Eiffel Tower in half an hour. Santos-Dumont's first attempt failed on the roof of the Trocadero Hotel, but in 1901 he succeeded to the delight of Parisians. The Aero Club, inspired by reports that the Wright brothers briefly had flown a heavier-than-air contraption in 1903, offered a prize to the person who could fly an airplane 200 meters. Santos-Dumont succeeded in 1906. He went on to make refinements in construction techniques, which he shared with everyone interested in aviation.

With World War I looming, he returned to Brazil. By that time he suffered from what is believed to have been multiple sclerosis. When the ship arrived in Rio, his admirers staged an ill-fated reception. A seaplane, the *Santos-Dumont*, crashed as it attempted to swoop low over the steamer's crowded decks.

The use of planes in warfare distressed him greatly. Even in Brazil he could not escape what he considered an appalling use of technology. From a seaside resort close to São Paulo he could see military aircraft engaging the rebels of the 1932 revolt. An ill and disillusioned Santos-Dumont eventually committed suicide. Nevertheless, the Brazilian air force considers him an honored precursor. Perhaps more appropriately, Rio de Janeiro's most popular airport bears his name.

Until the 1930s, airline routes reflected European needs and concerns. Government officials ruefully understood that the primary focus remained Argentina, not Brazil. Nevertheless, the time to introduce links in the interior had arrived. Condor, always the most venturesome, began the interior phase in 1930 with weekly flights from Corumbá to Cuiabá, the capital of Mato Grosso, with a touchdown at the river station of Pôrto Jofre, close to the Bolivian border. Two years later the route extended to Campo Grande (now the capital of Mato Grosso do Sul), with connections via the night train to São Paulo. Typically, Condor established a long route, then filled in the gaps.

In the Amazon basin, Pan American's subsidiary Panair began mail service from Belém, Pará, to the port of Santos in 1930. The following year, passenger service to Rio made it possible to travel from the north to the capital in five days, with restful overnight stops. Eventually, Panair extended the route to Buenos Aires. In 1933 regular service from Belém to Manaus, in the heart of the Amazon basin, opened up a route from one of the most isolated parts of the nation to the capital and beyond.

The army's mail system, the Correio Aéreo Militar (CAM), also played an admirable part in aviation history. Major Eduardo Gomes, head of the air force when it became a separate entity in 1942, played a formative role in many aspects of the network. CAM delivered the mail to small towns and outposts, many now forgotten, and ferried officials, supplies, and news across the interior. The navy operated another much smaller mail network.

A significant step forward came with the establishment of Viação Aéreo São Paulo (VASP) in 1933 by the city and state of São Paulo with money from the Municipal Bank of São Paulo. Public money made for a well-funded and quickly successful enterprise. In 1936 two 17-passenger planes began service between São Paulo and Rio. The less than 2-hour flight made the alternative 15-hour train trip seem nineteenth-century in comparison. The following year, a second daily flight had to be added. VASP began what today is the Ponte Aérea (Air Bridge) between the two cities, with flights in both directions every half-hour.

Another milestone occurred in 1940, with the construction of the Barreiras cut-off. Pan American built an inland airport midway between Belém and Rio in the backlands of Bahia, reducing distance and flight time dramatically. The old, much longer coastal routes favored seaplanes; the new approach ended that era.

Improved and larger aircraft equipped to carry more passengers and cargo steadily reduced costs. While such transport was still expensive, remote areas enjoyed better access in a matter of hours rather than weeks. Moreover, airmail, like the development of radio, helped to end the sense of national isolation that came with seemingly unconquerable distances. Mato Grosso and the Amazon no longer appeared so far away. The army's CAM provided the military with familiarity and at least the illusion of some control over the vast territory they sought to defend.

A Trial Dictatorship

Immediately after assuming control, Vargas consolidated his position, dissolved congress, and exercised federal powers by decree. He removed all state governors, except in Minas Gerais, and appointed federal interventors (acting governors). This action amounted to a direct attack on state oligarchies—a move heartily supported by the military. Vargas already had prudently forced out officers who had failed to support the Revolution of 1930. All guarantees under the Constitution of 1891 were suspended. The old republic had been toppled, but its parts remained, and certainly the displaced oligarchy hoped and planned to put it all together again. Vargas engaged in a flurry of activity, issuing decrees and regulations that created the image of a government not only in control of the crisis but also marching toward the future. As for elections, the president set up a series of commissions to suggest electoral codes and other reforms. Vargas called the process "reconstitutionalizing Brazil." Talk about the nature and drawbacks of the Constitution of 1891 made it obvious that the new document would place more authority in the executive. Vargas appeared to be tightening his grip with a firmness that alarmed the elite, particularly of São Paulo. Vargas appointed a non-Paulista as the interventor of the state, an indication he intended to keep a tight rein, although his choice proved inept.

The Paulista political elite conspired with their counterparts in Minas Gerais and Rio Grande do Sul to confront the regime. Believing they had a deal, they launched their challenge, led by former army officers whom Vargas had forced out. To their unwelcome surprise, no other state joined them—they stood alone against the federal army. The Revolution of July 9, 1932, as they preferred to call their reactionary revolt, fizzled out, but not without some high drama. Fearful that Vargas might bomb the city, the Paulista elite feverishly rallied their resources. Wealthy matrons donated gold jewelry; local machine shops constructed homemade tanks; and volunteers reinforced defenses, dug trenches, and stockpiled supplies. When the enemy arrived at the gates, they declined to engage the defenders; instead, troops encircled the city. São Paulo under siege crumpled without much of a struggle—the political theater and bellicose posturing in the end made the Paulistas look slightly ridiculous. Subsequently, when the city dedicated a boulevard in honor of the Revolution of July 9, President Vargas attended, calm, relaxed, smiling, and shaking hands, further humiliating the Paulistas. The president even authorized the federal treasury to assume 50 percent of the rebels' debt. In grateful recognition of the army's support, he increased its budget by 15 percent. The three-month rebellion discredited the Paulistas and made Vargas appear stronger than ever. The elite realized that they faced a skillful politician who instinctively knew how to turn the situation to his advantage. Not a verbal man, Vargas left everyone to guess his plans and political objectives.

The Revolution of 1930 had widespread, but not unified, support. A confusing conglomeration of groups welcomed the end of the agricultural elite's domination, but each had its own agenda and vision. The absence of well-organized political parties made it impossible to realign expectations to create a predictable political direction. Vargas indeed may have preferred an ad hoc governing style unbounded by restrictions on his freedom of action. Consequently, the president continually surprised everyone as he reacted pragmatically to immediate events. Nevertheless, it is clear he also planned ahead.

Afro-Brazilians, a large percentage of the lower class, believed that a new era had dawned. While they yearned for the monarchy during the old republic, now they enthusiastically endorsed the new regime, supposedly cleansed of the lingering notions of unreconstructed planters and resentment over the end of slavery. Within a month, Vargas created a Ministry of Labor and promised reforms to directly benefit workers. A year later the Law of Nationalization of Labor required industry and commercial establishments to have a work force made up of at least two-thirds native-born employees. Protection from immigrant competition appealed to blacks, in particular, who felt they had been pushed aside by foreign labor. The new government also reduced the number of immigrants allowed entry and made negative comments about foreign influence in the country.[5] The Legion of Black Men and other civic organizations rallied political support for Vargas. This may not have been necessary. Afro-Brazilians overwhelming backed Vargas and continued to do so until the end. The first national black rights group, the Frente Negra Brasileira (FNB), organized in 1931, was the most important. Within the FNB, a woman's section promoted the rights of women of color. The FNB succeeded beyond expectations. It became clear that the pent-up frustrations of the old republic had burst through with the Revolution of 1930.

The organization and several others like it became important in São Paulo, Minas Gerais, Espírito Santo, Bahia, and Rio Grande do Sul. The FNB offered literacy courses and vocational training. A credit union encouraged members to buy lots and build their own homes. Medical, dental, and legal assistance rounded out an impressive list of self-help activities. The group understood the importance of political organization and carried out voter registration campaigns with mixed success. The FNB became a legal political party in 1936, just in time to be abolished when Vargas eliminated all political parties.

While it never became a political force, the FNB did succeed as a pressure group. The organization's agitation ended the exclusion of blacks from places of public amusement, such as roller skating rinks. A high-profile success came when Vargas, in response to the group's complaint that blacks had been excluded from the civil guard in São Paulo (the state militia), immediately ordered the guard to recruit two hundred Afro-Brazilians. Part of the explanation for its political failure lies with the FNB's difficulty in recruiting middle-class blacks and black professionals willing to run for public office. Many of them preferred to identify by class, not race. Moreover, the organization became increasingly authoritarian and pro-fascist. After 1933, the leadership repeatedly praised Adolf Hitler for rescuing Germany from liberal democracy and alleged Jewish cosmopolitanism. Italy's dictator, Benito Mussolini, also had ardent admirers within the organization. Internally, the FNB's operations depended upon a self-perpetuating cadre that held all leadership posts. A strong-arm group modeled along fascist lines enforced discipline. The FNB, perhaps carried away by success, missed the opportunity to be a unifying force. Unable to influence the closed leadership, disenchanted groups formed small splinter organizations that acted to sap its strength. Its authoritarian reputation deterred its revival after the removal of Vargas in 1945.

A new electoral code in 1932 lowered the voting age from twenty-one to eighteen and extended the vote to working women. Literacy remained a requirement for voting, excluding the majority of the populace. Nevertheless, the changes broadened the electorate substantially. The Constituent Assembly elected under these rules drew up the Constitution of 1934. Not surprisingly, it contained measures distasteful to the oligarchy. It gave more power to the executive and included sections on labor, family, and culture pointing toward a new social responsibility to be exercised by the federal government. Fifty delegates representing corporate interests—labor, industry, the professions, and the civil service—joined 250 traditional deputies in the assembly. In spite of its new provisions, the constitution remained a tentative, even timid document. It did represent, however, the president's slowly evolving thinking about how Brazil should be governed. To the surprise of many, the new constitution restricted the president to a four-year term without immediate succession. Vargas, elected by the Constituent Assembly, now became constitutional president.

The left, disdainful of bourgeois politicians, failed to fully appreciate Vargas's political ability. Similarly, the extreme right underestimated him as well. Both eventually learned, but too late. The Brazilian Communist Party (PCB) functioned at the direction of the Comintern, an arm of the Soviet state, although the extent of Soviet control remained hidden from the public. The PCB's strengths and activities were centered in the cities—Rio, São Paulo, Pôrto Alegre (the capital of Rio Grande do Sul), and Recife in the north. Because Brazil remained largely rural until 1975, the PCB scarcely had any organized presence outside urban areas. The party counted on urban workers to be the vanguard of a socialist revolution. On the right, a fascist party emerged in the early 1930s. The Integralist Party (Ação Integralista Brasileira) copied, but far from completely, European fascism. Nationalistic, with an attachment to order, hierarchy, obedience and religion, the party's motto encapsulated its philosophy, "God, Country, Family." Party members adopted the usual fascist symbols, wore green shirts, carried banners, and used the traditional fascist salute, with a mystical twist. With the right arm extended, they uttered, "Anane." A Brazilian Indian word, its exact meaning is unclear, although it appeared to imply family or tribal unity. In common with fascism elsewhere, the Integralists forthrightly named those whom they considered enemies of the nation—democrats, communists, Masons, and Jews. In reality, all their alleged enemies combined constituted a very small minority in the Brazil of the 1930s.

The Green Shirts attracted individuals who believed that the Great Depression had ended the era of liberal capitalism. The fascism of Italy and Germany seemed to be its replacement. Their notion of a Christian nation based on God and family appealed to many clerics, including the hierarchy. A small number of military officers supported the group, but it drew mainly from middle-class civilians. Plínio Salgado, the dreamy intellectual who had played a role in São Paulo's Modern Art Week a decade earlier, emerged as the unlikely leader of the Integralists. He received some limited financial support from Italy. Berlin, however, preferred to build up Nazi support among German immigrants. The contacts, sympathies, and values the Integralists had in common with European fascism worried the liberal democracies of Europe and the United States. President Vargas appeared to share many of their values, as did some of his supporters. Missing from the Brazilian variety were two elements central to European fascism—overt racism and aggressive expansionism. Nevertheless, the similarities seemed close enough to be deeply troubling.

The two extremes provided Vargas with the political equivalent of the Great Depression. The Integralists and the Communists appeared to find street fighting useful. Violent clashes, marches, demonstrations, counterdemonstrations, and highly exaggerated rhetoric characterized the style of both groups. Each believed it was fighting for the soul of the nation and represented the future, as events in Europe appeared to demonstrate. Brazil and Vargas, in the view of both the left and the right, could be pushed into crisis. The level of violence produced anxiety out of proportion to the actual threat. The police kept both the Integralists and the Communist Party under close surveillance while Vargas awaited his opportunity. It could come from the left or the right—it mattered little.

The pretext for Vargas to take action came from the Communists. The Comintern instructed Luís Carlos Prestes during his Moscow residence (1931–1935) in the art of a coup. He now intended to apply that lesson, slipping into the country with a false passport along with his wife, Olga. From a secret hideout, Prestes assumed control of the Communist-front organization, the Aliança Nacional Libertadora (ANL), and issued a manifesto in preparation for his planned coup. As president of the ANL, Prestes called for land reform, nationalization of public utilities, and the creation of a revolutionary regime. Political action ended when the government used the National Security Law of 1935 to outlaw the ANL.

The next step for Prestes, the November Uprising, failed miserably. Seizure of military bases in Natal and Recife in the north and in Rio, the capital, failed to trigger a general revolt. Loyal army commanders crushed all three attempts with minimal difficulty. Vargas moved into action to counter the "Bolshevik threat." The geographically dispersed revolt made it easy to circulate wild rumors. Congress declared a state of siege, suspended civil rights, and augmented police powers. Meanwhile, rumors of cold-blooded killings of loyal army officers in their beds by the Communists outraged the nation. It still is unclear how much fantasy had been mixed with the facts. Predictably, Vargas's propaganda machine pulled out all the stops to create a continuing crisis. Suspension of the Constitution of 1934, the arrest of ANL supporters, and the capture of Prestes ended the threat.

For Vargas the moment of truth had to be faced before the scheduled election of 1938 and the end of his presidential term. The Paulista elite planned to coordinate anti-Vargas interests to oppose the government's candidate. Because the president could not run for reelection, they appeared to have a winning strategy. Vargas, however, moved up the moment of truth to November 10, 1937. Confident of army support, he ordered troops to seize the congressional building and turn away stunned congressmen. On radio, a relatively new political tool that he learned to use effectively despite being a poor speaker, Vargas announced the formation of the Estado Novo (New State) and a new constitution. Radio suited him well. It concealed his lack of charisma. Had television been available, it might have been fatal.[6] He promised to hold a plebiscite at a later date. Vargas then decided that a vote would not be necessary.

Vargas had taken the name Estado Novo from the dictator of Portugal, Antônio Oliveira Salazar. In many respects, Salazar served as a model, although Vargas borrowed freely and added his own distinct touches. The similarities between the two men are striking. Salazar lived modestly, talked when necessary, and preferred to indirectly intimidate, but would use force when required and relied upon the police to maintain a disciplined sober society. Both Salazar and Vargas led seemingly unexciting lives except for the time they spent carefully laying their plans and springing their traps. Both men rose to power in spite of a total absence of charisma.

The announced constitution included a state of emergency, which, while in effect, suspended the constitution—a slight of hand that left constitutional law experts gasping in disbelief and others in admiration. In fact, the constitution had some symbolic utility, although Vargas intended to govern as he thought best. He employed nationalism as his basic political tool to cut across class, interest groups, and region. Plínio Salgado expected that the Integralists would play a role in the Estado Novo, perhaps even controlling several ministries. Before his auto-coup, Vargas had implied as much. Now, however, he imposed a ban on Green Shirt demonstrations and made it obvious that he intended to squeeze them out of politics, as he had done with the Paulista elite and the Communists. Facing their imminent demise as an organization, a group of Green Shirts mounted a night attack on the presidential palace in March 1938. Vargas and his daughter Alzira returned fire from the windows. The shoot-out at Catete Palace had all the elements of a Wild West movie. Nevertheless, it allowed Vargas to round up allegedly dangerous Green Shirts. Salgado fled into exile in Lisbon—leaving the regime without an organized opposition either on the left or the right.

Remolding Education

Ardent supporters of the Revolution of 1930 espoused middle-class values, including the importance of education. Virtue and merit, rather than family and wealth, could best be encouraged through reform of the entire educational system and expansion of higher education. Suddenly it seemed that progress had outstripped the ability of the educational structure to meet, even minimally, the needs of the country.

The most prestigious secondary school, the imperial Colegio Pedro II, founded in 1839, graduated bureaucrats. Private secondary schools ranged from the reasonably well regarded, such as the Colegio do Dr. Kopke and the Colegio Briggs, to the half-day Externato. A formal secondary education allowed students to enter the law, medicine, and engineering schools established in the earlier part of the century. Public primary and secondary education did not, nor could it, flourish in a society that had few extra resources to free children from the immediate need to help the family survive, or in the face of social attitudes. Research, almost nonexistent, with the notable exception of public health, medicine, and mining, lagged behind the country's needs. The Ouro Prêto School of Mines (1876), which conducted highly specialized research of acknowledged excellence, had an international reputation. From the empire through the old republic, a weak educational system retarded technological and scientific innovation.

In the 1920s educational innovators influenced by European and American ideas suggested reforms at the state level. Establishment of the Brazilian Education Association (ABE) gave them a platform to press for a new type of school able to address the needs of development. Called New Schoolers (*escolanovistas*), they issued the Manifesto of the Pioneers of National Education in 1932. Many of the reforms eventually would be adopted and much of the program remains to this day. They advocated decentralization to allow schools to deal with local needs as well as professional autonomy. The first eight grades would have a common curriculum, while the secondary level could diversify as needed to meet individual and national priorities. Government at all three levels (federal, state, and municipal) would spend a fixed percentage of revenues on public education.

With the Revolution of 1930, the ideas of the *escolanovistas* received some consideration. Vargas and others understood that education constituted a social and economic bottleneck. In 1930 some 75 percent of Brazil's population of thirty-five million was illiterate. Creation of the Ministry of Health and Education acknowledged the need for federal attention to the education issue. Francisco Campos, Brazil's first minister of education, emphasized teacher training, school construction, and curriculum reform. Some 40,000 new primary schools opened, and secondary school enrollment jumped to 227,000. While reformers envisioned top to bottom restructuring, the federal government sought immediate results in the most cost-effective manner. Thus, they focused on higher education in the belief that reform would more quickly contribute to development. Reorganization of higher education began earlier with the placing of professional schools under the newly created University of Rio de Janeiro in 1920. The same process resulted in the founding of the University of São Paulo in 1934. The very first article of its charter emphasized scientific research. Article Four instructed the institution to use all resources, including radio and film, to spread knowledge. In 1938 the University of Brazil opened in the then capital of Rio de Janeiro. In keeping with the importance placed on ideas of national identity, each university established chairs of Brazilian history. Vargas hoped to harness education to serve his own political needs as well as those of the nation. A pattern of inverse development, with expansion of higher education outpacing growth at the secondary and primary levels, became evident and would remain a feature of the educational system well into the 1990s.

Vargas Inventing Vargas

Vargas quickly grasped the political potential of radio. By the mid-1930s, radio had passed from a novelty to a commonplace amusement and a source of information that knew no class boundaries and reached everyone. It broke through the isolation imposed by space, social distance, and illiteracy. Linking the radio audience together (as well as the classes and regions) depended on nationalism, which in turn could be manufactured by Vargas's propaganda machine and relayed in many forms by newspapers and radio stations throughout the nation.

Molding culture and the population became a natural, almost unconscious, process that touched the arts, music, and social attitudes. Nevertheless, some bureaucrats suggested a more systematic and organized approach. Simões Lopes, part of Vargas's leadership group, visited Berlin to study the Nazi Ministry of Information and Propaganda. He returned thoroughly impressed and suggested to Vargas that a modified version could serve Brazil's moral and material progress. Several weeks later, on October 7, 1934, the president established the Departamento de Propaganda e Defensão Cultural. The new department controlled the press, radio, cinema, and culture. Troublesome foreign journalists could be discouraged and, if necessary, expelled by decree. A propaganda and technical high point came with the radio broadcast of Vargas's wife and son, Getulinho, from the General Electric plant in Schenectady, New York, during their goodwill visit to the United States in 1936. A reorganization of the president's propaganda machine resulted in the creation of the theoretically all-powerful Departamento de Imprensa e Propaganda (DIP) in December 1939. The DIP reported only to Vargas and functioned separately, without ministerial control.

Inadequate funding made enforcement of DIP directives difficult. While most understood what the censors had in mind, they could be selective in implementing their orders without much risk. Flouting DIP directives, however, provided a pretext for harsh measures if the regime needed one. Bureaucratic infighting also acted to blunt the DIP's effectiveness. Police officials, previously charged with censorship, resented the attempt to delegate these responsibilities to the DIP's director, Lourival Fontes. They mounted personal attacks on him, questioned his loyalty, competence, and ties with foreign agents, and, in what they must have viewed as a damning indictment, reported that he walked down the street with his fly unbuttoned. As with many stories connected with Vargas, a powerful illusion effectively concealed a far different reality. The DIP was not an exception.

While Vargas may have admired Nazi propaganda methods, he preferred the approach of Rio's populist mayor Pedro Ernesto, who mobilized support by subsidizing samba and Carnival clubs and employed ward heelers and minor patronage to manipulate and direct his lower-class supporters. Vargas officially recognized these largely Afro-Brazilian groups, which had the effect of excluding spontaneous groups from entering satirical floats in Carnival parades. He also organized a float competition judged on criteria set by the state. In their pursuit of a government prize, samba groups modified their behavior and constructed "acceptable" floats. The first such competition attracted nineteen samba groups. The rules required the clubs to adapt historical themes or depict national figures. In 1939 judges disqualified a group that chose Snow White and the Seven Dwarfs. By including blacks in history, as presented by approved floats, the regime implied the equality of all regardless of class or color. Emotional inclusion seemed an acceptable replacement for politics.

The Estado Novo ended women's political participation. Ironically, Vargas extended suffrage to women in 1932. Women fared better than expected, particularly at the state level. On the verge of a political breakthrough, the Estado Novo stopped them dead. A devastated Bertha Lutz wrote the American feminist leader Carrie Chapman Catt in 1940 that all their hard-earned gains had been lost.

Vargas's radio broadcasts to the remote corners of Brazil and the "Hora do Brasil" (Brazilian Hour) stimulated a useful sense of nationalism. Radio loudspeakers placed in central locations by the government made sure people got the message. Propaganda stressed that all had something to offer their country, whether poor or rich, without reference to race. For the first time, the lower classes received instruction in civic virtues and national and international politics. Albeit distorted by the DIP, such propaganda formed a base for future political participation.

The Estado Novo rested on three main pillars—the army, bureaucrats, and urban workers—while propaganda smoothed over any contradictions. Vargas saw to it that all had a vested interest in the regime. Social welfare programs and government unions gave Vargas a core base reinforced by the imaginary radio community. Propaganda created an amorphous mass constituency, while the unions served to demonstrate actual social progress for the working class. The DIP depicted Vargas as the father of the people (O Pai do Povo) indulging his charges, the head of the family who knew what was best for its members. Brazil's patriarchal tradition made this portrayal acceptable. His wife, Darcy, became the nation's mother and a symbol of the wholesome family. In fact, the couple led separate lives, coming together when necessary for certain functions more as a political team than as husband and wife. The army, beyond a substantial budget to keep them happy, endorsed nationalism as the unifying theme for a modern Brazil. Vargas's desire to create a larger international role for Brazil as well as to monitor the dangers of a world where the strong—imperial Japan, fascist Germany and Italy—preyed upon the weak, seemed prudent.

Restructuring the administration began immediately, in December 1930, and, understandably, with the Ministry of Agriculture, Industry, and Commerce, which was transformed into Labor, Industry, and Commerce. Other changes followed in short order, including the reorganization of the Finance Ministry in 1934. Government bureaucrats took on an increasingly important role. At the end of 1936, Vargas established a central personnel agency, job classifications, and pay scales. Entrance into the civil service henceforth would be by competitive examination. A senior-level bureaucrat could be appointed directly by the president. In the Estado Novo the states functioned more as administrative departments. An interventor, who served as an agent of federal executive power, governed each state. State Departments of Public Service (DASP) reported to the national DASP. The same structure applied to the various ministries of justice. At the local level, mayors exercised powers equivalent to those of the state interventor. In theory, the structure extended the president's authority across the nation. While the structure did not function exactly as intended, it provided unprecedented authority over virtually every aspect of administration. Vargas's three pillars seemed to stand on an unshakable foundation.

To deal with those who could not be convinced by nationalism or co-opted in some fashion, the regime relied upon the police, detention camps, and strong-arm techniques. The notorious chief of Rio's police force, Filinto Muller, used the National Security Law of 1935 to its fullest extent to justify his sadistic treatment of political prisoners. Muller had a secret working agreement with the Gestapo and exchanged information with a number of foreign intelligence agencies. Such contacts led to the extradition to Germany of Luís Carlos Prestes's German-born Jewish wife, Olga, then seven months pregnant, who subsequently died in a gas chamber.[7] Little could happen in any city without the police being aware of it. Nevertheless, the police served only as an auxiliary to be used when all else failed—generally it did not. The dictatorship had sufficient popular support to make harsh measures unnecessary. When selective action appeared necessary, people like Muller took the initiative.[8]

Of the three pillars supporting the regime, the army was the most important. Without the army, the dictatorship would not have been possible. The president's objectives generally matched those of the officer corps. He articulated what military leaders could not. President Vargas understood that the army distrusted ideology, other than the lingering strands of positivism so deeply embedded in military thought. They desired national unity, a respected international role, industrialization to make the country more independent of foreign interests, and, above all, a spiritual fusion of the army with the people. This objective, deeply rooted in the previous century, appeared to have reached its pinnacle. Nationalism, coupled with radio, finally achieved the army's public relations objectives. Vargas, the DIP, and the Ministry of Education created the environment the army felt appropriate. Bringing all citizens together in a cooperative effort to achieve the country's inevitable greatness appealed to the army.

In the short run, the Vargas regime had a negative impact on politics. A long-term assessment must be more ambivalent. Clearly, Vargas believed that a patriarchal-authoritarian regime, not necessarily a harsh one, reflected tradition. Thus, his governing techniques represented a return to the country's historic political style. He did not see himself as cultivating the growth of liberal democracy. The concealed damage of his approach to politics escaped Vargas as much as it did most of his victims.

Notes

1. Paulo Prado wrote *Paulística: Historia de São Paulo* (1925) and *Retrato do Brasil: Ensaio sôbre a tristeza brasileira* (1928) in search of a Brazil he believed had been deformed by colonization and European and American influences. Ironically, historian Capistrano de Abreu, reading Prado's work in draft, advised him to drop some foreign words and phrases with the comment that in Brazil people often liked to "eat French and belch German." Quote in Darrell Levi, *The Prados of São Paulo, Brazil: An Elite Family and Social Change* (Athens, GA, 1987), 134.
2. Patriarchal notions assumed that wives, dependent servants, and retainers could not be independent voters quite apart from the issue of literacy or age restrictions. The subject of independent judgment progressively became moot as more women entered the work force, access to education expanded, and eventually the secret ballot was instituted.
3. To place Brazil in context, it became the fourth country in the Americas to do so after Canada, the United States, and Ecuador.
4. The company's continuing interest in the Brazilian market is evidenced by a partnership (2001) with VARIG, possibly including buying 20 percent of the stock.
5. The Constitution of 1934 established a quota. Previously, port authorities classified a foreigner who arrived in the country on a third-class steamship ticket as an immigrant. New regulations required a permanent residence visa.
6. An experienced deputy from São Paulo, realizing that the young Vargas, then a federal deputy, needed a prop in the absence of charisma, advised that "a leader such as you must smoke a cigar—start right now." Chermont de Britto, *Vida luminosa de Dona Darcy Vargas* (Rio de Janeiro, 1984), 55.
7. Prestes himself lived to be 92. He died in Rio in 1990.
8. Filinto Muller later became president of the federal senate during the military regime, a post he held until he died in a plane crash.

CHAPTER FOUR

The Vargas Regime and Its Legacy

Brazil Confronts the World of the 1930s

The 1930s underscored the importance of industrial strength coupled with military power. Japan, Germany, and Italy sought to end the economic and political uncertainty that followed the onset of the Great Depression by attempting to control markets and resources. Other powers, slightly more restrained, nevertheless pressured what they viewed as semicaptive suppliers to enter into unfavorable trade agreements. Even the United States worked to expand its influence in South America. Aggressive diplomacy, trade pacts, and eventually military force constituted the tools of the 1930s. A predatory nationalism swept Europe, validating naked self-interest with little consideration of the consequences. In Rio alarmed officials grimly assessed the nation's weakness.[1] Their concerns had a foundation in reality. The possibility of a generalized war in Europe and Asia concerned all to varying degrees. A diplomat, writing from Europe perhaps, only half seriously observed that if the Italian conquest of Ethiopia (1935) could not be undone, the Amazon might be next. The general staff in 1936 observed that a new division of land could be a possibility.

Threat, or actual force, might effectively transfer control over the country's resources to foreign overlords. Nor could direct colonization be ruled out. Closer to home, the danger seemed equally serious. Many believed that the Chaco War (1932–1935), in keeping with the 1930s pattern, constituted a contest over Bolivia's potential petroleum wealth. It pitted Paraguay, strongly but informally backed by Argentina, against Bolivia. Brazil's inadequate defenses along the eastern border with both belligerents posed a danger. The possibility of the war spilling over the border seemed an immediate threat. Argentina, militarily superior to Brazil, might welcome a generalized conflict. Vargas privately expressed the opinion that Argentina wanted to greatly expand its sphere of influence and funnel all of the Southern Cone's resources, perhaps including those of Brazil, through the port of Buenos Aires.

In the event of war with Argentina, policymakers and planners believed that they could not count on support from any Spanish-speaking republic. Neighboring states might seize the opportunity to take back territory they thought Brazil had despoiled them of in the nineteenth century. A geopolitical approach suggested that Brazil needed to become more active in the region. Colonel, later Marshal, Mario Travassos argued that the country had to project an east-west axis, or longitudinal Brazil, rather than the existing north-south coastal development pattern. He identified a strategic triangle, consisting of the Bolivian cities of Cochabamba, Sucre, and Santa Cruz, that formed the South American heartland. If the heartland could be controlled, it would neutralize Argentina's hold on the Río de la Plata network and end that nation's attempt to dominate Uruguay, Paraguay, and Bolivia. Travasso published his highly influential book, *The Continental Projection of Brazil*, in 1935. In the 1940s he served in the Brazilian Expeditionary Force, and then returned to the Army Staff College to mentor another generation of leaders.

In the meantime, only the historic relationship with the United States offered some protection from Brazil's envious and resentful neighbors, yet Washington had its own interests to tend to, a point made obvious when Argentina's objection to the sale of six obsolete U.S. destroyers to Brazil resulted in cancellation of the transfer. Fear of Argentina's military might ran high. The navy prepared for the worst and the army placed the frontier with Argentina on alert for a surprise attack. What needed to be done seemed obvious. Besides the need to arm itself as fast as possible, Brazil had to accelerate industrialization, increase exports to fund development, reduce coffee dependency, transform agriculture into agribusiness, and link the interior, particularly the north, with the rest of the nation through roads and settlement. Such an agenda necessarily would have to be long range. Nevertheless, an aggressive start had to be launched, which required strong state direction and intervention in the economy. National security fused with industrial and interior development.

Pressure on Vargas by the United States and Britain to distance himself from the fascist powers in the end could not be resisted, but a deal could be cut—cooperation and military bases in return for the financing and construction of a modern steel complex. The fact that Germany also indicated it might be interested in the project helped spur the United States to come forward. Washington believed that military officers unsure which partner offered the most advantages could be brought around by the willingness of the United States to finance a steel plant. Volta Redonda, symbolically built on exhausted coffee land, promised to be the core of another wave of industrialization. In reality, the army worried more about having sufficient arms to ward off the immediate threat, although it appreciated the long-range possibilities of a steel industry.

Nevertheless, Vargas attempted to cling to neutrality as long as possible. He sent his wife, Darcy, and one of his sons on a goodwill visit to the United States in 1936. Eleanor Roosevelt offered a luncheon in Darcy's honor. Subsequently, when Benito Mussolini's daughter visited Rio in 1939, Darcy hosted a reception, while Vargas remained discreetly in the diplomatic background. The Spanish Civil War put almost irresistible pressure on Vargas to join Germany and Italy in recognizing General Francisco Franco's regime. Diplomats in Spain reported every atrocity committed by republicans against the clergy. Vargas promised to recognize Franco once he captured Madrid and established effective control. In the face of pressure, Vargas managed to avoid agreements that limited his options, expressing support to be formalized at some vague date in the future. Meanwhile, José Joaquim de Moriz de Aragão, Brazil's envoy in Berlin in 1936, worked to maintain close ties with the Gestapo in order to keep track of Communist activity.

Fence sitting suited Vargas and served him well, in spite of the irritation of both sides and from less cautious diplomats. Positive neutrality appeared to be the best Germany and Italy could hope for until it became clear who would win the impending war. Reasons for sympathetic neutrality came over the airways. Radio Berlin's shortwave broadcasts, aimed at German-Brazilians—some one million in the south—made the case for Hitler, while broadcasts from Rome reached Italians and their descendants. Singer Helma Planck's selections of favorite German songs drew an appreciative audience. Berlin and Rome skillfully mixed propaganda and entertainment to stir up a sense of cultural nationalism. Both used much more powerful transmitters than the United States.

Just which power would come out the winner in the conflict remained unclear. Trade with Germany had been in the range of $170 million per year and, depending on the outcome of the war, it could be jeopardized by hasty action. Moreover, the United States could not supply armaments in the quantity needed. As a result, desperate for arms, the army turned to Germany. The British blockade ended that option, although one shipment from Germany was permitted to proceed to Brazil, paid for before the outbreak of hostilities.

In 1941 the government agreed to allow Pan American Airways, under a contract with the U.S. army, to modernize airports in the north and northeast, creating a thinly veiled, ready-to-use chain of air bases able to control the South Atlantic and reach into North Africa. Washington worried that the German-controlled airline, Condor, had routes that could facilitate Nazi activities throughout the Southern Hemisphere, perhaps even an invasion. To allay such fears, Brazilian businessmen, with the support of Vargas, bought control of Condor in 1942. The following year, the airline became the Cruzeiro do Sul.

With the Japanese attack on Pearl Harbor in December 1941, Vargas immediately voiced support for the United States and in January 1942 broke off diplomatic relations with the Axis powers. In the latter part of 1942, German U-boat attacks on shipping forced Vargas's hand—Brazil entered the war.

Vargas's somewhat reluctant, ambivalent support for the Allies stemmed from concern that the balance of trade between Germany, Britain, and the United States, which had served Brazil's interests, could not be sustained. Inevitably, war would result in American commercial domination. Along with trade and security concerns, Vargas worried about cultural influence. As a member of the elite, he shared their disdain for American crassness and what many viewed as its crude culture that acted to reduce everything to the lowest common level. Their ideal remained French—an influence unlikely to be absorbed by the lower classes. The elite understood that traditional Brazilian culture legitimized and reinforced patriarchal control. To allow the introduction of competing cultural structures risked fragmenting control and shifting social allegiances in unpredictable ways. American culture in virtually all aspects targeted the middle and working classes. A culturally isolated elite might well lose their directive control.

The newly established Office of Inter-American Affairs (OIAA), directed by Nelson A. Rockefeller, established an energetic presence in Brazil prior to the country's entry into the war.[2] Besides engaging in low-level espionage, the OIAA attempted to shape public opinion in favor of the Allies. A good deal of its activities revolved around cultural exchanges at the middlebrow level with some attention to high culture. The OIAA wanted to reach as many people as possible. Thus, the United States dispatched movie stars, directors, and filmmakers Errol Flynn, Orson Welles, John Ford, and Walt Disney to Brazil. A few stars made unfavorable impressions. Henry Fonda, dressed casually in old clothes, appalled the elite, who much preferred Errol Flynn's elegance. Fascination with Hollywood stars drew over 3,000 fans to greet George O'Brian on his arrival at São Paulo's Congonhas airport.

Disney produced cartoons calculated to delight audiences, while sugarcoating the actual propaganda message. Donald Duck's good-will screen tour of Latin America may well have been the most successful. Brazil's cartoon representation in the film *Saludos Amigos* (Greetings, friends) of Zé Carioca, a fast-talking pro-American parrot, amused and convinced at the same time. The elite, predictably, attempted to co-opt Orson Welles, the most intellectual film director of the time. Welles developed close ties with a number of high officials. When Brazil declared war, photographs of Welles seated next to Foreign Minister Oswaldo Aranha circulated throughout Latin America. Government officials wanted to win Welles over to their own views and did their best to show him around and entertain him. To the elite, Orson Welles represented the social and political dangers of North American influence, while Walt Disney exhibited the banal and infantile nature of American culture.

Nevertheless, Welles remained incorrigible. Even before arriving in Rio he had developed a keen interest in black themes and actors. His all-black *Voodoo MacBeth* incorporated African drums and used Haiti as the setting. Welles directed its Harlem performance in 1936. He went on to stage Richard Wright's *Native Son* in 1940, denounced by critics as Communist propaganda. He intended to film segments of his movie project, *It's All True,* for RKO in Brazil. RKO, the OIAA, and the Departamento de Imprensa e Propaganda (DIP) conspired to control Welles's use of favelas as backdrops and tried to eliminate scenes that suggested racism. RKO assigned an artistic director to watch Welles and cooperate with the DIP. It is not clear whether RKO worried more about screening a film in the United States that portrayed Afro-Brazilians or about alienating the Brazilian elite and the government. Officials insisted that plans to incorporate macumba scenes emphasized ignorance and superstition and instead pushed for scenic shots of Sugarloaf and Copacabana Beach.[3] The film was never finished. While the OIAA understandably congratulated itself on the overall success of its efforts, the elite and Vargas viewed their approach as overbearing, childlike, dangerous, and distasteful. Under the circumstances, it would have to be tolerated.

For all of the OIAA's efforts, the Portuguese edition of *Reader's Digest* may have been one of the more effective propaganda tools. The editor had previously decided that the subscription price was beyond the means of many Latin Americans, and, moreover, that distribution through newsstands seemed too disorganized. Nevertheless, alarmed that Axis influence appeared to be growing in Latin America, the U.S. government asked the magazine to reconsider. DeWitt Wallace rejected turning his publication into a propaganda mouthpiece or accepting financing. The solution, devised in 1940, was to accept advertising in order to cut costs, but only in the Spanish edition. The company expected to run at a loss. To everyone's surprise, the first issue sold 125,000 copies, far more than the 20,000 the publisher had predicted. Within two years, circulation reached 400,000 per month. In 1942 sales of the Portuguese edition exceeded sales of the Spanish edition in Latin America, and a year later monthly circulation was more than 300,000.[4] The Portuguese edition republished articles from the American version after the staff in Rio reviewed the content to ensure it would be of interest to their Portuguese-speaking readers. Not all the articles from the American magazine appeared in the Brazilian edition. From its inception, the *Reader's Digest* adopted a positive uplifting outlook. The people in its pages embodied stereotypical values of honesty, helpfulness, strength in difficult times, compassion, devotion to community, and ingenuity, among others. Its humor dealt with spouses, dogs, children, and personal reminiscences. Articles on medical breakthroughs, health issues, and personal loss, written in a style acceptable to a broad range of readers, informed and instructed. The positive image of the United States that the *Digest* presented probably exceeded anything the OIAA or the Office of War Information would have dared to publish.

The United States also engaged in reverse propaganda, suggesting to the American people that the Allies, worthy of gratitude and respect, were valuable partners in trying times. President Franklin D. Roosevelt encouraged cultural exchanges and tours by performers, with the idea of creating a positive impression among those who knew little about Brazil or its culture. The message suggested that the country had more to offer than coffee. Visits by entertainers tended to reinforce stereotypes but also reassured the American people that they had sympathetic friends in distant South America. Entertainer Carmen Miranda became the most widely known representative of Brazilian popular culture in the United States during the war years.

Interestingly, within Brazil, Miranda also served as a cultural bridge. Born in Portugal to a poverty-stricken family that had immigrated to Brazil when she was only two years old, Carmen seemed to know instinctively how to merge musical forms into socially acceptable adaptations. Afro-Brazilian and lower-class rhythms became the foundation of her success as the "Queen of Carioca Radio" and the "Ambassadress of Samba." A white performer, she reassured middle-class fans and delighted the largely black and mulatto lower class. A movie role completed her conquest of Brazil. Eager to become an international star, she went to New York in 1939, then on to

California, promising her fans she would not forget her roots, perhaps not understanding just how many adjustments Hollywood
would demand.

Her first recording, "In the South American Way," mixed Portuguese and English lyrics to blur the line between relaxed and lazy in
a way that offended and at the same time attracted Brazilians. Her
outlandish headdresses (she learned to trim hats before she broke
into entertainment) featured exotic fruit piled impossibly high on
her head. She returned to Brazil to encounter hostility after enjoying
almost a year and a half of success in the United States. The elite
resented her representation of Brazil abroad. Suddenly, her Portuguese birth became an issue. Her application for a Brazilian passport was denied. Rejected by Brazilians as having become too
Americanized, Carmen returned to Hollywood. Between 1940 and
1947, she appeared in nine films. She succeeded in creating a sympathetic image of Brazil in the United States, but one crafted in Hollywood that had little relation to reality. Two years before her death,
the Brazilian government finally relented and issued her a passport.
Carmen Miranda died in Hollywood in 1955, but would be buried
in Rio. Cultural sensitivity claimed an unnecessary victim.

A Guerra Atual (The Actual War)

The issue of active involvement in the war on the ground, not just
passively patrolling the coastline, had in effect been resolved in the
aftermath of World War I. In fact, a small naval group dispatched to
Europe unfortunately arrived too late to see action. All understood
that having not seen combat, Brazil had little standing at the peace
conference. Vargas did not intend to repeat that mistake. Nevertheless, senior generals expressed ambivalence about a European venture. At the time, the army numbered some 60,000, mostly in the
south. The possibility of an attack from Argentina worried many
planners, as did the fear of an Axis invasion. Vargas would not be
deterred. He made it clear to Washington that while the country
would allow bases on its territory and provide raw materials, the
government insisted upon an active, on-the-ground combat role.
President Roosevelt went to Brazil in 1943 to negotiate with Vargas
on his part in the conflict. Roosevelt had first met Vargas in 1936
during an earlier trip. Under pressure, Washington reluctantly agreed
to a force of 25,000 soldiers—far short of the number originally proposed. The problems of language, logistics, training, and the physical condition of Brazilian troops concerned the U.S. army command.[5]

Vargas intended that the soldiers of the Brazilian Expeditionary Force (Força Expedicionária Brasileira—FEB) be drawn from every state and region. He envisioned the involvement as a nationalist crusade—Brazilians, arms in hand, going to the rescue of Europe, in many respects like the American Expeditionary Force that went to France in World War I, an effort that dramatically altered the position of the United States in world affairs. Drawing soldiers from throughout the country required the FEB to form new units. It took time to create a smoothly functioning force. Competition within the officer corps to be part of the FEB became intense. All realized that participation represented a career-making opportunity—indeed, those who led the country in the postwar era would be FEB veterans. Meanwhile, General Eurico Dutra, the minister of war, selected officers who appeared disinterested in politics.

A series of miscommunications marred the initial interaction. The Brazilians believed they had been assigned to the North African theater and issued the troops the appropriate lightweight uniforms. In fact, the force was placed under the U.S. Fifth Army, then locked in a vicious wintertime assault against German positions in the mountains north of Rome. Brazil's first engagement resulted in heavy casualties and an ignominious retreat. Retraining, reequipping, and better liaison turned the FEB into a creditable combat force that took part in the assault on the historic Monastery of Monte Cassino, among other significant battles. FEB soldiers, called Zé Cariocas, acknowledging Walt Disney's contribution as well as their solidarity with American GIs, developed a reputation for dependability. The FEB's newspaper carried the same name. A German propaganda cartoon of a bedraggled Zé Carioca on crutches, with an amputated leg, in a backhanded way acknowledged the FEB's importance. On the home front, photographs of officers accepting the surrender of German officers filled the front pages of newspapers. The prestige of the army had never been higher.

A young U.S. army officer, Vernon Walters, served as the liaison between the FEB and the American army. A linguist and one of the very few Portuguese-speaking U.S. officers, Walters helped forge strong ties of friendship and respect between the respective militaries. He later became military attaché in Brazil in the early 1960s, immediately before and during the military coup of 1964. He later became deputy director of the U.S. Central Intelligence Agency. His friendship with top Brazilian military men led to wild rumors concerning the extent of American involvement in the events of 1964.

The experience of serving in the FEB, for those officers lucky enough to be chosen and even luckier to return alive, proved a formative one. Veterans referred to the conflict as the actual war (*a guerra atual*), dismissing all other engagements as trivial. They grew uneasy about their own government and admired the surprising strength of what they had previously viewed as an indecisive liberal democracy. Undoubtedly, the FEB officers absorbed American propaganda, including the virtues of and prospects for democracy in the postwar era. Brazil, under a dictatorship, might well be a pariah in spite of the sacrifices of the FEB. Vargas had no answer to this legitimate concern, nor could he easily transform his regime. The president had promised elections in 1938, then again in 1943, but the coup preempted the first and the wartime emergency the second. Indications of civilian disenchantment became increasingly evident. A manifesto in 1943 signed by prominent citizens in Minas Gerais called for the restoration of a liberal constitutional government. With the war over, Vargas could find no excuse for not holding elections.

In early 1945 a constitutional law provided for the popular election of the president. Vargas may have believed he could rally public support for his election, in spite of the end of press censorship and the now-open criticism of his government. To be on the safe side, the government encouraged the founding of several new political parties, among them the Partido Social Democrático (Social Democratic Party) and the Partido Trabalhista Brasileira (Brazilian Worker Party), and strengthened local political bosses. The opposition formed the União Democrático Nacional (National Democratic Union). To make sure the capital remained in friendly hands, he appointed his brother Benjamin as Rio's chief of police.[6] Clearly, Vargas had no intention of going quietly into history. Adolph Berle, the American ambassador, made a point of praising Vargas's "promise" to hold elections, hoping he could be embarrassed into doing so. Normally, Berle's statements would have created an uproar. Despite Vargas's efforts to capitalize on nationalist sentiments over foreign interference, the public did not rush to his defense. The country's weariness with wartime shortages and inflation explained the lack of reaction. The cost of living soared in São Paulo, while in the rest of the country it doubled between 1939 and 1945. Many believed that the Vargas policies could not be adjusted to postwar realities.

A great deal of Vargas's remaining support rested on a debilitating uncertainty. Labor feared that a new president might dismantle the pro-labor legislation put in place in the 1930s. Union leaders, urban workers, and the middle class worried that the oligarchy might be on the verge of regaining power. While the middle class fretted and workers envisioned a darker future, their mutual antagonism ruled out an alliance. Others who had prospered under the Estado Novo, sometimes under shady or preferential circumstances, wondered if they could retain their wealth. Out of a mixed bag of fears and emotions sprang the Queremistas (We Want Vargas) movement. No single person or group controlled the movement. As usual, Vargas did not make his wishes known. The president hoped to keep his options open, while the Queremistas wanted him to declare his candidacy. The background questions also created uncertainty. Would the military permit him to run or did Vargas prefer a 1937-style coup rather than an election?

Hugo Borghi emerged as the most effective and notorious figure in the pro-Vargas movement. A wealthy man, Borghi's bounty resulted from an injustice profitably remedied. Formerly, cotton producers labored under an arrangement where buyers, acting collectively, bought low, then exported at the much higher international market rate. Borghi persuaded Vargas to set a minimum producer price, then purchased all the cotton he could before the new scheme became public. Almost instantly he became a very rich man, but one with many enemies. He used his money to lavishly promote the Queremista movement and fanned it to a fever pitch. When Vargas allowed the deadline for announcing his candidacy to pass, a desperate Borghi came up with another scheme to write a new constitution with different rules. In the end, he threw himself into the Dutra campaign in return for protection.

The failed Queremista movement damaged Vargas. Convoluted politics at a crucial moment in history resulted in lasting suspicion of his every move. Vargas's practice of never letting anyone share his thoughts, or giving a straight answer, clearly backfired. The president probably could have survived, but for the almost total collapse of the regime's military support. The army demanded he resign. A realist, Vargas returned to his ranch in Rio Grande do Sul, worried that he might be forced into exile. Nevertheless, one final chapter remained.

Dysfunctional Democracy, 1945–1964

The election of December 1945 reflected growing political complexity. The oligarchy's power seemingly had been submerged into a political mass with six million votes cast in the election of 1945, compared to the rigged election of 1930 in which only two million people voted. Both the working and middle classes benefited greatly from industrialization, and Vargas's propaganda, as noted earlier, had an inclusionary political impact. Vargas, in fact, had presided over a transformation that was now beyond his control.

Expectations ran high, particularly after the predictability of the former regime. Not immediately evident, however, was the military's role in the new democracy. In the euphoria of the moment, few understood that the army intended to monitor democracy and determine its utility. Another problem, also not fully appreciated at the time, involved the formation of political parties, a central fixture of any democratic system. Of the three major parties, Vargas had formed two during his manipulations before the elections in 1945, and the opponents of Vargas a third. Clearly, the former president cast a long shadow over party politics. Moreover, he returned to public life with a ready explanation for his removal from office. He sidestepped the tricky business of the military to attack dark international forces intent on keeping Brazil a backward country with resources to be plundered with abandon. Vargas, long convinced that urban industrial workers provided the ideal political constituency, turned increasingly to labor for support. The army, with one eye on working-class demagoguery in Argentina, became wary of the new democratic Vargas. The speed with which he rehabilitated himself concerned his opponents. Nevertheless, as long as he remained within democratic bounds, they could not object too strenuously.

The first election since 1930 revealed the institutional popularity of the military. General Eurico Dutra, Vargas's former war minister, ran against Major General Eduardo Gomes, the head of the air force (established in 1942). Gomes had participated in the Copacabana revolt of 1922 and helped suppress the Communist revolt in Rio, but he opposed Vargas's coup of 1937. Both men proved to be turgid campaigners. Dutra liked to digress into homilies and stories about minor events of military history, while Gomes seemed remote and cold. During the campaign Gomes made remarks his opponents used to tar him as an elitist. With the reluctant endorsement of the former dictator, Dutra won handily as the candidate of the PSD, one of the parties founded by Vargas. Vargas himself won election as a senator from two states and as a congressman representing six states and the federal district. He chose to represent his home state of Rio Grande do Sul as a senator, but wisely limited his attendance in the capital. Clearly, the former president might be down, but far from out.

The Constitution of 1946 changed the political equation dramatically. It borrowed major elements from the pre–Estado Novo Constitution of 1934. A reactionary document, it decentralized authority and reversed the balance, established during the dictatorship, between the federal government and the states. It seemed to be a return to modified oligarchic politics without the oligarchy. A literacy requirement and exclusion of military enlisted men limited the size of the electorate. State bosses, schooled in trading favors, thrived. Political bosses encouraged the personal loyalty of party members, who seldom insisted on principle. The absence of an ideology to provide political direction led to short-term deal-making and unlikely alliances, which, if the parties had a guiding ideology, would have been embarrassing. An immature party system made politicians appear to be irresponsible opportunists.

The constitution allowed states to run their own affairs without much intervention from Rio. The president retained the right to intervene under certain, but restricted, conditions. It also restored the office of vice president. To the armed forces went the task of guaranteeing the constitution and law and order. After the dictatorship, everyone wanted to play politics and plenty of room would be provided. The document's weakness, unfortunately, would be compounded by an inexperienced constituency. The former authoritarian regime discouraged independent civic responsibility and the process of developing it would be a long one.

General Dutra had little democratic experience. He supported the Estado Novo, served it in high positions, and had won as the nominee of a party founded by the ex-dictator. He had some political advantages. Because of the inability to import consumer items during the war, the government had accumulated a large horde of foreign exchange that provided economic and political capital. Moreover, the strong demand for primary product exports in the United States and the seemingly endless demand for materials needed to rebuild Europe promised to keep prosperity going into the foreseeable future. On the negative side, allocating resources had become an issue of negotiation with a large number of equally inexperienced interests. The hope of restraining pent-up demand for foreign consumer goods vanished as imports flooded into the country, rapidly drawing down foreign reserves. State purchase of foreign-owned public utilities, combined with the import frenzy, left the pot empty by 1948. Some $800 million had disappeared.

The old themes of the 1930s could not be used to provide political cohesion. Developing new democratic ones appeared beyond the ability of postwar politicians. The Estado Novo relied upon nationalism to adjust the tensions between the classes, along with some limited attention to the welfare of urban industrial workers. Nationalism glossed over the real problems but worked well politically. Issues long unattended now had to be addressed. Unplanned urbanization had already become a problem by the 1920s. At the time of the Revolution of 1930, Rio de Janeiro had a poor population of some 70,000, still small by today's standards, living in makeshift shacks without sanitation or water. São Paulo, Recife, Santos, and other cities experienced a similar influx of the rural poor. Favela settlers represented a marginal subclass, without skills or education and often in poor health and suffering from malnutrition. No longer able to survive in the rural economy, people flooded into the cities drawn by an imaginary good life conveyed over the airwaves. They forged their own economy as ragpickers scouring the streets for debris, rummaging through trash, or working day jobs where they could find them. The changing nature of city life made poverty and the social gap all too obvious. How to incorporate the migrants into the city's social fabric and political life in other than a superficial fashion troubled the authorities, but no ready solution seemed at hand.

Industrial workers also felt themselves under pressure. Inflation, the inevitable lag of wages behind prices, and an economy that seemed to be booming for others increased worker discontent. A series of massive strikes in São Paulo in 1947 unnerved industrialists and rattled the Dutra regime. The Communist Party (PCB), revitalized by Luís Carlos Prestes's return from exile, actively recruited workers, providing an explanation of their present condition and suggesting the solution. Prestes, now a senator, and fourteen PCB deputies hammered away at the government. Senator Prestes undercut his position by declaring that in the event of war between Brazil and the Soviet Union (it was very unlikely), he would support Moscow. Aggressive worldwide communism and the advent of the Cold War acted to undermine worker demands. Industrialists readily labeled every demand and every assertive leader as Communist—true in some cases, but not in most. Dutra correctly viewed the PCB as antidemocratic but overestimated its strength. State elections in 1945 seemed to indicate the growing popularity of the PCB, when, in fact, it represented worker frustrations. The insistence of the United States on building an anti-Communist bloc to counter Soviet expansionism provided Dutra with international support for outlawing the PCB in 1947, and expelling Communists from congress as well as ending diplomatic relations with the Soviet Union.

In 1949 the army established the Superior War College (Escola Superior de Guerra—ESG) modeled after its American counterpart. The War College instructed both civilian leaders and military personnel in a broad political fashion often justifiably critical of the current political process. The ESG projected the army's notion of the direct connection between security, politics, and development. The college elaborated a Doctrine of National Security, which emphasized the danger of Communist subversion as well as the nation's geopolitical role in South America. Army self-confidence stemmed from the fact that Brazil had emerged from the war as the dominant

Latin American military power. The Argentine threat seemed under control. Within South America the Inter-American Treaty of Reciprocal Assistance (Rio Pact) appeared to limit the danger of traditional regional conflicts. Internal subversion and broader Cold War threats posed another problem. ESG graduates, both civilian and military, internalized a critical, analytical, suspicious, and mildly paranoid worldview. They accepted the need for internal and external vigilance. War College graduates played an important role in the military regime after 1964.

As Dutra's term staggered to a close, Vargas once again stepped forward. The situation seemed to favor his return. The Estado Novo's formation of government-controlled unions and limited labor reforms had worked well. With a few adjustments, it could do so again. A democratic structure required rhetorical appeals, patronage, and a more aggressive pro-labor policy, all of which could provide a solid political base. Industrial growth from 1930 to 1950 made industrial workers, along with the managerial middle class, the two fastest growing segments of the country's urban population. From 1945 to 1950 industrial output doubled and could be expected to double again in the next decade. Industrial workers had well-defined interests easy to appeal to and were of growing importance to the modern economy. In the proper organizational context, their political muscle could provide a base. Ties could then be established with the managerial and professional middle class by adopting economic nationalism. Vargas still enjoyed support from political bosses who had benefited from his regime. Even São Paulo's industrialists and coffee producers admitted that Vargas's economic policy in the 1930s had saved them and that, in fact, they had prospered. The military, wedded to democratic forms if not to the actual spirit of democracy, agreed it could not oppose a democratically elected ex-dictator. His embrace of populism could be accepted or discounted by those who remembered that Vargas generally agreed with everybody, and that what he said and what he did often seemed quite different. His flexible sincerity could not be disputed; thus, many expected to thrive under a democratically elected Vargas regime. Not surprisingly, he received 49 percent of the vote.

Vargas Returns

President Getúlio Vargas took office on January 31, 1951—it seemed a personal vindication. Yet he now had to govern under a constitution in large part written to make sure the perceived abuses of the Estado Novo did not repeat themselves. Congress had assumed the power to budget and promptly acted irresponsibly. Printing money erased deficits once accumulated, but at the expense of the currency. Brazil's currency lost value rapidly; in 1952 inflation reached 22 percent. Plummeting wages and a rising cost of living impoverished the lower classes and worried the middle class. Here was the opportunity for a pro-labor strategy to come into play. The president appointed João Goulart his minister of labor and raised the minimum wage, which had remained unchanged since 1943. In 1954 Goulart recommended doubling wages to offset inflation. At this point, the military stepped in to pressure Vargas to dismiss his minister of labor. Vargas did so, but then pushed through Goulart's wage increase. A watchful military intended to blunt, if not stop, the attempt to build a political base among the workers. Without a sufficiently powerful constituency behind him, Vargas could not move congress, nor did he have sufficient patronage to hold on to the political bosses.

The combination of an uncontrollable congress and a deeply suspicious and watchful military made Vargas appear politically incompetent. People talked about the old Vargas and suggested that age (late sixties) had diminished his political skills. Moreover, the entire government seemed corrupt. Inflation, the rising cost of living, and lagging wages encouraged bureaucrats at all levels to demand bribes, charging the user for their services or for a favorable ruling. Vargas presided over an ugly situation he could do little to change, while the press held him personally responsible.

Vargas envisioned a new stage of accelerated industrialization in order to conserve foreign exchange, increase the country's self-sufficiency, and create industrial jobs as well as expand middle-class managerial positions. The plan was reminiscent of his 1930 program. The bottleneck appeared to be in energy. Nationalized and foreign utility companies alone could not provide the massive amount of electricity required. Petroleum resources needed to be developed in order to reduce demand on foreign sources. Moreover, high energy prices retarded industrial growth. Vargas proposed a joint private- and government-financed monopoly to be called Petrobras. The project clearly fell into the category of infrastructure development. Unfortunately, the economic merits fell victim to partisan politics.

The debate raged for two years as congress tinkered with every aspect of the Vargas proposal. The right-wing opposition assailed the project as statist, while the left demanded full state ownership. The United States expressed its disapproval and even the military appeared divided between the nationalists, who approved, and the conservatives, who wondered whether the plan represented incipient socialism. To complicate the situation, the conservative opposition party flip-flopped to demand total state ownership in order to deny Vargas any claim to being a nationalist. In the end, congress crafted the project as it desired. The plan and the president had been battered beyond recognition. Vargas's new industrial strategy, in retrospect a sensible one, was stillborn. Coffee prices declined, causing balance-of-payment problems that required intervention by the International Monetary Fund (IMF). As usual, the IMF insisted on a stabilization program, which ended any hope of accelerated industrial growth. The economic stalemate intensified the political impasse. The president's enemies rushed in for the rhetorical kill. Although at the time few understood it, the episode indicated that democracy without democratic principles could not work.

The Assassination of a Regime

Although Vargas was returned to power in 1950 by a landslide, he knew his effectiveness depended on building an actual constituency. Aware that the democratic political system precluded the use of state propaganda, the president cast about for an acceptable vehicle to get his message across to the public. The obvious solution, a pro-Vargas newspaper, required money and a skillful editor—both could be arranged. Samuel Wainer, an experienced journalist and gifted editor, established *Ultima Hora*. A favorable loan of questionable legality from the Bank of Brazil, backed by wealthy friends of the president, provided more than ample resources. Preferential access to important stories, coupled with Wainer's expertise, soon made it the most popular newspaper in the country. Advertisers, aware of the newspaper's semiofficial status, poured money into the publication. Competing newspapers struggled for readers and ad revenue. Francisco de Assis Chateaubriand, who controlled a newspaper, radio, and later television empire, joined forces with Roberto Marinho of Globo Publishing, Rádio, and later TV Globo. Together they launched a campaign to destroy Wainer, and at the same time aim a few body blows at Vargas. They probably would have been only marginally successful had it not been for the convergence of several factors.

Globo Rádio, established at the end of the war, created a niche for itself in news programming and, as an extension of the news, in investigative reporting. In a program called "Family Conversation," a group of journalists played family members gathered around the kitchen table to discuss the interesting events of the week. A companion program, "Congress in Action," featured interviews followed by commentary. Both programs blurred the lines between hard news, rumor, and opinion. A relatively unsophisticated audience could not separate fabrications from actual events. Complimenting Globo's reporting, an outright opinion program drew upon already doubt-ful news reporting to make entirely outrageous charges. The host, Carlos Lacerda, later called "the Crow," picked over his victims—Wainer and Vargas. Lacerda, a complex personality, brilliant, good-looking, and with a charisma he could project over the airways, had a mixed journalistic career before attempting to launch his own news-paper, *A Tribuna*. Marinho and Chateaubriand, who accidentally stumbled upon his talents, almost immediately understood they had found their hatchet man. He could, and did, talk for hours far into the early morning. Pathologically obsessive, Lacerda never let up. Telephoned-in questions added fuel to his virulent attacks and also suggested the existence of a large community of right-thinking people who endorsed his views. He steered his conservatism to ap-peal to the middle class with a healthy dose of Catholic morality. According to Lacerda, the family, housewives with their innate moral superiority essential for child-raising, and similar values expressed all that was good about Brazil. Many of his techniques and homilies came from American bishop Fulton J. Sheen, at the time a popular conservative commentator and personal acquaintance of Lacerda.

Lacerda's attacks increasingly concentrated on Vargas, the former dictator now brought low by democracy, with Wainer a subordinate servant of evil. It appeared that Vargas had been elected for the sole purpose of stripping him of all respect. Wainer, his alleged creature, suddenly became a Romanian Jew (he was born in Romania and came to Brazil at the age of two). Moreover, his brief flirtation with com-munism now became an issue, while Lacerda's connection with com-munism, soon severed, would be overlooked. The grand finale of his vitriolic campaign came as he called on the military to end the anomaly of an honorable people governed by thieves. The central importance of one individual, and his unrelenting mission to de-stroy Vargas and Wainer, made Lacerda an obvious candidate for assassination.

Returning to his Copacabana apartment early on the morning of August 5, 1954, along with an air force major, a volunteer bodyguard, Lacerda was shot and wounded in the foot—the major died. A fe-verish investigation led to the presidential palace. Without Vargas's knowledge, his bodyguard, incensed by Lacerda's attacks on the president, had contracted the bungled assassination attempt. The air force, outraged together with the high command of the army, demanded that Vargas resign. Three weeks later the military ousted him from office. Shortly after his removal became clear, the presi-dent committed suicide, putting a bullet through his heart. The small, unadorned room in Rio's Catete Palace, now a museum, became his last monument. Vargas clearly had been under great mental strain for some time, although perhaps only his daughter realized the degree of his distress.

A presidential suicide is a major national trauma in any society. In Vargas's case, the effect was to shift the blame for the tragedy to his enemies. His suicide note, published throughout Brazil and read incessantly over the radio, shocked and saddened the nation. The note seemed like a message from a crucifixion: "I cannot give you more than my blood. . . . I choose this means to be with you always. . . . Now I offer my death. . . . I leave life to enter history." Vargas blamed sinister international financial groups and internal antiworker coalitions for the failure of his presidency and made an oblique reference to Lacerda, the Crow, as one of the "birds of prey." Even in the last minutes of his life, he could not bring himself to directly accuse the army, which had deposed him twice, this time mortally.

Overwhelming Brazil: Making the Unworkable Work

Vargas's vice president, Café Filho, who was supported by the military, now insisted on following constitutional practices and put together a caretaker government. All eyes turned to the upcoming 1955 elections. A resurgence of postmortem popularity for Vargas embraced the very much alive "Vargas gang." The two political parties formed by Vargas in 1945 joined to nominate Juscelino Kubitschek for president and João Goulart, the former labor minister, for vice president. They swept to victory on the wings of an angel, but just barely. The army grumbled about Kubitschek but made its dislike of Goulart obvious. Rumors of yet another military intervention circulated, especially after a sick President Café Filho turned the office over to the president of the chamber of deputies, an archenemy of the two elected to executive office. Fortunately for Kubitschek, a group of officers allied with high military officials formed the Constitutional Military Movement and took preventive action to guarantee the inauguration of Kubitschek and Goulart. This step represented the second extra-constitutional intervention by the military in the short ten-year existence of the new democracy.

Kubitschek, very much a product of the Vargas era, delighted in deals, loved politics, particularly the interaction with people, and went for the grandiose. He reached back into his family tree for the name Kubitschek, dropping his name Oliveira on the assumption his adopted one would make him stand out. His central European ancestors indeed served him well. Kubitschek became mayor of Belo Horizonte, the capital of Minas Gerais, and later governor of the state.

Yet the skills that made him a successful politician caused unease among the anti-Vargas opposition, including the military. At the very moment Kubitschek's presidency began, a small group of air force officers in Amazonia attempted to ignite a revolt against the government. The fact that he had won the presidency with only 36 percent of the vote did not give him an overwhelming mandate. Missteps, bad luck, or unexpected external blows would not be tolerated. The post–World War II era had been a major disappointment. The possibility of democratic failure already cast a dark shadow across the country. Cinema Novo's pessimism, while reflecting that of the left, captured the country's generally gloomy mood. Kubitschek understood, intellectually and politically as well as instinctively, that the nation needed a psychological jolt—a collective electrical shock to jar the population into a more confident stance.

Well aware that his tenure might be short, President Kubitschek wasted little time in getting started. On his second day in office, he created the National Development Council and the Program of Targets to set objectives for both the government and private capital. While many dismissed the plan as a rhetorical scheme, Kubitschek linked it with the building of a new capital city, to be called Brasília, in the interior state of Goiás. The proposed new capital's central location in the heart of the country, away from the historic pattern of coastal cities, indicated the southeast's willingness to have a truly national capital. An unbelieving congress approved the project during Kubitschek's first year in office. Work began in 1957 on a twenty-four-hour-per-day basis, as the president hurried to keep his promise of "fifty years of progress in five." Few believed Kubitschek's dream would come true when he made that now historic boast. The president drew upon his political experience in Minas, his understanding of why the elected Vargas had failed, and his own personality to devise his survival strategy. While the decision to build a new inland capital assured his continuation in office, he hoped to end a negative era and inaugurate a new positive one.

The break with the past and the bold move into the future would be symbolized in concrete. Brazil's most renowned architect, Oscar Niemeyer, along with the brilliant city planner, Lúcio Costa, seemed up to the task. The project was far more ambitious than Napoleon III's inspired remaking of Paris, resembling more the construction of Washington, DC. Yet, while the American capital evoked the glories of ancient Rome, Brasília looked to the future. A ceremonial city, its overscale buildings projected strength and permanence, cast in an unmistakably futuristic mold. Uninterrupted by traffic lights, streets flowed throughout the city, passing by seemingly magical glass buildings, reflecting pools, and decidedly modern statuary. Indeed, the entire city might have served the Jetsons better than those still earth-bound.

To accompany the president's national therapy, a new musical form emerged. The bossa nova fused *samba-canção*, a slower samba, into a pleasing but distinctively Brazilian sound.[7] The movie *Black Orpheus* established the bossa nova's international reputation. Filmed in Rio, with an emphasis on the city's sensual beauty, it won the Grand Prize at the Cannes Film Festival in 1959. João Gilbert, Sergio Mendes, Antônio Carlos (Tom) Jobim, and Vinicíus de Moraes became internationally known performing artists. Subsequent collaboration with American musicians infused the bossa nova with cool jazz. It recalled the 1860s cultural interchange between early New Orleans ragtime and classical composer Louis Gottschalk and his Brazilian friends. The Brazilian rhythm influenced American pop musicians and singers. Even Elvis Presley sang "Bossa Nova Baby." An enduring composition, "The Girl from Ipanema" (1962), by Tom Jobim and Vinicíus de Moraes, came with a romantic story attached that contributed to its popularity. As the story goes, two men who frequented a corner bar, the Veloso, daily observed a beautiful young girl on her way to the beach. A perfect and gentle male fantasy expressed in music resulted in the most famous bossa nova tune. The bar changed its name to "Garota de Ipanema."[8]

A bossa nova concert in New York's Carnegie Hall in 1962 marked a high point for the musical form, Brasília, and the "bossa nova president," as some called Kubitschek. As the music faded, the capital began to be retrofitted for human beings. The dehumanized, clean, and crime-free environment of the new capital, with its better schools, still seemed too artificial for bureaucrats, who now faced transfer from Rio to the backlands of Goiás. The future in concrete and marble did not compensate for the loss of a socially comfortable city. The triumph of reality over fantasy came with the installation of traffic lights—Brasília had become the accident capital of the country as well as the political one. Brasília remains a source of architectural pride, but its principal importance is geopolitical. The city's success marked the psychological passing of the frontier. Roads, spidering out from the new capital, touched all parts of the country—a new era, indeed.[9]

Financing rapid development, including the new capital, required the creative use of virtually every last monetary and fiscal device. By this time, many developmentalists accepted the idea that inflation could be used as a tool. Few people saved money—it had to be spent before it lost value. Those who could afford to buy a condo in the high-rises that transformed Copacabana did so. Many of them poorly built, with inoperable elevators and barely functioning plumbing, they nevertheless increased in value and offered protection from inflation. The less well to do bought soap, toilet paper, and other items before prices went up. Suddenly empty shelves in supermarkets indicated an imminent price increase. The rapid spending of money created jobs in construction as tangible property offered some protection from skyrocketing prices. Printing money, while it increased inflation, nevertheless bought development. Kubitschek, in fact, used everybody's money—domestic, foreign, borrowed, taxed, and finally printed. The amount of paper currency in circulation jumped over 300 percent before he left office and the country's foreign debt reached staggering levels.

Construction activity benefited a wide range of groups and interests. The government agency in charge, the Urbanization Company of the New Capital, directed to be as innovative as possible, responded with enthusiasm. Road building spread the wealth far beyond the new capital. More than 11,000 miles of new roads and an international airport connected Brasília with the rest of the country and the world. Some 1,400 miles of roads reached north, 1,060 to the northeast, and 400 to the south along with a web of feeder roads and links. Although unpaved, scarred with potholes, sometimes becoming a sea of mud or nearly lost in clouds of dust, they made transportation possible to previously isolated parts of the nation. Settlements appeared along the new roadways and stimulated the creation of feeder communities and economic activity of all kinds.

The vast amounts of money flowing in all directions bought people and cooperation as well as labor and material. Money flowed over obstacles both political and regional. Corruption, payoffs, inflated costs, and land speculation inevitably accompanied the rush to development. Kubitschek understood the use of corruption but made no moral judgment about it—to him it was simply the cost of doing business. It could be disagreeable, distasteful, and ugly, but to the politically experienced president, it was how things worked. Kubitschek enjoyed the power to convince and make things happen, no matter what the cost. He left the country broke, in debt, and emotionally drained.

Kubitschek's program ignored agrarian problems and did little for education. While development was unbalanced, it broke through several important barriers. Although Vargas had understood the need for more energy to support industrialization, Kubitschek succeeded in providing it. The massive Furnas hydroelectric project and the Tres Marias dam on the São Francisco River increased hydroelectric power from three to five million kilowatts, and improved transmission lines delivered the power efficiently to industrial consumers. The road system brought new areas into the national economy, and the new capital turned all eyes to development of the interior now that Kubitschek had so publicly demonstrated the possibilities. The number of industrial plants grew by 33 percent, employing close to two million workers.

While President Kubitschek had little time for foreign affairs, Brazil began to make a sustained impression, thanks to its national soccer team and the talents of star player Pelé. The Brazilians won the World Cup in 1958. Maria Bueno's win at Wimbledon in 1960 made her an international tennis celebrity. Brazilian women consistently reached the finals of the Miss Universe beauty pageant. During the Kubitschek presidency, VARIG introduced the first jet aircraft on the route to New York via the capital and later to São Paulo and Buenos Aires. REAL, soon to merge with VARIG, began service to Los Angeles in 1960 with an extension to Tokyo.

Despite being primarily involved in internal affairs, the president attempted to interest the United States in the development process throughout the hemisphere. Latin Americans had long resented the rush by the United States to rebuild Europe after World War II. Kubitschek saw his opportunity when the United States became preoccupied with the Cuban Revolution of 1959 and Cuba's rapid leftward drift. He suggested to President Eisenhower that Operation Pan American could do for the Western Hemisphere what the Marshall Plan had done in Europe. Well aware of Kubitschek's reputation as a big spender, Eisenhower rejected the notion but withdrew his opposition to the creation of the Inter-American Development Bank.

Over the course of Kubitschek's wild ride he progressively alienated the middle class and worried the army. The mad race to conserve modest assets in a time of inflation required constant attention and there appeared to be no end in sight. Entire extended middle-class families, including adult children and on occasion their spouses, crowded into small condos and shared a modest car and expenses, all the while barely holding on to their lifestyle expectations. The military, pleased with the various national projects and the great leap forward in industrialization, nevertheless worried that Kubitschek had bankrupted the country. The IMF said as much but, of course, had been dismissed by Kubitschek. Moreover, the army, as part of the middle class, shared its civilian colleagues' distaste for corruption and the day-to-day struggle with inflation. The gradual, but progressive, antagonism of the army and the civilian middle class would have serious consequences. Nevertheless, the positives continued to be evident. Politically, the new capital represented an important step in the country's history. Economically, industrial modernization, symbolized by the national automobile industry, pushed Brazil into a new era.

Driving toward Progress: The Automobile Industry

In the first half of the twentieth century automobiles represented the pinnacle of manufacturing technology, epitomized by Henry Ford's success in the United States. Moreover, the auto industry created demand for a wide range of raw materials and caused supporting industries to appear and prosper. It became a powerful economic engine for more advanced countries and could do the same for Brazil with its underutilized raw materials and potentially important market. The automobile embodied an irresistible, seductive combination of technology, progress, and modernity.

Brazil's experience with the automobile industry traversed a number of evolutionary stages, beginning with the importation of fully assembled cars and trucks called CBUs (completely built units). The CBU stage provided a basic understanding of the mechanics of the industry and suggested the potential of the market. The Model T's success encouraged Ford to establish a presence in Brazil in 1919, and General Motors followed in 1925. Meanwhile, Ford began to import parts and components to assemble completely knocked-down units (CKDs) at its Brazilian plants using local labor supervised by Ford technicians. Ford had an assembly capacity of 4,700 units per year. Almost a decade later, experimentation with building motors began with the state-owned National Motor Factory (FNM) in 1938. At the time, the FNM produced light aircraft engines for the National Postal Service.

By the late 1930s the severe limitations of the transportation system became glaringly evident. The country relied upon a railway network laid out to service the coffee industry, not the new demands for minerals and agricultural products. Railways reinforced regionalism rather than connectivity, tying one region directly with its export point. To compound the problem, railways deteriorated along with the fall in coffee prices. By 1945 the cost of track and rail car replacement exceeded $150 million. Over all, the needs of the rail system would absorb a minimum of sixteen months of the production of the steel complex at Volta Redonda. The other option, roads and trucks, seemed preferable. Moreover, trucks and cars, unlike railways, had the flexibility to go in any direction as economic needs changed. The primacy of railway towns, in fact, ended at the same time in Brazil and the United States.[10] Consequently, in 1949 the FNM began truck production with foreign-made parts. In addition, 60,000 trucks had to be imported and it was estimated that the need would increase by over 10 percent each year into the foreseeable future. Moreover, demand for cars grew rapidly, surpassing trucks in 1961. Clearly, Brazil had a sufficiently large market to move to the next stage.

Vargas, in the first year of his postwar elected term, created the Commission for Industrial Development and a Subcommission for Jeeps, Tractors, Trucks, and Automobiles under the chairmanship of the commander of the navy. The Subcommission investigated the possibility of manufacturing cars with domestic-made parts. Before much progress could be made, Vargas's presidency ended tragically.

Mercedes Benz ordered the first Brazilian-made motor block in 1955. It became an industrial icon, trumpeted as proof that casting motors in a "tropical country" was perfectly feasible.[11] Pressure to use only Brazilian parts became intense during the Kubitschek years. Official guidelines and policies pushed companies to use as many domestic parts as possible. A semiofficial Automobile Executive Group (GEIA) suggested new projects, plants, and suitable locations and recommended government approval or disapproval of plans by the companies. In response, General Motors constructed a plant on the General Dutra Highway, which links São Paulo with Rio de Janeiro, with the stated goal of producing light trucks with domestic parts. President Kubitschek, never one to miss a photo opportunity, personally inaugurated the new plant in 1959. Donning a heat- and flame-resistant suit, he poured molten steel into a motor block mold. By 1962, Brazil manufactured 200,000 automobiles, making it the world's seventh-largest producer. Many of the vehicles traveled on the new road system, but the country also began to export cars, trucks, and tractors to other Latin American countries.

Recounting official desires and political pressure, while important, nevertheless misses the almost epic struggle to establish an auto industry. The major challenges that confronted the automotive pioneers fell into the category of human and infrastructure deficiencies. The shortage of suitable workers, suppliers with sufficient skills to ensure reasonable quality parts, distributors, and mechanics able to service increasingly complex units initially appeared to be almost insurmountable obstacles. Fortunately, or perhaps unfortunately, most foreign companies, particularly those that arrived in the postwar period, underestimated the day-to-day difficulties. They knew little about the country's history, social conditions, or political system. As a consequence, they were unprepared for the extent of government intervention in decisions they viewed as purely business ones.

How individual companies met the challenges offers a view of industrial Brazil in the postwar period. Scandia, a Swedish truck and bus company, began operations in 1957. As to be expected, the firm assembled CKD units, which barely met the legal requirements for completely knocked-down units. Officials, eager to see Scandia succeed, initially gave the company plenty of slack. For several years Scandia trucks arrived on the docks missing only tires and batteries. At some point, Scandia would have to move toward utilization of domestic parts. In 1962 the company opened a plant in São Bernardo do Campo, now part of greater São Paulo. Reaching full production took much longer than constructing the plant. After fruitless efforts to find experienced workers, Scandia lowered its requirement to simply the ability to read and write. It soon became clear that even that standard could not be met. The labor pool included a high percentage of newly arrived, unskilled rural migrants. A by-now desperate management devised a training program to teach functional literacy. In addition, the poor physical and nutritional state of the employees required new company initiatives.

Other companies took different measures. Karmann-Ghia dispatched thirty-six trainees and a translator to Germany for a two-year program. All but one returned after completing the course—the remaining worker married a German woman and began his career in the European plant. Mercedes Benz created a first-class training institute in Brazil that became the industry standard. The federal government also trained potential workers through the National Industrial Apprenticeship Service (SENAI). SENAI was reminiscent of a similar program the empire had designed to meet the needs of the imperial shipyards.

Making parts to meet the domestic-content requirement called for some ingenuity. The government set the requirement according to weight, not value, so that some of the more intricate parts could be imported. Nevertheless, suppliers of domestic parts could not be easily identified.[12] Mercedes Benz sent a team to scour the streets of São Paulo for small metal shops, even individuals using a lathe. On spotting a likely candidate, a company representative tried to convince the shop owner or individual to try making parts—often they refused. Interested parties received technical support, working capital, and materials. While on the surface a wonderful opportunity, it required bookkeeping and, most difficult, a reorientation from a comfortable small business with well-understood advantages, to the depersonalized demands of a multinational company. The impact on an individual's family, friends, pace of life, and values had to be considered. Reliability proved to be a constant worry. Scandia stationed a full-time employee in machine shops to monitor quality and to make sure that agreed-upon delivery schedules were met. An unexpected delay could have expensive financial consequences for a company. Volvo initially shipped domestic parts back to Europe for testing before installation.

A service network to repair engines and transmissions became ever more necessary as units became more complex. Volvo dispatched a factory mechanic within twenty-four hours directly to a customer who needed repairs. Eventually, the company set up a hotline and arranged for the necessary service. The more primitive models, such as the Model T, could be serviced by any mechanic familiar with rudimentary farm machinery, even to the extent of making custom replacement parts. Not surprisingly, the Model T remained a common sight through the 1940s.

Service problems inhibited both market expansion and the introduction of higher priced models. Scandia's L75 truck, known with affection as the Blowtorch because of the tongue of fire that shot out of the exhaust when changing gears, delighted drivers who refused to accept the more complex improved models. When hydraulic steering arrived, it took five years to overcome buyer resistance, even though this feature made navigating around the many potholes easier. Many considered it nothing but an unnecessary innovation that posed yet another service problem. Easier to repair vehicles, invariably lower priced, found a ready market. General Motors, Ford, and Volkswagen met this demand with the Chevette (1973), the Ford Maverick (1973), and the Beetle (1950), renamed the Fusca in Brazil. Following handy instructions, the car owner supposedly could repair the Chevette and Maverick. The Beetle's simplicity beat them all. Service progressively improved, making for lower costs, marketing of higher priced cars, and increased profits.

Unexpected difficulties hampered production. Assembly and manufacturing plants, generally situated on the outskirts of the city because of space requirements, found that the unpaved roads turned to mud during certain seasons, making transportation of workers from the city impossible. Communication could be frustrating. In the 1960s it sometimes took three days to connect with a functioning telephone line to place a call from São Bernardo do Campo to São Paulo, a mere ten miles away. The then state-owned telephone company could not compete with couriers sent back and forth. Mail delivery could also be erratic until company personnel established a personal and paternalistic relationship with the postal clerks. Overcoming inconvenience became a minor commodity paid for in a variety of ways.

Only the most innovative survived the stress of coping with an industrial frontier every bit as challenging as exploring the backlands. Flexibility, a vital attribute, would again be demonstrated when the oil shocks of the 1970s hit Brazil. In rapid order the industry developed cars, light trucks, and vans able to burn sugarcane alcohol. A recent innovation (2000), clustering of independent parts suppliers around the main plant, would have seemed something akin to a miracle to the early auto industry pioneers.

The Decline of Democratic Brazil

President Kubitschek had overwhelmed the system instead of attempting fundamental political reforms to make democracy actually function. Moreover, the merit-based directive bureaucracy of the 1930s vanished in a sea of political patronage. In fairness to the president, the battle to achieve reforms probably could not have been won. Perhaps reasonably, he settled for development and indeed pulled fifty years of progress out of the hat. Nevertheless, after Kubitschek, the political problems remained unresolved, the country was broke and exhausted, and the middle class was disgruntled and alienated. Brazil's weak party system and personal politics made the weary electorate vulnerable. The individual who stepped forward, Jânio da Silva Quadros, set up the inevitable collapse. He served badly and briefly. While a candidate for the anti-Vargas party, he made it clear he was his own man and campaigned on a personal platform with scarcely a nod to other politicians. His platform, simple and easy to understand, called for the end of corruption and government inefficiency. He adopted a broom as his campaign symbol to the delight of the middle class and traveled to every corner of the country making innumerable speeches. On economic questions he appeared somewhat fuzzy, but against inflation and for progress.

Quadros, a popular mayor of São Paulo (1953–54), went on to be governor of the state (1955–1959) before running for president. He had a reputation as a builder, due more to Kubitschek's money than his own actions, but at the time that was not obvious. A former teacher, he preferred to wear informal open shirts and encouraged citizens to wander into his office to discuss problems or make suggestions. They usually found him with his feet on the desk. A populist in boom times, Quadros did not have a very taxing role to play—being a president in hard times demanded more. Unkempt, his clothes rumpled and shoes scuffed, an unattended shock of black hair partly covering his lined face broken by a bushy mustache,

Quadros looked like Groucho Marx. Clearly, he represented a break from the Vargas gang in power, although his vice president, the nominee of another party, João Goulart, continued to cast the Vargas shadow over the presidential palace.

Jânio Quadros's approach to economic stabilization followed the IMF blueprint. In general, the IMF favored ending subsidies for basic foods such as rice and black beans, higher taxes, and strict control over the amount of money in circulation along with other measures designed to shock the economy into health and break the inflationary psychology of consumers. The IMF tended to ignore the political ramifications of its policies on the well-founded notion that irresponsible politics had gotten the country into the mess in the first place. In a developed economy, harsh measures cause political problems, but in a country with a large, desperately poor population and a middle class barely holding on to its status, they spelled disaster, riots, perhaps even a collapse of the state. Quadros had not adequately considered the impact of his approach to managing the economy; when he did, he quickly reversed himself. Clearly, he had no workable plan in mind.

Foreign policy seemed like a task he could handle. The president decided that he had a role to play in Third World politics. Marshal Tito of Yugoslavia and others had increased their influence and prestige by separating themselves from the two Cold War warriors—the Soviet Union and the United States. Brazil would be neutral, which required reestablishing diplomatic relations with the eastern bloc, including the Soviet Union. Quadros, asserting that trade, not ideology, was the objective, sent a trade mission to China and bestowed the Cruzeiro do Sul (the highest award for foreigners) on guerrilla icon Che Guevara. Given the previously close ties with the United States, most of his balancing went to the left. Quadros envisioned a Brazilian-Afro sub-bloc based on a shared demographic history. He ignored the fact that many of Africa's products competed with those of Brazil. While Quadros's foreign policy irked the United States, President John F. Kennedy liked the Brazilian president, identifying perhaps with a decided outsider.

Quadros soon found himself at odds with congress and effectively stymied. The frustrated president publicly talked about the country's unworkable system and insisted that only a Gaullist solution could work. Charles de Gaulle had rescued France from chronic political turmoil and had created a powerful presidency to monitor a functional prime minister, a structure Quadros believed could do the same for Brazil. In retrospect, his analysis of the situation and the solution seem sensible, but few envisioned Jânio Quadros in the role of Charles de Gaulle. If during the presidential campaign the public overlooked the bizarre aspects of his behavior and focused on his charisma and honesty, they now realized that he was out of his depth, unable to cope effectively with the day-to-day political struggles and certainly not with the challenges of long-range planning. A weak political structure and a politicized bureaucracy could not carry him along. Once the public began to question his sanity he lost the game.

His quirky behavior became the subject of barroom jokes. The president's attempts to ban the unstoppable seemed mind-boggling. Banning bikinis on Copacabana Beach appeared equivalent to reversing the tides, and about as popular. Prohibiting perfume bombs at Carnival was equally fruitless, as were attempts to limit the length of civil servants' coffee breaks. His chauffeur reported that the president carefully calculated the exact middle of the back seat of his limousine and shifted around until he found it. Compulsive behavior and inappropriate use of authority suggested a mental unraveling. The stress drove the president to retire to his private screening room with a bottle of Scotch whiskey to watch movies.

Muddled by stress and alcohol he resigned the presidency. His logic, easy enough to follow, assumed that the army would not accept Vice President João Goulart as president and would press for a solution along the lines Quadros had suggested already. A panicked congress then would adopt the Gaullist solution and grant him emergency powers. Nothing went according to plan. Congress accepted his resignation, but the army decided to deal with the issue of resignation and succession as two separate items. Quadros, shocked and disappointed, left for Europe, making a parting statement that verged on the incomprehensible. Claiming that he had been forced out, he would return "to show everyone who is the scum in this country"—presumably, those who had accepted his resignation. Having been president for less than a year, Jânio Quadros left Brazil in shambles. If he had stayed longer, he would likely have been removed.[13]

The End of the String

The not accidental timing of the resignation came as Goulart toured a hog farm in Communist China. The vice president decided to fly to Paris rather than risk a return until the situation stabilized. Goulart's brother-in-law, Leonel Brizola, the governor of Rio Grande do Sul, cleverly set the stage for a compromise. The commander of the third army, stationed in Rio Grande do Sul, sided with Goulart and the governor, agreeing to repel, if necessary, any federal force sent to the state. Goulart then returned to Brazil by way of Rio Grande do Sul. The split within the military ensured his political survival, but the conditions of his return would have to be worked out. The top military officers in the cabinet had made it clear they would not accept Goulart as president—now they had to compromise. The arrangement saved face, but did so by drastically altering the constitutional structure establishing a parliamentary system. A symbolic president with actual power vested in a prime minister seemed a brilliant solution. A hastily passed constitutional amendment made it all legal, while doing great damage to the notion of democratic constitutional procedures. Tancredo Neves, who later became the first elected president after the military regime ended in 1985, served as prime minister. A plebiscite set for January 1963 allowed a vote on whether to retain the parliamentary model or revert to the old system. Goulart had been placed on probation.

By the time the plebiscite returned full presidential power to Goulart, it was too late. A three-year economic plan in 1963 promised a return to fast growth while controlling inflation. Few besides economist Celso Furtado, the plan's author, and Goulart appeared willing to take the gamble. In the absence of confidence, many foreign suppliers demanded payment in advance, and investment virtually stopped. Those who could transfer assets out of the country did so. A host of small-time currency exchanges functioned illegally. Many accepted personal checks in hard currencies, which in turn they sold to travelers. The public ignored price and rent controls. By early 1964 inflation exceeded 100 percent. Both the left and the right began planning for a sudden collapse of the state and an opportunity to seize control. It seemed a replay of the late 1930s.

Goulart appeared to be losing legitimacy as fast as inflation accelerated. A similar process had undercut Jânio Quadros in his final months. Rumors that his wife was in the midst of an affair made the point that, never mind the country, Goulart could not even control his own household. One of the president's legs was shorter than the other, which now became the butt of cruel jokes. Moreover, his mother died, allegedly opening the way for his brother-in-law, Lionel Brizola, to dominate and direct the floundering president. Goulart found himself transformed from the heir to Vargas into an ineffectual, pathetic figure. Politically, he had become an orphan. Neither the left nor the right seemed willing to take him in, but the left thought he could be used.

A desperate Goulart moved to the left, lured by the hope of finding a political base and holding off the military. He began to talk in generalities about reforms including land reform, expropriation of oil refineries, and broadening the electorate to include illiterates. The vagueness of his plan suggested he intended to institute radical measures. Rural violence in the northeast revolving around peasant leagues organized by Francisco Julião alarmed landholders. Many feared imminent revolution. Talk of Goulart becoming a Communist led to further hysteria. Allegedly, he had in mind a godless, Communist society and a Soviet-style economy. Mothers, priests, and the faithful marched in protest over actions that threatened the foundation of the Catholic family. The president's plan to unionize enlisted military personnel indicated the level of desperation. Without control over the enlisted men, the officers could not direct military force against the state—unfortunately for the president, an obvious and transparent ploy. Meanwhile, the radical left also believed it could infiltrate the enlisted ranks and immobilize the military—again, a little too obvious. If anything, these plans moved up the inevitable military intervention before the officer corps lost control. Goulart's address at the Rio de Janeiro Auto Club, where he spoke to a meeting of sergeants, represented the final straw. An angry and alarmed military began to move.

Through various channels the position of the United States would be ascertained. President Lyndon B. Johnson, fearful that Brazil hovered on the verge of collapse, civil war, and a possible Communist takeover, threw in the towel on Brazilian democracy. Indeed, there seemed to be few in Brazil itself who supported its continuation. The United States prepared to assist if necessary, including sending oil tankers to keep the army supplied in the event of prolonged fighting. Colonel Vernon Walters, the U.S. military attaché, picked up hints as to the timing but not the exact moment. Walters understood that any interference from Washington might backfire. Many expected armed resistance. The left declared that the working and lower classes would fight in the streets if the military intervened—the army expected at worst an ugly confrontation. Military conspirators believed, correctly, that the coup would succeed or fail within days.

The army moved in force on March 31–April 1, 1964. Rio and other major cities found tanks at all the appropriate choke points. Teargas drifted across likely demonstration sites. Troops occupied government buildings and radio and television stations. Brasília became a political island cut off from the rest of the country. Military and civilian police arrested union leaders, peasant league organizers, radical students, ex-president Kubitschek, and any politicians who could rally resistance. Within forty-eight hours the military had established physical control. Mass demonstrations and street fighting never materialized. A relieved President Johnson quickly recognized the new regime. João Goulart prudently fled to Uruguay.

Notes

1. The work of Stanley E. Hilton (see Bibliography) neatly captures the tenor of the times.
2. Originally the Office for Coordination of Commercial and Cultural Relations between the Americas created on August 16, 1941. The name changed the following year.
3. Macumba is the popular term for any Afro-Brazilian religion. Originally, it referred to a sect in Rio de Janeiro.
4. Arranging for ads or buying large quantities of the magazine without the *Digest's* knowledge may have occurred, although no evidence has been found to support my suspicion. For a company history, see James Playsted Wood, *Of Lasting Interest: The Story of the Reader's Digest* (New York, 1967).
5. Brazilian winter issue could easily be mistaken for German uniforms—a detail not fully considered. Soldiers of the 10th Mountain Division on several occasions fired on Brazilians in the confusion of battle.
6. Benjamin Vargas represented the family's dark side. An incident at the Copacabana Palace Hotel illustrated the problem. Drunk and losing money at roulette, he laid his revolver on the table and loudly announced his bet, "black seventeen." The ball dropped into nine. As he reached for his gun the quick-thinking croupier announced in a loud voice, "black seventeen." Ricardo Boechat, *Copacabana Palace: A Hotel and Its History* (Rio de Janeiro, 1999), 71.
7. Bossa nova may be translated as the new trend.
8. The girl later identified as Heloísa (Pinto) Pinheiro did not enjoy an easy life. In her late fifties (2002) she opened a boutique named after the song title, only to have the heirs object and take legal action. In the legal battle the Cariocas supported the still beautiful "Helô."
9. The contrast with the passing of the frontier in the United States is striking. Rather than isolated homesteads, Brazil put down a capital city.
10. In the United States the interstate highway system, begun after World War II, ended regional isolation and changed the relationship between city and countryside. It would do the same in Brazil.
11. "Tropical country" is a code term for perceived Brazilian incapacity.
12. Many amusing stories are told about attempts to meet the weight requirement. One well-known company slightly misjudged and solved the problem by adding a nonfunctional iron bar to the chassis.
13. Quadros attempted a comeback, running unsuccessfully for governor of São Paulo in 1962 and 1982. Then, to everyone's surprise, he was elected mayor of São Paulo in 1986.

CHAPTER FIVE

Under Army Command

The Military Technocrats

Ten days after the coup, a three-man junta made up of military cabinet members issued an Institutional Act giving the executive overwhelming authority. Francisco Campos, the intellectual father and drafter of Vargas's authoritarian Constitution of 1937, drew up the key Institutional Act; others would follow. These Acts automatically became part of the then-current (1946) constitution. Campos declared it an "authentic revolution . . . [that] embodies the interest and will of the nation, not the self-interest and will of a special group. . . . In the name of the people they [the military] exercised the Popular Sovereignty, which ultimately rests solely with the people. The new government . . . will assure the exercise of power in the exclusive interests of the Nation." Vargas would certainly have appreciated the sleight of hand, particularly the claim of popular sovereignty by the military. The Revolution of 1964 chose General Humberto de Alenças Castelo Branco as president.

Castelo Branco, a veteran of the FEB, entered the army in 1918 from a military family in the northeast. Physically solid, short in stature, with a calming manner, the general carried with him an aura of stability in clearly unstable times. He presented himself to the nation as a man of middle-class values. To demonstrate, he made public a list of his property—indeed, a modest accumulation. The list included a three-year-old Aero-Willys car (an inexpensive automobile), an apartment in Rio purchased with a deposit from his wife's inheritance and ten years of monthly payments, and a few shares in Brazilian companies. Who could doubt his middle-class standing and virtues of patience, thrift, honesty, faithfulness, and, to top it off, his trust in Brazilian companies as an economic nationalist?

How Castelo interpreted events could not be ascertained immediately. His generation of army officers had been schooled in anticommunism at the Superior War College (Escola Superior de Guerra).

The War College tended to overestimate the efficiency and danger of Soviet influence. While now-open Soviet archives are filled with accounts of plots, conspiracies, and attempts to gain influence in South America, ideological rigidity made them much less effective than the army feared. They understood, however, that grinding poverty, maldistribution of wealth, and vast numbers of landless peasants made the political system vulnerable to the extent it might fall into the hands of the Communists. In short, there was plenty of harsh reality mixed with paranoia to meet everyone's needs. Castelo Branco had two major objectives, seemingly interrelated: stop the spread of communism and restore the economy. Unimpeded by politics, the president proceeded to stabilize the economy. Initially, his regime cranked up the printing presses, flooding the country with huge amounts of paper money. The currency fell on international markets and exports and imports declined. In early 1965 the government restricted currency in circulation, reducing inflation progressively so that by 1967 it fell to 24.5 percent.

The government's carefully calibrated measures revived the economy, which grew by 4 percent in 1966 and by 5 percent the following year and produced a trade surplus of $200 million. Significantly, manufactured products constituted the second most profitable export after coffee. Castelo Branco encouraged foreign investment, believing it would stimulate industry and technology transfer. He rejected the idea of nationalized industries, fearing this action would open the door to communism. Foreign investment in 1968 constituted only 8 percent of all industrial investment, but to many the proportion appeared to be much more. The United States and Europe supplied the bulk of investments. Castelo's economic policy could not have been implemented other than by an authoritarian regime, a point made clear when the 1965 elections returned candidates hostile to the government in nine out of eleven states, including Minas Gerais and Rio de Janeiro (then the state of Guanabara).

Democracy Training

To the president, the 1965 election results showed that the electorate still needed to learn responsibility. Their backhanded rejection of the military government angered Castelo but did not deter him. The second Institutional Act dissolved all political parties and initiated indirect election for the two highest offices. It also allowed the president to pack the Supreme Court with five new judges and restrict the scope of the court's activities. The amendment authorized military courts to try subversives, permitted the government to cancel political rights on an individual basis, and increased federal powers to intervene in the states, among other restrictions. A third Act (February 5, 1966) authorized the state legislature to select the state governor, who in turn selected the mayor of the state capital. The regime set out to destroy the traditional role of state governors as the mediating force between the federal government and the people, represented by the municipal level. Civilian politics remained alive, even vigorous, at the lowest organized level, except for the municipalities in the state capital. The intent—to centralize control—freed municipal officials from domination by state governors and the political influence of the capital city. Those interested in politics found municipal office and local issues one of the few areas where they had freedom to move within the well-understood limits of the military regime. With this important exception, only the superstructure of democracy remained in place. The restrictions eliminated most aspects of direct democracy while permitting controlled indirect participation. The formation of an official party, along with an official opposition party, strengthened the notion of being retrained in democracy. A predictable joke distinguished between them on the basis of their response to authority—the official party responded with a "Yes, Sir!" while the opposition answered with a "Yes." The new Constitution of 1967 legitimized the authoritarian regime. A National Security Law in the same year permitted the government to arrest and imprison anyone deemed to be a threat.

Castelo Branco did not attempt to name his successor. He also rejected pressure to remain president. Nevertheless, Marshal Artur da Costa e Silva, who declared his candidacy, clearly would not have been his choice. Congress went through the motions and elected Costa e Silva. Castelo Branco died in an aircraft accident shortly after the new president took office. Costa e Silva, a milder individual, allowed more freedom, setting off a wave of demonstrations and demands and a resurgence of congressional independence, all of which ended when hard-line (*linha dura*) military officers forced the president to declare dictatorial powers, disband congress, impose censorship, broadly suspend political rights, and permit the arrest of suspected individuals. The fifth Institutional Act also suspended the recently crafted Constitution of 1967. Subsequently, the Constitution of 1969 incorporated further repressive modifications. The police took ex-president Juscelino Kubitschek, Carlos Lacerda, and a number of journalists into custody. Foreign correspondents had to submit their dispatches for approval. The president, a reluctant convert to the *linha dura*, declared the new restrictions necessary to deal with subversion and corruption. The long shadow of fear and intimidation, including self-censorship, fell across the land.

The Dirty War

The easing of restrictions by Costa e Silva, before the internal coup of the *linha dura*, identified individuals and organizations potentially able to challenge the government. These included the Brazilian Mothers' Union, the various university student federations, and advocates of land reform and peasants' rights. The National Intelligence Service (SNI), a secret police agency, directed the social purges considered crucial. A network of paid informers plunged into their work with vigor to supply voluminous but often inaccurate information. Military intelligence monitored the correspondence of suspects, even potential suspects, as well as telephone usage. Agents sat in on university classes and reported allegedly questionable views. A purge of unreliable university professors removed those considered left-wing. Fernando Henrique Cardoso, one of many driven out, dismissed, or abruptly retired, went on to become president of Brazil in the 1990s.

In 1968 student protests soon drew in other elements opposed to the regime. A massive demonstration in Rio of thousands of protesters, clerics, professionals, artists, students, and others, known as the March of the 100,000, alarmed the army. The number of protesters made the use of force to break up the march impossible, but the government now prohibited all public demonstrations. Pro-regime students at the private Colegio MacKenzie later attacked the University of São Paulo School of Philosophy leaving it in shambles. At the end of the year police arrested 1,000 members of the National Student Union (UNE) meeting in the interior of São Paulo. This left only a few possibilities for nonviolent opposition.

The music festival era begun a year after the military takeover served as a tolerated outlet for political frustration. Lyrics expressed dismay with the regime and called for social justice and toleration. The fine, but unpredictable, line between the tolerated and unacceptable acted to restrain all but the boldest singers. A protest song of Geraldo Vandré (Geraldo Pedrosa de Araújo Dias), "Not to Say I Didn't Speak of Flowers," which won second place in Rio's International Song Festival in 1968, rallied student opposition. A journalist, giving in to hyperbole, called it a Brazilian "Marseillaise." The military regime fruitlessly banned the song for ten years. A fearful Vandré wandered around the world, returning in 1973 only to be arrested, then released after he publicly disavowed the political use of his music. Not surprisingly, some protest music irritated the authorities more than others. Tropicalism (Tropicália), developed by Caetano Veloso and Gilberto Gil, mixed protest with style and humor. The performers dressed in lavish tropical costumes along the lines of Hollywood at its most imaginative, with outrageous hairstyles, in imitation of Carmen Miranda—in general, they had a lot of fun. Unfortunately, they failed to amuse the generals. Arrested by the police in December 1968, Veloso and Gil spent two months in jail and then were under house arrest before they prudently moved to London (1969–1972). Dealing with the organized and visible opposition proved relatively easy—perhaps too easy.

Inevitably, the opposition moved underground. Guerrilla groups, made up mainly of urban middle-class students, began to employ violence against the state. Carlos Marighella, a Marxist, offered guidance and encouragement in his widely circulated *Manual of the Urban Guerrilla*. Marighella wrongly believed that small, highly organized guerrilla units could topple a military dictatorship. The military had long claimed to be protecting Brazil from subversion; now it had proof. The existence of leftist guerrilla groups provided justification for the past and excused extra-legal and harsh measures to contain the threat in the present.

Money to finance guerrilla operations came from a string of bank robberies. The guerrillas took cover in the favelas on the ill-founded assumption that the poor and downtrodden would identify with them and shield them from the police. Making a big splash internationally could be achieved by high-profile kidnapping. They started with the ambassador from the country with the largest investments— the American ambassador, Charles Burke Elbrick, in 1969. In return for radio, television, and newspaper presentations of guerrilla manifestos and the freeing of fifteen political prisoners flown out of the country to Mexico, his captors released the frightened diplomat. The guerrillas went on to kidnap the Swiss, German, and Japanese representatives, in order of their country's rank in foreign investments— a subtle point missed by most. Military and civilian police authorities, unleashed to break up the guerrilla groups, resorted to torture, assassination, and simple disappearance without any trace. Students— in practice, middle-class individuals between the ages of eighteen and thirty, who appeared to be suspicious or who moved in questionable circles—became targets. Torturing individuals who then denounced others provided useful information, but at the expense of many innocent people. Direct orders to torture and kill, avoided except in rare instances, shielded superior authority from blame. Agents responded to vague orders by devising their own sweeps and deciding when and where to use extreme measures. Accountability became so diffuse that no one appeared to be in charge. Sadistic zealots inevitably committed atrocious acts in the interest of rooting out subversives and eliminating the guerrillas and their sympathizers.[1]

The poisonous residue of the aptly named "dirty war" continued to surface unexpectedly. For example, the unresolved Arena Riocentro incident came back to life eighteen years later. It involved an attempted bombing of a concert on April 30, 1981, that attracted some 20,000 believed to be antigovernment sympathizers. Just minutes before the show was to begin, with the arena packed, two bombs exploded in the parking lot that killed an army sergeant and severely wounded a captain. Both worked for army intelligence. An official investigation declared them victims of a terrorist attack. Most concluded that the two intended to bomb Riocentro. Nevertheless, the case would be swept under the carpet. In 1999 the Riocentro case was reopened, much to the anger of the army. In similar fashion, accusations threw into confusion the 1999 nomination of João Batista Campelo as chief of the federal police when a priest claimed he had been tortured under Campelo's supervision.

The dirty war's legacy remains to embarrass politicians understandably reluctant to complicate the present with a past that most prefer to forget. In the case of Campelo, President Fernando Henrique Cardoso, himself purged during the military regime, refused to withdraw the nomination. During televised testimony watched by the entire country, Campelo denied everything. A diligent reporter, however, found documentary evidence to the contrary, and Campelo withdrew. The use of state counterterror has left innumerable political land mines to haunt Brazil well into the twenty-first century. Significantly, the army rapidly regained its popularity, leaving the task of dealing with history to reluctant politicians.

Military Men and Clerics

The Cold War served to stimulate competition among the various systems pledged to address and remedy the social ills of Latin America. The Cuban Revolution shocked more than just Washington. The contention that the Catholic Church collaborated with the elite to ignore the subjugation of the poor disturbed churchmen. Many priests and bishops believed that such charges contained an uncomfortable element of truth. The dirty war posed a dilemma for the Church, which, fearful that communism threatened the nation, had supported the military coup of 1964. To complicate matters, the coup coincided with the Second Vatican Council (Vatican II), convened by Pope John XXIII in October 1962. Vatican II presented a new agenda and empowered lay Catholics to aggressively assist in the task of aiding the poor. In 1963 the papal encyclical *Pacem in Terris* incorporated the United Nations Universal Declaration of Human Rights (1948) as part of Church teachings. A bold new direction put the Church in open conflict with the state. Regional meetings in Medellín, Colombia, in 1968 and in Puebla, Mexico, in 1979 confirmed the new approach to social justice and identified concrete, practical help to Latin America's poor as a major objective. Vatican II, long on Catholic moral principles, provided few clear guidelines as to how individual priests were to respond. Serving the poor, downtrodden, and neglected appeared to require direct action to alleviate social and political injustice in the present for the existing generation, not long-term amelioration. Some 2,000 of Brazil's priests, or 15 percent, left the clergy to minister directly to the poor as they personally decided how best to do so. Bishops lost their directive ability as many chose to listen to what they considered to be a higher authority. Living among the poor, and bluntly condemning those who appeared to condone suffering, meant ending the Church's traditional spiritual and social alliance with the upper classes. The very people who controlled all the important temporal aspects of the country found themselves morally tainted. They reacted with anger and a deep sense of betrayal.

Christian Base Communities (CBCs) became the organizational representation of the new Catholic agenda. Lay leaders elected by the community shared responsibility with nuns and priests for the group's activities, theoretically bringing all believers to the same level. A community usually numbered from twenty-five to thirty members directed by grassroots lay leadership, reinforced by the moral support of the clergy. They sought to change the immediate situation. Fatalism and despair, common among the rural and urban poor, gave way to new and demanding activism.

Politicians, particularly in rural areas unaccustomed to aggressive pressure from below, viewed the communities as radicals and their plans as semi-Marxist or worse. Demands for land, medical attention, schools, cooperatives, and all the rights and privileges that seemed to be provided to the more favored classes made up the core of their demands for social justice. Direct action in the face of an unresponsive state challenged government control and legitimacy. The militant stance of the CBCs alarmed the government and local authorities. The military government's fear of Communist subversion and the use of Marxist terms by the communities contributed to official hostility. In the end, officials chose to view priests and nuns who worked with the poor as either Communist dupes or even hardcore Communists who had subverted the Church. The Catholic hierarchy, while somewhat ambivalent about the increasingly secular radicalism of a number of nuns and priests, hesitated to restrain their activities, being acutely aware of the moral dilemma posed by Vatican II.

Not all clergy became radicalized. A strong conservative element within the Brazilian Church felt that Vatican II had gone too far and struggled to regain control. Nevertheless, in the post-1964 political climate, a radicalized clergy seemed to be a serious threat to the regime. It became a self-fulfilling fear as state violence forced a divided clergy to unite against abuses. Arrests of priests and lay leaders, torture, kidnapping, murder, and lesser forms of harassment, such as monitoring sermons and false charges, including homosexuality and womanizing, aimed at embarrassing bishops and others, resulted in a state of clerical siege. During the successful hunt for and subsequent ambush of Carlos Marighella in São Paulo in 1969, the police tortured Dominican friars known to support the guerrillas. The authorities then used the episode to imply that the Church broadly supported terrorists. Unknown assailants murdered the assistant to Archbishop D. Helder Câmara. Even D. Helder feared for his life. In the past, the army had honored the archbishop. In Paris in 1970, when D. Helder publicly denounced torture, the government mounted a smear campaign that in the end denied him the Nobel Peace Prize. In 1973 the government shut down the radio station of the archdiocese of São Paulo.

The issue of betrayal provided much of the damaging tension that underpinned the military state's relationship with the Church. Many at the top levels of the military considered themselves devout, traditional Catholics who had been betrayed by a subverted Church and by a clergy all too ready to be duped. A number of clerics worried that alienating the state risked strengthening non-Catholic sects, many of which had become rabidly anti-Communist and strongly supportive of the regime. Such sects, particularly the Pentecostals, could quickly provide additional pastors and organize new congregations, while the Catholic Church had few priests and could not easily or rapidly train more. In order to avoid a complete, perhaps irreparable, break between the Church and the state, a secret informal group—the Bipartite Commission—brought the two sides together to talk, complain, and on occasion sharply protest. In the so-called leaden days, when a way out of the political and moral impasse could scarcely be envisioned, the group provided semiofficial contact. While never acknowledged officially, its existence during the worst days of the dirty war (1970–1974) tempered the extreme views of both sides, as the Commission sought to find common interests.

Brasil: *Ame-o ou Deixe-o* (Love It or Leave It)

Collectively, political exiles are symptomatic of the afflictions of the country they leave behind. Unlike forced expulsion, which is a physical act performed by others, voluntary exile is both a rational decision and a deep emotional response. Those who abandoned Brazil after 1964, and later during the years of repression and the dirty war, left with a dark vision and little faith in the future. They confronted some uncomfortable truths. That the coup succeeded with so little opposition and then consolidated power so rapidly could not be blamed convincingly on apathy or on the United States. The apparent acceptance of the generals and the ready extension of legitimacy by all the country's institutions stunned activists. They questioned their own role in the disaster. Many wondered whether, in their pursuit of a fantasy, they had betrayed themselves and the nation. Others, particularly in the creative arts, left because they felt they could not express their individuality in such circumstances. The number of political expatriates appeared relatively small and, indeed, the technocratic elite remained, rushing to staff the military's new agencies and to create the economic miracle, among other things.

Western and eastern Europe, Australia, Britain, Mexico, Chile, Cuba, and, to a lesser extent, the United States received the exiles. Those who chose to go to Chile moved on with the military coup of 1973 in that country. Fernando Henrique Cardoso, whose own moment in power could not have been envisioned at that time, returned from a Chilean and Paris interlude in 1968. He later declared that the military regime had done him an enormous personal favor by forcing him out of the predictable routine of a university professor. As a group, the exiles had diverse experiences ranging from the ideological rigidity of the eastern bloc, to the democratic welfare states of Scandinavia, the one-party regime in Mexico, and the personalistic regime of Communist Cuba. Events in Chile undoubtedly provided their own lessons. Many ended up in Paris, plunging into its vibrant intellectual milieu—the last of the Republic of Letters. In France, Cardoso joined a distinguished circle of social scientists that included Celso Furtado. Paris became a favorite stop on the exile circuit. A constant stream of visitors made for a floating seminar that engaged some of the best minds of Brazilian letters.

Cultural exiles, dependent on their roots for inspiration and acceptance, generally fared poorly. The London exile of Caetano Veloso and Gilberto Gil ended Tropicalism and what might have been a longer-running musical style. Chico Buarque de Hollanda, whose music had a substantial audience in Europe and the United States, found some temporary relief in Italy. Vandré suffered in exile. Most voluntary exiles returned in the late 1970s, as the military progressively eased itself out of power. Many returned to drop out rather than resist even symbolically. Although Tropicalism could not be revived, its championing of counterculture remained to provide a refuge for the disillusioned. Only a small percentage of artists became active guerrillas, and the violence did not create its own cultural icons.

Development, Wealth, and the Income Pie

Military planners, well aware of social problems, believed that poverty and income disparity constituted a phase common to all developing countries as they struggled to muster resources and modernize. The immediate debate revolved around the income pie. Industrial development greatly expanded the country's gross domestic product (GDP). From 1967 to 1973, as a result of the government's economic strategy and favorable conditions, the country experienced a boom. In 1970, 54 percent of the population lived in poverty; by 1980 the figure had fallen to 25 percent. Nevertheless, the gap between the rich and the poor widened in percentage terms. The argument against distributing income turned on the need to amass capital for development—premature distribution supposedly would leave everyone with an insignificant slice of the national pie. Meanwhile, real wages, adjusted for inflation, declined drastically in the northeast and drove internal migration southward, in turn retarding wages in the nonskilled industrial sector. Relative prosperity and continued poverty showed checkered regional patterns largely related to illiteracy and low levels of education.

Educational policy had short-term political and economic objectives. Improved access to education meant expansion of higher education, which could make a quick contribution to development. Primary and secondary levels would not be totally ignored. At the lower levels many of the reforms suggested by the New Schoolers of the 1920s technically became law, including compulsory education through eighth grade and professional (vocational) education at the secondary level. The attempt to end the quality gap between public and private schools and focus on primary and secondary education would soon be abandoned. New revenue in the form of a federal wage tax on employers (salario-educação) solely for primary school use recognized the need for a more stable financial base, even if it made only a marginal difference at the time. An adult literacy program (Movimento Brasileiro de Alfabetização—MOBRAL) had some impact. Nevertheless, transferring responsibility for primary and secondary education to the states and the municipalities underscored its low priority. Lack of standards, low salaries, and poor management produced predictable results. While much more of the population had access, as promised, less than half of those who started finished the primary level. Those who did could expect only to do marginally better than those who dropped out by the fourth grade. Social programs such as public health screening and training along with school lunches had a positive effect, but clearly the government did not expect much of a development contribution to come from this level. Public primary and secondary education funneled a relatively small number of students into federally funded universities.

The regime undertook a total restructuring of the university system in 1968. Entrance examinations, along with social barriers, effectively made the universities into middle-class institutions. Higher education received lavish amounts of funding especially after 1968. In addition, the government provided support for suitably prepared students to study abroad. The pattern of an inverted educational pyramid evident under the Vargas administration remained in place, much for the same reasons. The amount of funds devoted to education as a percentage of GDP declined under the military government, although in real terms spending increased.

Land reform, intended to hold desperate surplus rural workers in the countryside so they would not flee to the cities, conflicted with government efforts to stimulate large-scale commercial agricultural ventures using the latest technology. There were vast amounts of land, much of it fragile rain forest in the Amazon basin and elsewhere. Nevertheless, even in the rain forest the government promoted large-scale cattle raising, nonsustainable lumber operations, and mining. The transformation of agriculture into farm factories in many parts of the developed world provided support for favoring large-scale enterprises over landless peasants. In fact, breaking up large holdings seemed retrograde. Agricultural exports, from soybeans with an excellent market in Japan and elsewhere, to orange juice concentrate with demand in the United States, to chicken and meat products and other items, depended on an economy of scale in order to compete in the world market. It was said that one orange plantation had more trees than the state of Florida. In effect, landless peasants would have to wait until they could be absorbed into the modern economy as rural workers. Land reform as a matter of social justice had few proponents among planners. Moreover, the military regime tended to equate social justice with the radical left. To many officers, any concession in that direction opened the door to socialism and, more to the point, might derail development.

Pragmatism, rather than simple callousness or ideology, explained much of the regime's actions. Social programs in some areas received admirable attention. To make sure that the states and municipalities implemented policy decisions made at the top, the government set up revenue-sharing funds (*fundos de participação de estados e municipios*). Other funds provided welfare programs, such as a worker security scheme supported by a payroll tax that became a source for financing housing and public health. Virtually everyone received universal medical care in public facilities or in subsidized private clinics and hospitals. While underfunded relative to need, with often indifferent care, the system nevertheless established an important entitlement and state obligation. The National Social Security Institute (INPS) centralized pensions, welfare assistance, and health care on the national level and included rural workers in a universal pension plan. Planners met social needs while creating pools of money to meet capital demands. In the process they overlooked the danger of dependence on payroll taxes. The ups and downs of the economy could not provide predictable revenue. As a result, pension plans became a major problem in the 1990s, to the point of endangering the entire economy.

Rural Unions

A new rural labor structure emerged in the late 1950s and early 1960s. The spread of commercial agriculture beyond traditional crops and regions changed the relationship between landowners and peasants throughout the country. The old semipatriarchal arrangement, which mixed paid labor with nonmonetary privileges such as a right to farm small plots or use what limited machinery the landholder might have, could not be adapted to meet the needs of commercial agriculture. Landowners who shifted to commercial agriculture became employers, and the peasants, workers. In response to this reality, the last president before the military takeover, João Goulart, signed the Rural Worker Statute in March 1963. Under this law a 1 percent tax to be paid on commercial agricultural products went toward social services for rural workers. It served more as a symbolic recognition of the altered relationship. The law required operators to estimate and pay the tax. The absence of enforcement resulted in minimal collection.

The leaders of the coup of 1964 also realized the extent of the transformation of labor relations in the countryside. They brought to this understanding an ingrained sense of the utility of corporatism, absorbed into the military mind-set in the1930s. Once the consolidation-of-power stage ended, the military regime issued two decrees that modified the earlier statute. The 1 percent tax was now imposed on the proceeds of the sale of the crop. This change made it easier to calculate and collect the tax. Another decree established the Fund for the Assistance of the Rural Worker (FUNRURAL) to operate dental and medical clinics. An oversight directorate of FUNRURAL included members of the National Confederation of Agricultural Workers (CONTAG). Contracts with rural unions to administer assistance with government funding linked them with the regime. The strings attached could be loose, but remained strings nonetheless.

The government's approach to labor relations encouraged the formation of rural unions, which then provided medical and pension benefits. Unions were given the legal authority to determine who could be a member, in other words, to decide who was a rural worker. The fragmentation of the rural population into workers and others duplicated the situation in urban areas. Low levels of disposable income of members could be boosted noticeably with a relatively modest increase. Many organizations came to be associated with their medical clinical efforts, rather than with the traditional struggle for better working conditions and higher wages. Conservative union tendencies suited the regime, which always had the option of delaying the transfer of funds if it thought such a move would be politically useful. Rural union leaders built up their organizations, trained others, including Chico Mendes of the rubber tappers' union, and learned to manipulate and make deals within the system. State-level CONTAG leaders often seemed more interested in their own career enhancement than in improving the working lives of their members.

Development at Any Cost

The curriculum of the Superior War College drew its economic orientation from the Anglo-American experience and its apparent success in reinflating the economy to meet the challenge of World War II and the reconstruction of Europe. As a result, economists acquired enormous prestige as miracle workers, able to plan and execute rational long-range development schemes. The military government consequently placed geopolitical development above all else. In its view, underutilization of resources historically retarded the process of development, delayed the modernization of the nation, and endangered security. The army had supported Vargas's call for a "march to the west" to develop and protect Brazil's vast underpopulated interior. Little could be done at the time. Nevertheless, the idea became part of the grand scheme. The building of Brasília and the new road network opened vast areas to development. The government planned to continue and if possible increase the momentum but without what it believed to be the political irresponsibility of the past. With the completion in 1965 of the link between the new capital and Belém at the mouth of the river network, the government started construction of the Transamazonian Highway. A secondary network of roads branched out from the main trunk to open up previously isolated areas of the Amazon basin. Planners showed no concern for the extent to which economic projects ignored the preservation of nature. Economists thought of nature as awaiting transformation into some usable form, or as a storehouse of exploitable raw materials. The developmental mind-set, long evident, particularly in the army, remained the guiding paradigm.

With the coup of 1964, the time for action arrived. President Castelo Branco called for Operation Amazonia, established a new development agency, and reorganized credit resources to spur private development. Tax incentives transformed Manaus in the heart of the Amazon basin into a tax-free industrial port in 1967. The initiative, geopolitical as well as economic, was intended to attract people into the region as fast as possible. A development plan (1967–1971) encouraged private investment in large-scale agriculture, cattle raising, industry, and forest product projects. A second plan (1972–1974) assigned priority to roads and the immediate creation of smaller farms, followed by a return to large-scale projects with the resources to propel rapid exploitation.

Meanwhile, the lure of land served more as a social panacea than an actual remedy. The government planned to resettle 100,000 families. Under the Program for National Development (PIN) the regime organized the National Institute for Colonization and Agrarian Reform (INCRA). On the road network, INCRA planned a string of urban-rural settlements. Each settler would receive a plot of one square kilometer. In another location, forty-eight identical government-constructed houses would make up the *agrovila*, with a school, clinic, and community center. In theory, *agrovilas* combined urban living and a rural economic base. Clearly, social science planners forgot about Henry Ford's failed Fordlandia rubber plantation experiment and human nature. By 1978, INCRA had settled only 7,674 families. These people abandoned the *agrovilas*, often dismantling the assigned houses bit by bit, and moved to a preferred site. After the two oil-price shocks of the 1970s, the government could afford to make only nominal investments to resettle landless peasants.

Planned development in the Amazon, because of the notion of large amounts of land for the taking, also attracted squatters hoping to combine working the land with casual wage labor. A large-scale rice plantation in the Mayo River Valley lured so many desperate peasants that the area planned for development expanded threefold, much of it illegally cleared. The existence of unused land created a false psychological escape valve. Expectations ran far ahead of reality.

Deforestation—the burning of the rain forest by land speculators and large and small developers as well as by farmers—proceeded without regulation. International protests merely provided further proof that others sought to exert control over Brazil's sovereign territory. Lip service, hand wringing, and underfunded attempts to protect the rain forest did little to mask the geopolitical satisfaction of the government. By 1980 some 3,000 kilometers of primitive roads crisscrossed the region. The government hoped to pave at least the major ones, maintain bridges, and scrape dirt side roads. Plans underestimated the initial cost of paving and the expense of maintaining the road network. As a result, potholes, collapsed bridges, erosion, and washouts made large stretches of primary and secondary roads almost impassable. Once started, road building in the Amazon took on an inevitability of its own, far beyond the capacity of the state to control. Degradation of land along the road system further segmented the forest. In a desperate search for a better life, immigrants followed the roads to their dreams only to find that any agricultural or forest products they harvested had to be marketed at low prices because of high transportation costs.

To the military regime unplanned settlements, unregulated destruction of the rain forest, and other problems seemed a reasonable price to pay for development of an area long viewed as dangerously isolated. The population of the northern region jumped from some 2.5 million in 1960 to an estimated 8.5 million when the army relinquished power in 1985. Development reached a self-sustaining pace in the period between 1970 and 1985. As late as 1960 only twenty-two cities in the north had populations exceeding 5,000. Belém and Manaus, the two principal urban poles of the region, had 100,000 inhabitants. By century's end, around 150 cities had populations over 5,000, eight of them over 100,000, while Belém and Manaus exceeded one million.

The landless, poverty-stricken marginal collectors, small farmers, and Indians found themselves on their own in the face of government neglect and the hired gunmen of large-scale speculators and developers. Bishop D. Pedro Casaldaliga published a 120-page pastoral letter titled *The Church in the Amazon in Conflict with the Latifundium and Social Marginalization*, which detailed the impact and the atrocities against Indians and squatters. The presence in the state of Pará of a well-organized guerrilla group made D. Pedro's activities extremely threatening to the government. Some 5,000 soldiers and numerous security personnel struggled for several years to crush the guerrillas. Meanwhile, beatings, torture, and the murder of priests and suspected activists appeared to be part of the development process. Bishop Casaldaliga barely escaped death. A disapproving World Bank accused Brazil of encouraging economic growth at the expense of social justice.

The development process set in motion by the government brought new interests and settlers into cultural and economic conflict with the Indian population at an accelerated pace. Deculturalization—the reduction of previously isolated groups unprepared for civilized reality to urban misery, poverty, prostitution, and alcoholism—appalled the international community. To the government such reactions ignored the country's history. Miscegenation among Indians, Africans, and Europeans, beginning in the sixteenth century, had created the Brazilian people. International organizations generally took extreme positions, which the regime relatively easily shrugged off. In fact, not all indigenous peoples reacted helplessly in the face of illegal incursions into their territories by loggers and small miners (*garimpeiros*). Attempts to preserve the forest for sustainable development produced mixed results. The conflict between the old economy and that imagined by planners became personalized in the person of Chico Mendes. A rubber tree tapper who depended on the rain forest for his livelihood, he became an international figure. The World Bank and other transnational development agencies regularly consulted him on the preservation of what he called Brazil's "green inheritance." Late in 1988, as he stood in the doorway of his home in Xapuri, the hired guns of a large landowner ended his crusade.

The birth of the environmental movement, largely an urban movement with concerns far beyond the issue of rain forests, occurred, not coincidentally, along with the easing of political restrictions by the military regime. While there had been earlier muffled voices of protest by 1974, associations began to emerge in various cities. Perhaps most important, the Movimento de Arte e Pensamento Ecológico (Art and Ecological Philosophy Movement) in São Paulo encouraged a critical evaluation of environmental issues—reminiscent, as intended, of the Modern Art Week movement of 1922 that so profoundly changed the intellectual basis of the old republic. In 1978 the group began to publish the *Pensamento Ecológico*, which, in addition to reprinting translated articles of interest, also provided an outlet and forum for Brazilian authors and critics. José Lutzenberger, an early environmentalist, published *The End of the Future? A Brazilian Ecological Manifesto* in 1980, followed by another work titled *Atomic Nightmare*. Growing criticism of nuclear power led to an amendment to the state constitution of Rio Grande do Sul prohibiting the construction of such power plants.

Other groups, such as the one in the city of Lages in the state of Santa Catarina, quietly embarked on eco-development to show that a balance could be achieved between development and the environment. Two new environmental journals (*The Other* and *Alternative Life and Culture*) broadened the debate and reached a wider middle-class audience. University students also began to take up the cause. Exposure to the international debate had an impact on the middle class, now willing to consider the notion of a quality of life approach that linked environmental degradation to the individual on a very personal level. Eco-tourism strengthened the idea that preserving nature could be profitable as well as pleasurable. An ongoing marine conservation project, Tamar (sea turtle), attracts over 300,000 visitors per year. Tamar protects endangered species' habitat and raises and annually releases some three million hatchlings. Over twenty visitors' centers dot the coast, making a significant economic contribution to the local area and to the state of Bahia as well as to the survival of the sea turtles.

Pra Frente Brasil (Onward, Brazil): The Economy Turns into the Miracle

The military adopted the same crisis management approach to dealing with the industrial sector as it had applied to the issue of Amazonian development. In the late 1960s the government invited European and American industries to set up operations in Brazil where they would not have to invest in costly antipollution systems. International criticism condemned such opportunism. In 1972 the Brazilian representative to the International Environment Conference in Stockholm denounced calls for restrictive environmental regulations as an attempt to block Third World development. Brazil, not alone in this view, noted that the "pollution of poverty" could be addressed only by economic development. The regime, under pressure from lending agencies that insisted on at least some paper attention to environmental concerns, established a Special Secretariat for the Environment (SEMA) in 1973. Its main task was to prepare environmental assessments to meet loan requirements. As a marginal agency housed in the Ministry of the Interior, with few resources and an unspoken mandate not to hinder development schemes, it had, as intended, little impact.

The regime relied heavily on technocrats. It protected them against political pressure but otherwise gave them the freedom to do the job assigned. Castelo Branco's government did much of the difficult preliminary work to bring inflation down to 24.5 percent by 1967, rationalized debt repayments, and in general put the country's economic house in order. The economy revived in 1968, and to the surprise of many entered a period of rapid growth of some 109 percent over a six-year period. The technocrat largely responsible for the recovery, Antônio Delfim Neto, a young and innovative economics professor in São Paulo who assumed the post of finance minister, introduced reforms and several new financial devices. By easing credit in 1967, Delfim Neto revived the manufacturing sector, stimulating the growth that eventually turned into the miracle. Establishment of a central bank allowed for more control, monitoring, and, when necessary, financial manipulations. To encourage savings, an indexing scheme adjusted accounts upward to compensate for inflation. Increased savings reduced inflationary pressures and generated investment capital. Brazil still needed external sources of capital, but a start had been made. The introduction of the crawling peg, a series of modest but frequent currency devaluations, brought a welcome degree of predictability. Foreign investors could now rationally gauge currency values over time. Delfim Neto became a celebrity among international capitalists and remains so today.

How long the boom could have lasted is anyone's guess, but it undoubtedly would have been much longer except for the OPEC price shocks of 1973 and 1980. Brazil, 50 percent dependent on oil imports, suddenly faced a massive import bill. To pay it, the government encouraged exports, held down imports, and borrowed money abroad. Following the second OPEC price shock, and an even larger bill, more money had to be borrowed. The government reasoned that if the economy continued to expand, it could stay one step ahead of its debt. The worldwide oil crisis encouraged plans to develop alternative sources of energy as rapidly as possible. The military regime approached the oil price crisis as a national emergency requiring virtually wartime measures to ensure national survival. Under such conditions, the impact on the environment mattered even less than usual. The silencing of public debate, inherent in the nature of an authoritarian regime, led to what political scientist Eduardo Viola characterized as a sense of environmental impunity. Nuclear power, sugarcane alcohol, and dams became the panacea. Time for planning seemed short, and the result was some hastily and ill-conceived projects. The nuclear facility of Angra dos Reis created a potential ecological time bomb, while it added to the country's energy supply. Constructed on a geologically risky site, with questionable technology and almost nonexistent planning for an accident, it remains a symbol of development at any cost. Soon after it came on line in 1985, Angra dos Reis earned the nickname of "firefly" because the electric power it produced flickered on and off.

Unfortunately, the worldwide credit squeeze of 1981, with its high interest rates, called the gamble. Brazil was unable to pay its debt and the economic miracle ended. Delfim Neto began to scramble for every centavo, using any available device to increase tax revenues, particularly the important federal tax on industrial products (IPI). Instituting price increases greater than the rate of inflation bolstered IPI collections and retail taxes at the municipal level. Squeezing resources meant survival, but not much more. Once again the country had fallen victim to external events, which undercut the independent struggle for modernity.

Arms Industry Diplomacy

In 1964 the new regime sought to portray itself as having rescued the country from a possible Communist takeover. It needed both the assistance of the United States in material terms and the extension of legitimacy by the acknowledged leader of the Western world. Washington required little urging. It recognized Brazil's new government even before the military had decided who would be the president. In order to consolidate international support, the military government made it clear that it would assume a regional role in the ideological struggle based on strong bilateral ties with the United States tempered by a degree of bargaining power. This arrangement took the form of secret logistical support for pro-Western groups and assistance in suppressing radicalism in Uruguay, among other clandestine operations. In 1965, Brazil participated in the American intervention in the Dominican Republic, although the army insisted it did so not to please Washington but to strengthen the Organization of American States. Subservience from the Brazilian perspective did not last long. In 1969, Brazil refused to sign the Nuclear Nonproliferation Treaty in spite of pressure from the United States, and by 1974 announced a policy rejecting automatic alignment with Washington. Brazil reestablished diplomatic relations with the People's Republic of China that same year. Diplomatic and trade contacts with the Arab world involved pushing aside Israel, Washington's Middle East ally. The government further irritated the

Carter administration by recognizing the Palestine Liberation Organization (PLO) in 1979. Increasing criticism on human rights issues by the United States annoyed the generals, although Washington pressed the regime privately.

Military presidents emphasized that the doctrine of national security required an independent self-reliance to deal with communism both internally and externally. The army did not want to be dependent on American protection alone. The withdrawal of U.S. forces from Vietnam in 1975 made this even more urgent. In many ways, the army theorists of the Superior War College returned to the country's traditional quest for self-reliance, which may be traced back to World War I and later the Vargas administration.

Security, viewed broadly, demanded economic and social development. Technical modernization of the armed forces and industrialization seemed to be a promising combination. Military preparedness could supply the engine to drive the economy. In the 1970s technological warfare capability became a central goal. To break the control of the superpowers over weapons seemed desirable as well as feasible. Brazil's defense industry thus lay at the center of the broad notion of national prestige, security, and development. In 1969 the government established a mixed (public and private) enterprise (EMBRAER) to produce both military and civilian aircraft. Finally, in 1975 the government created the Industry for War Material (IMBEL) as a state holding company to direct the private- and public-sector defense industry (other than aircraft). IMBEL received money to make weapons that could not be manufactured profitably by private firms. Exports would enable it to produce far beyond domestic needs. IMBEL enjoyed exemption from tariffs and taxes, and, in addition, state agencies gave priority to its needs. All of IMBEL's workers were classified as army employees.

The international arms market soon had a new player with a range of reasonably priced products seemingly comparable to those offered by the traditional dealers. Brazil, unlike the Soviet Union and the United States, claimed it did not attach political conditions to arms sales. General Arnaldo Calderari, then president of IMBEL, put it neatly: "The sale is purely commerce . . . we're looking to the Third World, and we'll sell to the right, the left and the center."[2] In fact, Brazil maintained both formal and informal embargoes. Fear of jeopardizing sales to Iraq, which bought 20 to 30 percent of arms exports, meant that Iran had to be excluded. The outbreak of the Iran-Iraq War provided the opportunity to test weapons. Some 2,000 IMBEL armored vehicles and tanks took part in the conflict. Brazilian tanks outperformed inexpensive low-end Eastern Bloc and Western models, thus enhancing their reputation. Angola and Nigeria, both oil suppliers, also acquired tanks in extensive oil-for-weapons exchanges. An important part of the success of the industry may be traced to the fact that IMBEL provided basic technology at reasonable prices. Extensive use of standard off-the-shelf items made repairs inexpensive and parts easy to obtain.

Problems began with the move to more sophisticated, higher priced technology. The market preferred proven reliability. In the end, the Gulf War–Desert Storm in 1991 destroyed the illusion of the defense industry as the engine of growth as well as a dramatic means of projecting Brazil onto the world stage. The overwhelming superiority of American technology, vividly flashed around the world by CNN along with photos of Brazilian-made Iraqi equipment littering the battlefield, damaged the industry's earlier reputation. The one undeniable success of the venture, the aircraft industry, continued to enjoy a commercial market in light and medium planes into the present century.

Returning to the Barracks

Signs of growing civilian restlessness convinced many military officers that the time had come to conclude the process of reforming democracy. To delay much longer even the hope of a return to civilian rule seemed too dangerous. Moreover, many officers believed that the dirty war had undermined the previously close relationship between the civilian population and the army. Military officers increasingly appeared to be the enemies of civilians and democracy, rather than patriotic defenders of the nation. Many officers avoided wearing their uniform in public. Violations of human rights, murder, indiscriminate violence, and torture had progressively sapped the regime's claim to legitimacy. The politics of violence and fear directed by security forces seemed out of control, appearing to contaminate and corrupt the military itself. The warning signs could not be ignored. In 1973 the arrest and fatal torturing of student activist Alexandre Vannucchi Leme caused a month-long protest. The regime believed, correctly, that the victim was a contact for the underground ALN, a nationalist splinter group of the Communist Party. Whether the intent was to kill him or merely extract information cannot be determined. Some 3,000 students and clerics ignored riot police and security agents to attend his memorial service.

How to let go of the tiger's tail without being eaten posed the obvious problem. By 1974 a growing consensus in favor of a controlled and progressive easing had emerged. The change became evident in press and media censorship in particular. Church, union, and business interests became aware of the withdrawal strategy through indirect contacts. The death in 1975 of journalist Vladimir Herzog, while being tortured, caused public outrage and complicated the easing already under way. President Ernesto Geisel (1974–1976) nevertheless continued his policies. The Herzog case ended the widespread use of torture. Hard-line anticivilian elements in the military found themselves increasingly isolated but still able to cause trouble.

In many respects the easing resembled reinflating the tires on a bicycle.[3] All the civilian political institutions remained in place; it was now necessary to give them some substance. Slowly, the Brazilian Bar Association regained its voice while influential business leaders spoke out in favor of a return to civilian rule. Clerics no longer lived in constant fear. The major condition for military withdrawal was that there would be no questioning or punishment of those involved in the dirty war, directly or indirectly.

Finding just the right degree of easing without losing control proved difficult. A series of decrees in April 1977 assured sufficient control to make the process, in the words of General Geisel, "slow, gradual and certain." To further set the stage, his successor, President João Batista de Oliveira Figueiredo, issued a general amnesty in 1979 of all political prisoners, including involuntary exiles and those who had committed abuses during the dirty war. Luís Carlos Prestes, among other political exiles, returned. It remained to ensure that the amnesty would hold when civilians returned to power. The "gradual" arrived with the presidential election of 1985. An ill Figueiredo and senior officers failed to name a candidate and the contest fell to civilians.

Ironically, the campaign for direct elections for president, demanded by an overwhelming majority of the public, allowed the military to exit without excessive embarrassment. Although defeated, but just barely, in the chamber of deputies, the military won in a de facto sense in the streets. The support for a return to direct elections undercut the legitimacy of the actual indirect mechanism used by the regime and still in place. The government's failure to put forward a military candidate in effect conceded the point. The civilian opposition put up Tancredo Neves, governor of Minas Gerais. Neves, a skillful, likeable individual well known to the generals, quietly reassured the army that if he won the election, he would treat them with respect—in short, they would not be held responsible for their activities, including the dirty war, during their twenty-one years in power. Willingness to forgive, partly tactical, also rested on the realization that the number of victims was far less than the number of people killed and tortured in the dirty wars of Argentina and Chile.

Innocent individuals who had paid the ultimate price and their families now paid a further political price. To sweeten up the army, Neves promised to increase the military budget. This was the soft landing the army had hoped for. It had taken all of ten years to let go of the tiger's tail.

Notes

1. For an account of methods used and the individual experiences, see the compilation now in its 30th edition, *Brasil Nunca Mais*, Arquidiocese de São Paulo (Petrópolis, 1985).
2. Quoted in Patrice Franko-Jones, *The Brazilian Defense Industry* (Boulder, 1992), 170.
3. The process began with *distensão* (decompression) and moved toward an *abertura* (political opening).

CHAPTER SIX

Resurrection

Resurrecting Civilian Politics

President-elect Neves disappointed everyone. He collapsed on the very eve of his inauguration, was rushed to a military hospital, and later died without ever assuming office. Vice President José Sarney took over as provisional president while the stricken president-elect underwent a series of futile operations. Neves died on April 21, 1985, and the country went into shock. President Sarney, virtually no one's choice, would have to direct the revival of the democratic political system. Sarney, from the northern state of Maranhão, had little experience with broad-based national politics. He supported the military government and had functioned well in the small pond of Maranhão, but he had none of the stature of Neves and little time to learn on the job. Nevertheless, President Sarney should not be dismissed as a failure. Even a seasoned administrator could have gone down given the enormity of the task. In fact, he did much better than is generally conceded. He also governed in an understandably reactionary political environment. The imposed centralism of the military regime provided much of the motivation to go in the opposite direction. An inexperienced congress and an as-yet unclear political dynamic presented difficulties and challenges quite apart from unaddressed problems facing the nation.

A new monetary scheme, the Cruzado Plan, introduced a different currency unit and various fiscal restrictions. As inflation came under control, restrictions would be lifted. It worked, but it required fiscal responsibility to be sustained. The inflation rate fell to 2 percent monthly, consumer confidence returned, the economy recovered, and tax revenues rose. A grateful people rewarded Sarney's political party by sending many of its nominees to the chamber of deputies and the senate as well as important governorships. Sarney disregarded the advice of economists, however, and did not attempt to moderate economic growth or wage increases. By 1987 the Cruzado

Plan broke down entirely, unleashing hyperinflation that reached 1,038 percent the following year. Without any other options, the government declared a unilateral moratorium on payment of its foreign debt. While an impatient president lost the promise of the plan—its potential undermined by misjudgment—the concept nevertheless laid the groundwork for the much more successful Real Plan in 1994.

Sarney took action on other problems with far-reaching consequences for the country. A series of reciprocal presidential visits between Argentina and Brazil began the process of defusing potentially dangerous nuclear competition between the two countries. Had the issue remained unchecked, the possibility of an arms race in the region or at the very least a vast waste of scarce resources would have become a reality difficult to undo. The decision to open up previously secret installations for presidential visits also made economic and political cooperation possible, including, subsequently, the creation of Mercosul. Without doubt, tensions in the Southern Cone would have frightened away foreign investors and discouraged capital and technology transfers. Sarney's initiatives also demonstrated civilian authority over the pro-nuclear military lobby, although the armed forces remained divided on the program.

The president successfully pushed through a law guaranteeing AIDS sufferers state-of-the-art treatment. As a result of his foresight, dire predictions of an AIDS public health disaster remained unfulfilled. President Sarney also decreed an annual National Day to Combat Smoking in 1986. With financial help from the World Bank the government launched a smoking prevention program intended to reinvigorate the national antismoking program inaugurated by the minister of health in 1979. As the first postmilitary president, Sarney performed beyond expectations.

The New Fiscal and Political Reality

The military regime concentrated fiscal resources in federal hands, while distributing funds to the states and municipalities to implement policy. The process of strengthening municipalities came at a crucial moment as urbanization gathered momentum. The new Constitution of 1988 continued the pattern, but altered the balance of revenue and restricted the supervisory role of the federal government. The modified arrangement allocated 44.6 percent of revenues to the federal government and 55.4 percent to the states and municipalities. On the surface it did not seem like a drastic change, yet it plunged the federal budget into chronic deficit. The greatly diminished supervisory role of the federal government altered the central locus of political power that characterized the military government. The states and cities resisted and then reluctantly accepted the need to assume some (but not all) formerly federal responsibilities, not just absorb more money. Predictably, the change set off a wave of municipalities created to get a share of federal revenues. In the next five years 650 new ones, with populations of 10,000 or less, came into legal existence. In all, 885 municipalities appeared, each entitled to a share of tax revenues.[1] The Constitution of 1988 mandated a minimum distribution regardless of size. Equally important, it also reemphasized the pre-1964 structure of politics. It should be kept in mind that traditional politics in Brazil depended on state and local political bosses who directed their national-level colleagues. The Constitution of 1988 provided them with resources they were unlikely to surrender.

Widespread urbanization, not just in the major capital cities but across Brazil, coupled with the progressive strengthening of municipal governments under the military regime, had to be accommodated. The Constitution of 1988 recognized municipalities as federal entities, placing their legislation on a par with state and federal enactments. On a practical level, the new constitutional status of urban centers made it difficult and technically impossible under normal circumstances to challenge municipal governance. The municipalities received exclusive control over the organization and provision of public infrastructure services—water, sewage, sanitation, and transportation. In the case of social services, education, and public health, the federal constitution made the municipality the principal policy executor. State governments and federal authorities supplied technical recommendations and financial resources if necessary and available. Primary control of the delivery of services lay with local authorities backed by state officials. In general, the federal level allocates resources when available; the lower level decides how the money is spent.

In addition to constitutional authority, the shift of revenue gave municipalities a high degree of autonomy. Theoretically, constitutionally mandated transfers eliminated political pleading. Automatic deposit of funds also provided a degree of predictability depending on tax revenues and economic conditions. The deliberate shift from discretionary (political) to automatic federal transfers strengthened municipalities and to a lesser extent state governments, while it weakened the federal regime. Predictably, a continually cash-strapped federal government either underfunded or stopped providing nonmandated resources completely. The social security system, responsible for pensions, public assistance, and universal health care, became a fiscal, social, and political time bomb. The Constitution of 1988 included some five million rural workers without regard for previous payments into the system. Moreover, men could retire after thirty-five years and women after twenty-five years in the work force, thus enabling many people to retire in their early fifties. Perceived political necessity led to special pension entitlements. Civil servants, including university professors, retired at full pay. Widely different benefit amounts provided handsome pensions for some people, but scarcely more than a welcome subsidy for the majority. The need to give priority to pension payouts forced severe cuts elsewhere.

Federal funding for health care declined by slightly more than $5 billion between 1989 and 1992, and along with poor management effectively destroyed the system. Under the provisions of the Constitution of 1988, federal, state, and municipal governments share responsibility for the Unified Health System (SUS). All three levels are theoretically responsible for funding, while the state and local governments are free to structure and manage assets and resources. In practice, the system depends on federal transfers. Declining resources resulted in impossible conditions, long lines, wasted hours, and refusals to admit patients as well as denials of costly life-saving treatment. Crumbling buildings and thefts of already scarce medical supplies by poorly paid physicians and staff completed the ruin.

Without transfer payments, municipalities cannot sustain a high level of expenditures, let alone expand their services. Some 75 percent of municipalities generate less than 10 percent of their revenues from their own tax base. Not even the largest cities are able to generate over 50 percent of their budget from their own tax resources. Housing needs remain unmet. Those able to organize into some sort of corporate body may be able to extract some resources. The poor understand very well the organizational requirement. For example, the Union of the Housing Movement in São Paulo, which encourages illegal occupation of abandoned buildings in the declining city center, is able to pressure officials, even the governor, to ignore such seizures. Their trophies include the once-grand Hotel São Paulo and unused federal property. Groups like this represent the organized homeless, not the entire population in need of housing.

Inefficient tax collection, tax avoidance, fraud, and a large informal sector provide a partial explanation for the limited resources available to address social problems.[2] The long tradition of trading in contraband goods has been updated to include counterfeit products smuggled in from Paraguay or the port of Santos on a grand scale. The federal tax agency estimates that billions of dollars of tax revenues are lost in addition to some $10 billion per year in lost sales to legitimate manufacturers. An estimated 34 percent of cigarettes consumed annually in Brazil are counterfeit. Cigarettes account for 74 percent of the important tax on industrial products (IPI) collected by the federal government. In addition, the lost sales tax directly affects municipal collections. Another significant drain is the common practice of kickbacks and outright theft of government funds that run into the millions.

The types of industries easy to tax are large, well-capitalized, non-family owned enterprises. Yet small enterprises account for most of the nation's businesses. Many prefer to operate in the informal economy to avoid restrictions on firing employees as well as to evade the taxes on social benefits that double the cost of employing a legal worker. Large companies, in order to protect themselves from taxes, negotiate a deal, threatening to move to a more accommodating city or another state. Predatory luring away of a tax-desirable industry pits municipalities and states against each other in the constant search for additional revenue. In the past, scarce tax resources could be dealt with by printing money. Unfortunately, such a measure caused major economic turmoil, heavily penalized the lower classes, and depressed consumption. In addition, the Cardoso regime's political popularity depended on a stable currency (the Real Plan) and controlled inflation, ruling out the easy if short-term solution. Revenue shortages and lack of capital for development endanger the fiscal stability of all three levels of government—federal, state, and municipal. Direct foreign investment is crucial, but it depends on a stable economy. Indirect investment in the stock market, while useful, can be withdrawn within hours with disastrous consequences for the value of the currency. Exports of non–value-added products and processed goods rise and fall on the whims of the world market. This reality partially explains Brazil's attachment to Mercosul.

Municipal power seems unlikely to decline in importance. Federal politicians in the senate and the chamber of deputies depend on the urban-sector politicians who control patronage, and, provided they have a reasonable record of accomplishment, who can mobilize voters and direct them as desired. Politics follows money, and social services and public projects follow both. Not surprisingly, many elected federal officials run for municipal office while in congress, thus reversing what in other countries would seem the logical progression of a political career. Tax collection and reform requires political will, acceptance by local and state bosses, and a change in public attitudes.

Mãe Preta (Black Mother) to Zumbi: The Decline of the Myth of Racial Democracy

The fear of racial conflict runs deep in Brazil's history. Dependence on forced African labor and the sheer number of slaves who powered the economy linked slave control with production and hoped-for prosperity. Most slaves worked under strict discipline reflecting the fears of their owners that violence could erupt at any moment. The actual number of slave revolts and the dangers they posed never matched the level of unease of owners, with the possible exception of the almost bungled process of abolition between 1870 and 1888. The existence of a substantial number of free blacks and their free-born descendants, along with mixed people of color, served to fragment the Afro-Brazilian population into levels of social privilege that differentiated them, adding a class element to the underlying reality of racial slavery.

Attitudes toward ex-slaves and people of color underwent a process of downward homogenization after 1888. While not completely socially leveling, it pushed them in general down into a putative marginal laboring class, regardless of their actual individual circumstances. Nevertheless, within the Afro-Brazilian community itself differentiation remained. The influx of European immigrants added the crucial element necessary to consolidate the new postslavery attitude among the elite. Exclusionary custom, not law, underpinned the largely informal system of prejudice and discrimination—one quickly understood by all.

The other important issue, the place of Afro-Brazilians in a non-slaveholding nation, had been addressed previously during the war with Paraguay. The recruiting of free black and mulatto soldiers, along with the freeing of slaves to join the army, had at that moment theoretically made them into citizen soldiers. Army attitudes toward slavery led to abolition in occupied Paraguay and the refusal to act as slave catchers. Afro-Brazilians, ex-slave or not, theoretically functioned in the same fashion with identical rights and restrictions as others of their class, but in fact the social reality held them in an inferior position. They lived a multitiered existence, included in society by their very numbers and economic activity, yet they also inhabited another shadowy plain, a realm of informal exclusion.

Change became evident in the 1920s and 1930s as a growing number of Afro-Brazilians refused to accept the gap between reality and social fiction. By the 1930s most black newspapers clearly challenged the myth. In 1925 the newspaper *O Clarim da Alvorada* called for the formation of a congress of black youth. Out of this idea came the Palmares Civic Center, named after the most famous runaway slave settlement, the Republic of Palmares. Besides being a self-help organization, it worked to remove restrictions on blacks with mixed success. Vargas received the support of the Frente Negro Brasileiro (FNB), the first registered black political organization. Vargas, however, did not spare the FNB when he abolished all political parties in 1937. Postwar recovery would be slow, retarded again in 1964 with the military takeover. Nevertheless, in 1978 the Movimento Negro Unificado (MNU) began to pull black groups together and inform them about events internationally. The MNU chose November 20 as the National Day of Black Consciousness in honor of the death of Zumbi, the leader of the Republic of Palmares.

Brazilian Paulo Moura, appearing with New Orleans jazz musicians during the Jambalaya Jazz concert series in Rio de Janeiro in November 2002—an indication of the richness of the African Diaspora that links Brazil with Louisiana. Moura wrote *Urban Fantasy for Popular Percussion* in commemoration of the 100th anniversary of the end of slavery in Brazil and conducted its performance by the Brazilian Symphony Orchestra in 1988. *Courtesy of Tom André, photograph by Lisa M. Robinson*

Several factors stimulated the formation of Afro-Brazilian organizations in the 1970s. The wave of independence movements in Portugal's African colonies and the experience of North American black power groups inspired a series of black pride cultural groups, such as the Quartonbo, an alternative samba school, the Senghor Institute, and the dance troupe, Olorum Baba Mim, among others. These organizations combined cultural pride and political activity.

Young Afro-Brazilians in Rio adopted various elements of the North American movement including a special handshake and soul music called *bleque pan* (black power). Afro-Brazilian soul music produced *bleque pan*, black samba in São Paulo, and black *maneiro* in the state of Minas Gerais. *Axé* music (samba-reggae) emerged as the music of black affirmation. By identifying with the African diaspora, Afro-Brazilians acquired legitimacy and placed cultural and political demands in a global context. At the same time, Afro-Brazilian themes became more acceptable in Brazilian cinema. A few directors dealt with stories that addressed racism despite the reluctance of some distributors to handle such films.

The turning over of political power to civilian politicians by the military in 1985 resulted in a rush of democratic experimentation. The new Constitution of 1988, which extended the right to vote to virtually everyone, including illiterates, put the structural mechanism in place for Afro-Brazilians to enter politics in more than token numbers. A surge of black representation, still far from matching the number of Afro-Brazilians in the overall population, rested on work by black organizations in the 1970s. Before the return of civilians to the presidency, only a few blacks had been elected to congress. Nevertheless, scholars, activists, artists, musicians, and writers drew attention to the political potential of the Afro-Brazilian population and, even more important, to the need to change social attitudes that hindered political advancement. In general, the states resisted any structural changes that threatened the authority of their political machines. Of all states, Rio de Janeiro sent the most Afro-Brazilians to congress.

The famous sociologist Gilberto Freyre, who, ironically, helped advance acceptance of the African contribution in Brazilian history, denounced the Afro-Brazilian movement as a pernicious North American import. He claimed that it threatened black revolt and brought unhappiness instead of what he called happy and fraternal sambas. Freyre and others worried that the racial polarization that characterized North American politics would destroy Brazil if it took root. Activists pressed for legislation to promote affirmative action, a black national holiday, and recognition of racism as well as penalties for discrimination. An indication that black consciousness had broad popular support came with the centenary of the abolition of Brazilian slavery in 1988. Critics derided official celebrations as merely self-congratulatory, rather than serious attempts to assess progress and deal with the problem of discrimination.

State and municipal governments, long aware of the intensifying issue of discrimination and worried about a potentially violent divisiveness, reacted with renewed efforts to portray black culture as incorporated into the general culture. In the process, aspects of historic black culture became points of interest to tourists and antiquarians. In much the same manner as Vargas's approach to Carnival groups and the commercialization of samba and Carnival in the larger cities, elements of black culture would be turned into a regulated national activity, disconnected from race. In the state of Bahia, officials turned to the Afro-Brazilian religion of Candomblé, *capoeira* (a martial-arts form with African roots), and *maculele* (a type of stick fighting) as the most promising. The city offered academic courses and sponsored expositions and parades featuring these aspects of Afro-Brazilian culture to market their interpretation and transform culture into folklore.

In the case of *capoeira*, the federal National Sports Council (CND) established a commission to institutionalize it, complete with standardized rules and competitions. Practitioners had to join a club recognized by a *capoeira* federation under the Brazilian Boxing Federation's (CBP) overall supervision. Set rules for apprenticeships and training completed the process. Certain types of *capoeira* became unacceptable. An attempt to require *capoeira* instructors to have a university degree in physical education caused an outcry from traditional lower-class teachers. The sanitized sport became popular with the middle class—once it had been separated from its black lower-class roots.

Organized tours profited those instructors and performers willing to modify their practices. Staged hotel presentations and escorted visits to approved sites shifted the original intent to entertainment. Tourism inevitably trivialized important elements of culture to the point that they became empty curiosities. The transformation of active culture into folklore is unlikely to be successful in the short term but in the long run may have a negative impact.

In opposition to cultural absorption, a re-Africanization movement emerged. Candomblé went through its own purification process and shed foreign elements, including the influence of Umbanda. Consultants from Nigeria reviewed their practices and pointed out unacceptable deviations. Both the federal universities in Bahia and São Paulo, responding to demand, offered Yoruba language instruction. Some Carnival groups in Bahia pulled back from commercialization and returned to perform in their own neighborhoods.

Politicians also came under pressure. Abdias do Nascimento, a leading activist for over fifty years who served as a deputy and later senator, claimed, perhaps correctly, to have been the first consciously black deputy. Benedita da Silva, one of three black women elected to congress in 1983, and reelected since 1986, shared Abdias do Nascimento's consciousness. During Benedita da Silva's second term

(1991–1995), she promoted, unsuccessfully, the formation of a racial caucus with the idea of trading votes en bloc.[3] Most of the black deputies who served with her hesitated to use race as a basis for political organization. Nelson Carneiro, whose political career spanned some thirty years as a deputy and senator, reflecting the nonracial politics locked into the electoral structure, preferred to remain invisibly black. Nevertheless, in 1990 three Afro-Brazilian governors took office.

Activists continued to press congress to take a more forceful stance on the issue of race. In November 1995, thousands from around the country gathered in Brasília to commemorate the death of Zumbi, the Afro-Brazilian leader of the Republic of Palmares, the largest runaway slave settlement in the Western Hemisphere (1600? –1695). Zumbi died at the hands of a Luso-Brazilian militia that overran Palmares. Deputy Paulo Parm proposed legislation to pay reparations to each slave descendant, in fact, to every living Afro-Brazilian. President Cardoso took the more modest step of creating a working group to study the situation and suggest policy reforms. Changing sociocultural values continued to offer the most hope, but this objective was clearly a long-range one.

Nevertheless, political pressure resulted in some advances at the very important local level. For example, the municipal charter of Belo Horizonte (capital of the state of Minas Gerais), in accordance with federal constitutional guidelines, declared racism a crime. Municipal law required, among other measures, that all official publicity include black models in proportion to their numbers in the city. Public schools must present material on African and Afro-Brazilian history. The municipal calendar recognized an annual Black Consciousness Day on November 20. The charter also addressed more serious attitudinal issues, such as prohibiting municipal agencies from sterilizing black women except for health reasons.[4]

Clearly, in the 1990s perceptions underwent some important changes. Nevertheless, insistence that Brazil is a racial democracy continues to obscure reality. The claim is true only if one separates the formal from the informal and political action from social reality. The difficulty of doing so explains the frustration of those who live in an almost Kafkaesque situation. Complicating black self-identification is the social reality that people use some 200 racial categories, and a number of regional variations, to describe themselves. As a consequence, at one point the percentage of the population officially identified as black dropped dramatically, defying belief but nevertheless with important social and political consequences. Recently (2002), willingness to self-identify as black has increased, an indication that many people see significant change. Deep disagreement over a winning strategy divides the country. Those who choose to reclassify themselves out of the contest, politicians who avoid racial politics, and activists who insist on re-Africanization and racial blocs all have their supporters. It is not clear which combination of these approaches, or if any of them, will bring about the desired result.

The Victory of Materialism: Radio and Television

The Estado Novo and its aftermath, from 1945 into the new millennium, coincided with the commercialization of mass communications, consumerism, and the eventual victory of materialism. All modern nations are materialistic, and developing countries have important subgroups that are avidly so. Broadening consumption is as much a social process as it is an economic one.[5] Stimulating demand for products starts with desire, which in turn depends on communication. Word of mouth and casual gossip are effective but slow methods of disseminating information. Technology revolutionized communication, making it almost instantaneous. Printed books and newspapers started the organized widespread purveying of information, but they depended on literacy, hand distribution, and some level of education. Radio changed all that by broadcasting to a mass audience across the country.

Radio came into its own from the late 1920s through the 1970s, and beginning in the 1950s television accelerated the process of mass communication and marketing. Earlier technological advances such as railways, steamships, submarine cables, and the telegraph, among others, had an important impact on wages, wealth, and consumption but in ways much different than radio and later television. Radio could not be ignored easily, nor did it depend on skills such as literacy or on wealth. It represented the first regional and national mass popular medium of communication. Its appeal to a largely illiterate audience quickly became evident. In the past, ignorance, great distances, and rural demographics isolated the population culturally. Between 1900 and 1920, only one in four Brazilians could read and a large percentage read at marginal levels. Radio made these obstacles unimportant—inevitably changing the sociopolitical balance and creating a new culture and material expectations.

Radio arrived in 1922. Westinghouse and General Electric exhibited at Brazil's centennial exhibition and installed equipment on Corcovado, the distinctive peak on which the famous Christ the Redeemer statue stands. Loudspeakers, scattered around the exhibition, attracted and amazed curious onlookers. Westinghouse and General Electric received grand prizes for their technological marvels. This public fascination indicated that radios would be adopted by middle-class consumers as soon as equipment costs became affordable.

Initially, government regulations limited public ownership of receiving and broadcasting equipment. As in many other countries, officials believed that radio technology should be restricted to the state's communication needs. The first step granted licenses to radio clubs. Finally, in 1924, the government eased restrictions on receivers but not on transmitters—the pattern generally followed around the world today. Outside intrusions could not be avoided. Broadcasts from Argentina and Uruguay and shortwave transmissions from Westinghouse's Pittsburgh, Pennsylvania, station KDKA shattered any illusion that the new communications medium could be controlled, at least at the listener level. In 1931 twenty stations transmitted regionally. A decade later, some one hundred served the public. Rádio Nacional acquired a shortwave transmitter to become the first station to broadcast nationally. Its ability to reach every part of Brazil made it the dominant force in radio.

After its introduction in 1922, most thought that radio would be a means to bring cultural and educational programs to an illiterate or poorly schooled audience in the more remote parts of the country. Moreover, urban professionals could polish their rough edges and aspire to elite levels of sophistication. Equipment companies sold the vision of families sitting at home listening with pleasure and profit to operas, lectures by renowned authorities, and the news. São Paulo's first station, Rádio Educadora Paulista, established in 1924, reflected this notion. Five years later, a São Paulo station completely dependent on commercial advertising began operations.[6]

In Rio the Rádio Sociedade do Rio de Janeiro based its programming on lectures on Italian, English, and French literature, science, Portuguese grammar, natural history, and geography, among other subjects. Experts from a wide range of fields who passed through the capital enabled the station to offer an amazingly diverse selection of programming. A 1,000-watt station that began broadcasting in 1926 from Manaus in the heart of the Amazon was followed the next year by a station in Pôrto Alegre in the southern state of Rio Grande do Sul. In 1933 the Rádio Escola Municipal do Distrito Federal (Federal District Municipal Radio School) soon received some 11,000 written assignments from its students. Listeners had to pay close attention to often difficult subjects. The programs could be boring and pedantic as well as beyond the ability of the audience to absorb them. The radio school soon moved down the cultural ladder, although educational programming remained part of the mix, as it is today.

A break in cultural tension came in 1932 when the first advertising jingle aired promoting a Botafogo (Rio) bakery. Before 1932 advertising consisted of a discreet mentioning of names. Creating a mass audience remained difficult because of the cost of individual receivers, which in 1932 represented from 15 to 20 percent of a working-class monthly salary. Nevertheless, in poorer districts and rural towns, local stores and bars provided access. The number of listeners grew as the price of receivers declined and the programs became more popular and lightly entertaining. Singers, humorists, and storytellers replaced classical music, operas, and lectures. On their own initiative, broadcasters toned down some of what they believed to be the more bawdy aspects of popular culture. Under cover of technology, radio became an anonymous cultural arbitrator. It determined without debate what was broadly acceptable across the republic. In the process, radio gave popular culture legitimacy and perhaps for the first time breached the cultural barriers between classes.

Radio advertising progressed from the reasonably refined, aimed at the middle class, to mass commercial advertising as producers and manufacturers became aware that the lower classes were also consumers. Advertisers pressed for programs that reached the broadest possible audience. Radio advertising soon included a regional mix of products, including Colonia milk, Tabarra soap, and Castellões cigarettes. In the 1940s radio advertising served as a principal means of introducing American products. The efforts of large American advertising agencies such as J. Walter Thompson and McCann Erickson, whose accounts included Ford Motor Company, General Motors, Coca-Cola, General Electric, Johnson & Johnson, Goodyear, and Colgate-Palmolive, reinforced the mass media's emphasis on consumption. Ad agencies determined content to a large extent. Only Rádio Nacional could negotiate a reasonable degree of artistic control. News programs, such as "The Esso Reporter" (sponsored by a multinational petroleum products company, today's Exxon), attempted to avoid all comment on the news and simply repeated local and United Press International (UPI) releases. Nevertheless, the five minutes allotted "The Esso Reporter" gave the program an authoritative urgency.

An important moment in the development of a mass consumer society arrived in 1948, with the magazine *Revista do Rádio*. Building on existing trends, the *Revista* mobilized tastes at the lower end, preferred by many advertisers. The magazine became a powerful adjunct to on-air programming. That same year, Auricelio Peneado, director of the major polling organization IBOPE, declared Coca-Cola "the symbol of the new economic, political and social order" and, moreover, a force for democracy. Its consumption, according to Peneado, brought with it progress, health, efficiency, and faith in the future.[7] *Donald Duck* (*O Pato Donald*) magazine arrived the same year the elected Vargas returned to the presidency. To those with more refined tastes, the *Revista do Rádio*, Coca-Cola, *O Pato Donald*, *Seleções do Reader's Digest*, and Hollywood movies seemed like the several horsemen of a cultural apocalypse.

Radio's cultural drift downward depended upon the extent that ad agencies used their power to enrich or starve a station. Rádio Nacional, able to resist such pressures more than most, nevertheless shifted more toward soap operas, beauty and body care programs, and cooking shows. IBOPE's polling showed that women made up 60 percent of the radio audience and, moreover, listened throughout the day as they went about their work. Perceived women's interests determined programming. Consequently, soap operas pushed virtually everything else aside. At this point, the *Revista do Rádio* entered the contest for advertising revenues by making itself the uncritical booster of radio. Soap operas created fans and the *Revista* went a step further by constructing a star system, complete with an aura of Hollywood, that made the star rating more important than the program itself. The magazine's popularity, second only to *O Cruzeiro* (similar to *Life* magazine), depended on the middle and lower classes.

The lifestyle depicted in the *Revista* was all about radio stars—how they lived, what they ate, the soap they used, the household products they insisted upon, the hair crème they chose, the cigarettes they smoked, and all the other products that made them so wonderful, glamorous, and successful. Advice columns appearing over a star's name discussed how women should dress, apply makeup, deal with romance, whether they should smoke—in short, a complete guide to life and its suggested consumer items.

The creation of radio stars predictably led to fan clubs. The clubs adopted the same basic open membership policy as soccer fan clubs (*torcidas*) and, to a lesser extent, religious groups. The only membership requirement was exclusive devotion to the star. Their points of contact with their idol, invariably a woman, included listening to programs, attending live performances, and reading the *Revista*, which reported on the star's daily activity. Members paid dues, most of which went toward expensive gifts usually presented backstage by club members after a performance. In return, fans expected their star to show gratitude—tears and modest statements of unworthiness. The *Revista* followed up in detail, reporting on the star's reaction—how overwhelmed, how pleased she was. Fans also expected to be invited to the star's home on certain occasions. Such gatherings resulted in a full report along with photos in the *Revista*. Fan club members insisted on a two-way relationship. Radio personalities who refused to meet such expectations did not reach the top of the profession or attract as many advertisers.

Emilinha Borba represented the archetypal *Revista do Rádio* creation. While she was a minor radio personality before its publication, the magazine elevated her popularity to a white-hot level. Her image, that of a poor girl grappling with success but still firmly rooted in her humble origins, suited her fans. Marlene, another top star, cultivated a non-elite refinement suggesting that such a virtue did not have to be class-based. Teenager Angela Maria radiated freshness along with vulnerability, while Dalva de Oliveira constructed her own soap opera life. She presented herself as a classic abused woman who suffered but endured. Fans saw their star as one of their own because of her triumph over adversity.

In 1950 television arrived in Brazil. To introduce the new medium, stores in the capital set up demonstration receivers and made lists of those interested in purchasing a set. TV Tupí in São Paulo formally began the new era as the first station in Latin America. Francisco de Assis Chateaubriand, who controlled twenty-three newspapers, twenty-eight radio stations, and other enterprises, financed the venture. TV Tupí-Canal 6 in Rio started to broadcast the following year. By the late 1950s, some twenty stations transmitted. Initially expensive because of the high cost of broadcasting and receiving equipment, television did not immediately challenge radio. Three years after its introduction only 2 percent of middle-class families in the capital owned a set. To most people the high price made television an exotic technical wonder. Nevertheless, by 1960 over 600,000 television sets had been sold. A decade later, television swept radio into the regional niche market. The government's decision to allow private ownership meant that television would become a medium for advertising without regard for region or class. Commercials used large slides accompanied by jingles, with the product pitched by an attractive young woman. Unintended humor helped, such as when the girl demonstrating the ease of opening a sofa bed had to wrestle with the mechanism. Early television followed the content model of radio. Programming began at six o'clock in the evening and ended at midnight. All shows were presented live until the early 1960s, when videotape became available.

Telenovelas, inspired by radio, appeared in 1951. The first, *Your Life Belongs to Me* on TV Tupí in São Paulo, aired at ten o'clock in the evening. Daily *telenovelas*, sponsored by Colgate-Palmolive and advertisers of light or nondurable consumer goods, cosmetics, soap, cleaning products, and food and beverages with mass market appeal, attracted a loyal daytime audience. Videotaped shows sent to stations throughout the country generated a countrywide audience that reinforced the national consumer market created by radio. From Mato Grosso to Rio de Janeiro, television characters and shows influenced popular perceptions of reality based on fantasy. In the 1970s television absorbed 50 percent of all advertising revenues, compared to less than 10 percent for radio. Only advertising of lower-priced items by small local shopkeepers and inexpensive transistors saved radio from disaster.

O Globo, created in 1965, dominated the industry almost immediately. A joint venture of the wealthy Marinho family and Time-Life modeled after television station WFBM in Indianapolis, Indiana, the company soon became profitable. The Marinho family bought out its American partner in 1969. TV Globo supported the military regime through news programming carefully crafted to appear professional and credible. Other television stations followed Globo's lead. In turn, the government facilitated the importation of the latest equipment and encouraged new stations by financing their expansion. With Intelsat, television stations in São Paulo and Rio become national networks able to send their signals in real time throughout the nation. Television presented middle-class values oriented toward consumerism. Programming followed the American standard of aiming for a general cultural level of preteen adolescents. Globo set up a research unit to monitor viewers' tastes. As a result, it charged high rates for commercials and guaranteed results. Television provided the means to fashion an ideal consumer society that reached across the nation to every class. As the movie *Bye Bye, Brazil* (1980) made obvious, every place, no matter how remote, was touched and changed by television. It is said that Brazilians of all classes watch more television than the population of any other developing country. Globo molded television culture and set the industry standard.

The victory of consumerism in Brazil mirrored the U.S. experience, but with some unique features. A high point of sorts came with the debut of the Xuxa Show. The invention of Xuxa represented one of the most successful and cynical manipulations of the national pathology in the interest of consumerism. Maria da Graça Meneghel, the daughter of a military family of German descent, became a media sensation as Xuxa. Starting out as a model, she quickly moved beyond selling chic clothes to selling her sexuality. Highly calculated alliances and a complete understanding of the ideal notion of femininity soon made her a blonde bombshell, the Brazilian Marilyn Monroe. Her well-publicized affair with renowned Afro-Brazilian soccer star Pelé clinched her success. Xuxa appeared on the cover of virtually every magazine. The December 1982 issue of the Brazilian edition of *Playboy* featured a lavish photo spread of Xuxa in suggestive poses.[8] The issue quickly sold out and is now a coveted collector's item. Her soft porn movie is a favorite selection in video rental stores. In carefully staged interviews, she affirmed her vulnerability and dependence on a man as a positive role for her and indeed for all women.

In 1983, Xuxa became the host of a children's program on Manchete Television before being lured away by TV Globo. The show combined erotic display with children's games that revolved around Xuxa. The camera always remained focused on her. The message suggested that sensuality, along with tenderness and love of children, represented the best of the modern woman. The show recruited blonde, prepubescent girls as *paquitas*—miniature Xuxas who served as her assistants on the set. The vast majority of women could not measure up to the standard of beauty suggested by the Xuxa Show—blonde, blue eyes, and an apparently perfect body. Afro-Brazilians rarely appeared on the set. Nevertheless, Xuxa denied any hint of racism, referring, when challenged, to her attachment to Pelé. In effect, Xuxa played on all of society's deep insecurities, including sexual and racial ones. In the end, she invited the audience to become a part of what Xuxa represented by buying the sponsors' products. Her audience left with at least a commercial token of a life they could never attain. At the end of the program Xuxa returned to a spaceship, blowing kisses as the audience begged her to stay. As the spaceship (an artfully contrived elevator) rose, the camera cut to a shot of Christ the Redeemer on Corcovado. Two small pink neon hearts glowed on Christ's chest. Not surprisingly, Xuxa's marketing abilities made her one of the richest women in entertainment. As early as 1991, *Forbes* magazine listed her wealth as thirty-seventh in the entertainment world, in the same company as Madonna.

Socio-Psychological Icons: Soccer and Carnival

In Brazil the two major emotional events are the soccer championships (World Cup and the Americas Cup) and Carnival. When foreigners are asked what they associate Brazil with, they respond without hesitation—soccer and Carnival.

Soccer in Brazil reflects a patriarchal society on the one hand and expresses class and race frustrations on the other. A spectator sport, soccer creates a sense of social unity in a nation with weak ties between the classes. The roots of the game in Brazil are relatively new. Charles Miller, a Scotsman born in Brazil but educated in England, returned to São Paulo in 1894 with, among other things, two soccer balls. His club, the São Paulo Athletic Club, originally a cricket club, soon had its own intramural teams. Members included English merchants, engineers, and company administrators along with a sprinkling of wealthy Brazilians. In Rio de Janeiro, Oscar Cox, an Englishman, established the Fluminense Club to encourage the sport. Soccer became an elite social pastime for the foreign community much like squash, badminton, and tennis. It distinguished its players from the surrounding native community. Young men impeccably attired in imported shorts, socks, and shoes demonstrated their prowess in front of elegantly dressed girls and lesser males.[9]

Soccer's social descent began with the founding of the Bangu Athletic Club in 1904 by English technicians. The Bangu Textile Company constructed a soccer field next to the factory, located at the time in an isolated part of Rio. In order to provide an opposing practice team, factory workers learned the game. They proved more than adept, giving the young Englishmen more competition than they had expected. Soon workers were given special privileges and time off to develop their skills. Bangu even hired employees on the basis of their soccer skills. Lower-class youths played pickup games with rag balls in any available open space. The sport spread rapidly in urban centers. Members of the snobbish clubs tried to ignore the high level of play among the lower class, but eventually they reluctantly conceded, becoming spectator-managers rather than players. São Paulo's Corinthians, organized by Brazilian railway employees in 1910, recruited players and paid them token amounts depending on their performance. Such crassness resulted in their expulsion from the soccer federation for breaking rules governing amateur soccer. Nevertheless, the success of the Corinthians on the field led to a general move to reward players. Unwilling to let go of their perceived superiority completely, the clubs did their best to select light-skinned athletes. Carlos Alberto, a mulatto who played for Fluminense, applied rice powder (*po de arroz*) to his skin to make himself acceptable. As a result, lower-class fans called the club *po de arroz*.

Afro-Brazilians formed separate clubs. In São Paulo the São Geraldo Athletic Association, founded in 1910, and the Cravos Vermelos, founded in 1916, became known for their superior skills. Smaller, more provincial clubs had little choice but to include players of all races. Rio's Vasco da Gama club, organized by the Portuguese community, fielded a winning team in 1923 that included black players, thus breaking decisively the color barrier among the major clubs. In 1933 the Vargas regime, through the Brazilian Sports Confederation, made players salaried employees regulated by the Ministry of Labor. By the 1930s soccer appealed to a mass audience. Radio created a national following as well as soccer stars and fans. A broadcast of the 1938 World Cup in France, with a full description of the national team's performance, transformed Leonidas da Silva, the "Black Diamond," into Brazil's first national soccer idol.

The first soccer match between São Paulo and Rio in October 1901. Newspapers reported the games in detail. The scores of 0-0 in the first and 2-2 in the second game indicated an evenly matched contest. Charles Miller is standing on the train just to the right of the smokestack, to see the Rio team off. Oscar Cox, the Anglo-Brazilian captain of the Rio team, is directly below the smokestack wearing a boater. The social high point, a dinner, included toasts to King Edward VII and Brazil's president. *Courtesy of Gregg Bocketti*

Players were club employees—not members. They did not have access to club facilities such as swimming pools and dining rooms, nor did they participate in social activities. Thus, although the sport became a lower-class passion, well-off dues-paying members owned and managed the teams. The clubs took in gate receipts, profits from the sale of player contracts, and advertising revenue. In recent times, for example, players wear the Coke logo. Some 5,000 clubs field teams, but only thirteen are considered important. These are the clubs from which the World Cup teams are drawn.

Lower-class supporters participated through the *torcidas* (fan clubs) under their control, with open membership totally independent of the team club. O Cruzeiro club in Belo Horizonte, the capital of Minas Gerais, has a parallel fan club called Mafia Azul (blue mafia). *Torcidas* offer a welcoming organizational structure and a sense of community for the lower class and new arrivals from the country-side. They frequently provide help in finding a job or housing, use-ful contacts with the often difficult urban bureaucracy, and even material assistance. Thanks to radio and later television, Mafia Azul has members throughout Brazil. Visiting members, or those who move to a new city, have access to an instant support network. Vio-lence, a less admirable aspect of team loyalty, helps to distinguish one group from another. It may also partly explain the 40 percent drop in stadium attendance over the last fifteen years.

Conceding that Afro-Brazilians demonstrate excellent soccer skills did not erase racial uncertainty. When Brazil lost the 1950 World Cup to Uruguay in Maracana stadium in front of a capacity crowd, jour-nalists made two black players the scapegoats and suggested that racial impurity lay at the heart of the failure.

During the military regime, President Emilio Medici manipulated soccer to increase support for the government. In the months pre-ceding the 1970 World Cup play-off in Mexico, he pressed for re-moval of the coach and even helped train the team. When the Brazilian team returned victorious, a picture of the president hold-ing the World Cup trophy appeared in every newspaper in the coun-try. Pelé, who won the World Cup in 1970 with a little help from the rest of the team, became a national icon—received by the president and exempted from income taxes. Pelé carefully sidestepped any discussion of race in sports. Further military meddling included tak-ing over training for the World Cup, which turned out to be a disas-ter for the 1974 and 1978 Brazilian teams.

A soccer victory or a defeat reflects on the nation. The populace is united in euphoria or shattered in defeat. When Brazil lost 3-0 to France in 1998, the disappointment briefly plunged the country into despair. When Senegal eliminated France early in the 2002 contest, Brazilians felt somewhat avenged. Nevertheless, in the initial rounds of the 2002 contest, President Cardoso observed that if the team failed to get into the play-offs it would be a calamity worse than an eco-nomic crisis. Brazil has been in every play-off since 1930. Cardoso lectured the team on its duty—fortunately, Brazil won the World Cup. A crowd of 400,000 greeted the team on its arrival in the capital. The celebration concluded with a ceremony led by the president on the steps of the presidential palace. Yet all is not well with the national sport.

Along with globalization, sports clubs have discovered that they can sell players' contracts to European clubs for exorbitant prices while their own limited resources make it difficult to hold onto players. Amateur management and widespread corruption have disillusioned and angered fans. The increasing primacy of business and financial skills may force a restructuring of the game and the end of club own-ership.[10] Whatever happens, it is unlikely that Brazilians will aban-don their bond with the game itself, but they will be sorely tested.

The same phenomenon of temporary social unity is evident in the rituals of Carnival. Common to all predominantly Catholic coun-tries, the annual festival is the final excess before the sober demands of Lent. Nevertheless, Carnival plays out in a manner unique to each culture, meeting social needs that have little to do with religion. Carnival requires an urban setting with a significant mass of people and a broad spectrum of classes.

The Portuguese introduced a rough and violent variety of Carni-val that pitted people against each other in mock battles that at times ended in real fights. The crude joke, the *entrudo*, challenged the victim's sense of humor and sparked revenge. Unwitting pedestri-ans coped with all sorts of refuse dumped on them from windows. In the street, eggs, mud, and buckets filled with flour, urine, or worse flew through the air. Pickpockets and petty criminals mixed with the crowd to take advantage of the confusion while attempting to avoid an unwanted barrage of flying objects. Bad taste and disorder replaced the normally reserved behavior of the Portuguese, all of which ended with the beginning of Lent on Ash Wednesday.

In the Brazilian setting African influences and slavery added their own distinct elements to Carnival rituals. Rural celebrations evolved as villages became towns and cities emerged. Modern Carnival de-veloped in the nineteenth century as an urban event. Free urban blacks mixed African notions with the *entrudo* to form a modified Carnival. When the French architect Auguste Grandjean de Montigny died of pneumonia after being soaked with water in 1853, the authori-ties banned the *entrudo* with limited results. In 1855 an elite group organized the first costume parade including D. Pedro and his fam-ily and other prominent members of high society—all marched to the music of the Cossacks of the Ukraine. Floats with representations of Chinese mandarins, among other exotic figures, followed by a troop of horsemen finely mounted for the occasion, delighted bystanders. Earlier in the century (1840) an Italian resident organized the first masked ball in the Hotel de Itália. Others followed his example. A masked ball held at a roller rink with everyone on wheels ended in lots of fun and many bruises. An 1890 ball scandalized and titillated the audience with the first performance of the French cancan in Rio.

As slavery began its long and lingering collapse, runaways sought refuge in settlements in surrounding cities, thus reinforcing African influences. In 1885 a group of Congolese Afro- Brazilians dressed as devils, old men, kings, and queens paraded behind banners directed and controlled by a whistle-blowing master. Drums set the beat for a series of dance steps and chants. The Sudanese began the *rancho* tradition, which included women and more elaborate musical accompaniment. Groups called *cordões* emerged to poke fun at authority, while prudently disguised in costume. At the lower end very modest individuals, "the dirty ones" (*sujos*), formed neighborhood *blocos de sujos*—a small handful of people identified by a distinctive dress or symbol. In 1889 twenty such *blocos* paraded in the capital. Unwilling to abandon the celebration completely to the "lower elements," in 1907 the well-to-do drove through the city in open autos filled with costumed passengers who tossed confetti and small trinkets to bystanders. By the 1930s traffic jams ended the practice and Carnival became a street festival that threw all classes together.

Musical innovations and dance steps came from below—the pace and spirit of Carnival depended on the lower classes. Samba music and dance became popular in the early 1900s. The term samba may be of Angolan origin derived from the Kimbundu word *semba* (invitation to dance), but, as in many elements of popular culture, no one can be sure. Samba schools provided a structure for increasingly costly and elaborate displays organized around a scripted theme (*enredo*). In the 1930s, as observed earlier, Vargas attempted to lower the level of satire by inaugurating a competition among groups for a prize. The Commission of Tourism subsidized samba schools and floats and oversaw the capital's entertainment. The elite and middle class sought to progressively control the level of exuberance—to a certain extent successfully. The *entrudo* no longer had such a mean streak, although perfume balls had their drawbacks. In Rio in 1984 the *sambadomo*, designed by Oscar Niemeyer, directed the parade along a corridor between concrete bleachers, in effect a controlled space. Commercialization and tourism now influence the celebration, while television coverage, prizes, and other inducements tend to reduce its spontaneity.

The one area that appears beyond external pressure is sexual license, nudity, exhibitionism, and cross-dressing. Sexual fantasy is by its nature not amenable to restriction. Role inversion, when the lowly become kings and queens and all are able to cross class lines without reproach, acts to defuse social tensions. Reversing gender roles and exaggerating femininity by male homosexuals became a noticeable feature of Carnival around 1900. Masquerade balls provided space in which to push the limits of sexuality before an elite and middle-class audience. In 1950, Elvira Pagã paraded through the streets topless in her golden bikini. She went on to win the first Carioca Queen of Carnival contest, the start of a popular tradition. Carnival master Joãozinho Trinta, a man ahead of his time, used a fully nude male group in the early 1990s, resulting in dismissal from the Beija-Flor samba school. Carnival appears to be evolving back toward neighborhood celebrations as a reaction to commercialization and the extravagant amounts of money required to mount a samba school production. The tourist industry's Carnival will continue, but the more interesting display will always be in the streets.

A Mass Democracy Messiah

Fernando Collor de Melo, a young, charismatic former governor of the state of Alagoas from a politically important family of considerable wealth, to many seemed like a Brazilian John F. Kennedy. After the disappointing events that elevated Vice President Sarney to the presidency, the electorate yearned for its own democratic icon, and Collor de Melo seemed the perfect choice. He used television to great effect lashing out at corruption and those who lived well off the long-suffering taxpayers. The candidate promised to shrink government and adopt a neoliberal economic policy that required privatizing state enterprises, liberalizing trade, and reducing tariffs. He faced some daunting problems. The military government had borrowed lavishly. The debt burden had reached almost $90 billion, among the world's largest. Collor became president in March 1990, amid high expectations.

President Collor de Melo immediately created a crisis atmosphere, easy enough to do, and then issued a stream of provisional decrees to deal with the alleged emergency. He froze savings accounts and prices and ended indexing for inflation. Business firms found their operating capital frozen. Thousands of federal workers, fired without regard to constitutional procedures, demanded reinstatement. Tariffs fell long before manufacturers had prepared themselves for competition. Collor's party, barely represented in congress, had just twenty deputies and two senators. Collor de Melo, a man in a hurry, failed to take the time to build legislative alliances, violated the spirit of the laws, and disregarded regulations and common sense. He successfully restructured debt servicing, providing some relief and new loans. Unfortunately, the corruption he promised to end soon enveloped his administration. Excessive payoffs and bribes, often offered to escape arbitrary action by officials, led to a congressional investigation and an impeachment vote. On September 29, 1992, the president resigned, hoping to avoid being removed from office. Nevertheless, an angry senate voted 76 to 5 to remove him and stripped him of political rights for eight years. On the positive side, it was the first time a president had been deposed constitutionally, rather than by the military. The episode also served as a warning to future presidents not to ignore congress.

Collor's negative record is balanced to some extent by an act of statesmanship. Building on Sarney's initiatives, he ended nuclear competition between Brazil and Argentina. Such a move required the acquiescence of the military. All three armed services—the army, navy, and air force—had their own nuclear programs. Just how extensive they were remains unclear. The armed services buried program expenses deep in the budget. It has been suggested that even military presidents had little notion of costs and developments. Following the nuclear agreement, the two countries exchanged annual visits by senior military officers, conducted joint naval exercises, and even cooperated on conventional weapons development. In 1991, Collor also signed the accord with Argentina that established the regional trading group Mercosul.

The impeachment of Collor thrust Vice President Itamar Franco into the presidency—the second vice president in a row to assume the highest office. After a low-key career in politics, he seemed out of his league. In fact, he functioned best as a provincial boss, not a national leader. Constant cabinet changes and a tendency to be against or doubtful about everything, rather than for something, seemed to promise a period of destructive drift. In 1993, Franco appointed Fernando Henrique Cardoso, an internationally respected academic and senator from São Paulo, to lead the Foreign Ministry and then moved him to the Finance Ministry. Cardoso brought a team of talented experts into the Finance Ministry, many of whom had been involved in the failed Cruzado Plan. A combination of expertise and daring along with large amounts of luck resulted in the success of the Real Plan (1994). Few expected the new plan, designed to address inflation (2,670 percent in 1993) and maintain a stable currency, to be any more successful than earlier attempts. Planners drew up a balanced budget and established a new currency, the *real*, to be phased in based on actual value. Inflation began to decline, falling to 21 percent by 1995 from 5,000 percent the year before. The poor benefited almost immediately. The poorest 50 percent of the population increased its share of income 1.2 percent, or some $7.3 billion, while the richest 20 percent lost 2.3 percent, or $12 billion. Cardoso, seemingly able to accomplish the impossible, won the presidential election in 1994 and took office in January 1995.

Mercosul: A Fragile Trading Bloc

The formation of trading blocs had long been viewed as desirable if Latin America were ever to escape the economic power of external markets. An early attempt, the Latin American Free Trade Association (LAFTA) of 1960, hoped to become a free trade bloc in twelve years. Brazil, Argentina, and Chile, the main supporters of the idea, envisioned that they would benefit from expanded trade in industrial goods by at least partially replacing European and American imports. The power of the external markets and wide variations in levels of economic development doomed the overly ambitious plan. In 1980 the Asociación Latinoamericana de Integración (ALADI) replaced LAFTA, functioning as a forum to work out tariff agreements. After both Brazil and Argentina returned to civilian rule, they signed a new agreement in 1986, the Program for Integration and Economic Cooperation (PICE). Negotiated in the full rush of the return to democracy in the region, the program suggested mutual support for civilian rule and security and implied that both countries would work toward a better life for their citizens—more of an emotional endorsement than an economic plan. The same year the Argentine-Brazilian Economic Integration Program (ABIP) sidestepped old trade differences and emphasized the importance of trade policy. Argentine president Raúl Alfonsín, who pressed for the agreement, acknowledged Brazil's leading political and economic role in the region. Nevertheless, little progress could be made until the accelerating integration in Europe forced both countries to contemplate a new international order that threatened to marginalize them. Collor and Argentine president Carlos Menem agreed that the time for serious action had arrived. On March 26, 1991, the Treaty of Asunción established the Common Market of the South (Mercosul in Portuguese; Mercosur in Spanish). Paraguay and Uruguay had little choice but to go along. Mercosul's long-range objective, the creation of a European-style economic bloc, seemed a bit too ambitious even then. Tariffs dropped dramatically—in many cases they were eliminated between member states.

Although Mercosul became the world's fourth largest trading bloc, its future success remained uncertain. Expansion to include Chile (1996) and Bolivia (1997) as associates, not full members, obscured some larger issues. Chile preferred the North American Free Trade Agreement (NAFTA) of 1994 and access to the large American market, as did others. President Bill Clinton convened the Summit of the Americas in Miami in 1994 with the idea that a hemisphere-wide free trade bloc would be in place by 2005. While little movement toward such a goal followed, the lure of the American market acted to blunt expansion of Mercosul much to Brazil's annoyance. The economic differences between the member states, as well as the long-standing financial instability of the two core members, also caused problems. Both Argentina and Brazil understood that in the event of some financial crisis they could not rely for assistance upon resources within Mercosul. Only the resources of the United States or Europe would be sufficient. Brazil, with its large population, dominates the group and produces 65 percent of Mercosul's output. As the larger power, Brazil frequently acts unilaterally. For example, in 1995, Brasília abruptly decided to limit Argentine car exports to 50 percent of the previous year's total. Then again in 1997, Brazil required payment in cash for imports, all without consulting its erstwhile partners.

Brazil views Mercosul as an important element of its political hegemony and as a counterweight to that of the United States. While Buenos Aires shares Brasília's antipathy for Washington's influence, it is just as concerned about Brazilian hegemony. In reality, Brazil cannot take the loyalty of its trading partners for granted. The long-range interests of the Spanish-speaking Mercosur are, in fact, different from those of Brazil, a point made when Chile, after months of deliberations over full membership in Mercosur, decided at the last moment to retreat. President Cardoso scheduled a triumphant summit meeting where all members would officially approve Chile's application for full membership. Before the event could take place, Chile announced negotiations with the United States on a bilateral trade agreement. Other Latin American states wanted the same arrangement. What should have been a celebration of Brazil's leadership looked like a possible wake for Mercosul as the Mercosur contingent looked for a profitable escape. The passage of the Trade Promotion Act by the U.S. Congress in August 2002 will likely lead to a hemisphere-wide free trade zone and the end of Mercosul.

The Military in the Democratic Era

The army managed the transfer of power in 1985 in an effective manner and on terms reasonably favorable to its interests. The immediate objective, to avoid accountability for dirty war tactics, obscured the important long-range strategy to maintain institutional integrity, secure access to its perceived share of resources, and ensure minimum civilian intrusion into the military's affairs. Senior officers understood that concessions had to be made in order to accommodate the new democratic reality. Moreover, Brazil had become much more economically and socially complex than when the military assumed power in 1964. Preserving core prerogatives mattered more than any cosmetic change required by the structural forms of democracy. The keystone remained the constitutional charge making the military the guarantor of the constitution, which in essence made it superior to the document itself. Ultimate military constitutional authority, a governing principle since the very birth of the republic, would be reaffirmed in Article 142 of the current Constitution of 1988. In the new era, military influence had to be exercised carefully, behind the scenes, and negotiated quietly with the president and congress. The military did not want to be seen as a destabilizing force in the early stages of civilian reorganization of the country. Military leaders, prepared to be patient, husbanded their assets. Intelligence agencies continued to function without legislative oversight, gathering political and social information on a wide range of topics and individuals, from politicians to those pressing for land reform. In Amazonia the army exercised directive authority in the region as it had during the military regime allegedly for security purposes. Just before the withdrawal from power, the military government undertook the Calha Norte project to promote the settlement of a strip of territory along the northern border. The army controlled directly some nine million hectares of land in the region. In effect, Amazonia functioned as a military preserve within a civilian state.

The reasonable economic success of the Real Plan and its new currency, as well as the subsequent political stability achieved under President Cardoso, allowed the army to strengthen its position. By fully supporting the Cardoso government the military became a political constituency entitled to patronage consideration. In 1995 the army indicated that it would not accept a salary policy that rewarded only the top generals, rather than an across-the-ranks adjustment. The impasse was overcome with Cardoso's suggestion that military personnel be classified as career state employees. A constitutional amendment shifted the issue of military pay to the executive. Both got something out of the arrangement. The army accepted the designation as employees, while the president avoided the appearance of having caved in to pressure, becoming in the process a patron of the armed forces. Military confidence in its position within the country and close standing with the president made it possible to accept civilian direction of the new Ministry of Defense in 1999.

The army's relationship with the Cardoso regime rested on more than pay. The president viewed the military as vital to his plans for a resurgent Brazil. Moreover, the country's dominant economic position in South America had geopolitical implications, which required the projection of power. A weak, demoralized army would neither serve nor meet the president's expectations. Significantly, a newspaper poll in 1997 gave the armed forces an 80 percent public approval rating. Modernizing the military took place in spite of budgetary restrictions. By 1998 defense expenditures topped $13.1 billion. In addition to the army, the navy and air force received attention. Brazil's navy is perhaps the most powerful in Latin

America, with the possible exception of Chile's. Military modernization, largely under the control of the various services, is not subject to public scrutiny. The Cardoso regime allowed the army to reactivate its graphite reactor program, which was capable of producing weapons-grade plutonium. The program had been closed down by President Collor.

President Cardoso did not hesitate to use the army for internal policing functions as permitted by the constitution. Both the military high command and the government largely agreed on the mission of the armed forces. According to General Benedito Leonel, the chairman of the Joint Chiefs, the army's role was to win or prevent war, confront insecurity, and maintain peace. Insecurity, defined as low-intensity conflict and further specified to mean racial, class, or religious strife, economic conflict, and urban violence, gave the army a strong internal mission. Factors contributing to instability, such as misconduct by civilian authorities, particularly the police, could also be addressed.

Reliance on the army to deal with labor and social problems began in Cardoso's first term with a strike of petroleum workers. Army occupation of four refineries carried out at dawn by soldiers armed with machine guns as well as rifles, on the direct orders of the president, made it clear that he would not allow union opposition to derail his privatization plans. The army's involvement in restraining the occupation of land by the allegedly radical Landless Movement (MST), as well as property claims by small miners, responded to orders from Brasília. Such civil actions often required a significant number of troops.

Land Reform from Above and Below

The difficult if not impossible task of land reform nevertheless needed to be addressed. The president sought not only to reassure large agricultural interests but also to meet the immediate needs of a land-hungry peasantry. An estimated 58,000 large holdings occupy 45 percent of active productive agricultural land. Much depended upon the meaning of "productive," as broadly defined in the Constitution of 1988, which exempted large productive holdings from expropriation.

A sizable amount of agricultural land is not in production and is theoretically available for distribution. Nevertheless, any large-scale redistribution effort required that resources be shifted from more immediately productive investments. Many economists regarded land reform as nonproductive and retrograde in the face of the modern trend toward large-scale commercial agriculture. An aggressive distribution program might well create a two-tier agricultural system. Small farms or cooperatives would need state funding to make them minimally productive and could not contribute to exports.

Pressure to address the issue of land comes from a number of sources, but the most effective is the Movimento Sem Terra (MST, Landless Movement) established in 1985. Its slogan, "Occupy, Resist, and Produce," masks a complex grassroots process. MST leaders plot the seizure of land, make sure that their chosen target meets the legal requirement for unproductive land, organize their forces, and provide food, water, and transportation. Immediately after the takeover, schools and medical facilities are set up. A group of several hundred to 1,500 individuals quickly plows the fields and plants crops. In effect, an instant village appears. While the government often sends in police or troops to displace the peasants and reverse illegal land seizures, it must do so carefully or risk political damage. Lawyers and politicians, including MST deputies in congress, stand as the first line of defense for the seizure, but if they fail, the settlers resist removal. Ill-trained police have massacred squatters in several incidents. The same piece of land may be occupied a number of times before the government concedes, expropriates the land, and compensates the owner. Not all successful MST seizures result in viable settlements. Inexperience, transportation difficulties, and lack of sufficient agricultural credit can be fatal. The MST also attempts to generate publicity by occupying the land of prominent individuals. President Cardoso's farm in Minas Gerais became a constant target for activists, and in 2002 they succeeded in gaining entrance only to be removed by troops and federal police. While clearly an effort to embarrass Cardoso in a presidential election year, the brief seizure produced uncertain results.

A pilot project called the Banco da Terra (Land Bank) in the northeastern state of Ceará in 1997, later extended to other states, seemed to be a positive step. The government and the World Bank pledged to provide $1 billion to buy farmland over a five-year period. The scheme required peasants to choose the land, negotiate with the owner, and after several years begin to repay the loan. The Banco da Terra scheme functioned together with the compulsory purchase of underused land by the government on which to settle landless peasants. The two programs combined provided land for 285,000 families, only a dent in the estimated 2.5 million landless peasants but a long-delayed start after decades of much talk and no action.

Indian land policy posed a similar dilemma for the government. Reserves for the native population seemed necessary because the international community equated rain forest survival with Indian survival—the guardians-of-the-forest notion. In 1988 the Federal Indian Bureau designated some 11 percent of the country's land—an area larger than Spain and France combined—for native Brazilian groups. This dramatic action supposedly resolved the issue. In 1991 the government designated forest reserves for the seventy-three indigenous groups. That same year the Union of Indigenous Nations was formed to provide a rights lobby. A dramatic moment came at the Global Forum in Rio de Janeiro in June 1992 when Indian leaders, in indigenous dress and carrying traditional weapons, arrived to make their case to an international audience. Laying aside huge tracts of land for Indian groups placated critics at least temporarily.

The inability to preserve the integrity of some land set aside, as well as the failure to establish recognizable boundaries, undercut the stability of a number of reserves. Violence, in the absence of enforcement of rights to the reserves, began almost at the moment of their creation. In 1999 the Poiguara lost land to sugar producers backed by the federal minister of justice, who cited the more important economic benefits. Logging, mining, and agricultural and cattle interests routinely violated indigenous property rights with the tacit support of local politicians. When violence breaks out, the police generally do not support indigenous claims.

It should not be assumed that all indigenous groups are powerless to protect themselves. The Kayapo of the southern state of Pará collect taxes on gold production in their Gorotire reserve and use light planes to patrol their lands. Members of other indigenous groups work in the outside wage economy and mine and log within their reserves. The key factor is the level of familiarity over time with the surrounding society. Missionaries, traders, rubber tree tappers, and others have in good ways and bad helped instruct Indians. Despite problems, the government has declared its reserve program a success, noting that the number of native Brazilians has increased, as more claim that status. Others countered that most of those demanding land are in fact not Indians, but opportunists. General reluctance to see the survival of Indians as a group explains the attitude of the authorities and the low official count of the number of Indians. Out of a population of some 174 million the government acknowledged only 330,000. Those who speak Portuguese, dress in modern clothes, and attend school are viewed as assimilated and thus no longer eligible for special rights. Differing definitions and the often romantic desires of North Americans and Europeans to ensure the cultural survival of Indians as Indians (the ecological noble savage) present political difficulties for the government.

The dilemma, as well as the historical and cultural contradictions, became evident with the Pataxo tribe's occupation of Monte Pascoal National Park, the site of Pedro Alvares Cabral's landing on the coast of Brazil in 1500. Conflict with the tribe began in the 1940s when the park was created. The Pataxo refused an offer to move to another area and survived by selling handicrafts to tourists at the park entrance. They gradually lost their language and culture to the point that the government considered them assimilated. In 1999, on the eve of the 500th anniversary of the Portuguese arrival, they occupied the park and claimed it as their homeland. The tribe demanded the return of the 138,000 acres originally set aside, most of which is now owned by ranchers and others. The Pataxo insisted that they needed more land because their number had grown to some 6,000. Environmentalists also faced an unexpected reality. Usually, they supported Indian rights as a way of preserving the rain forest, but the Pataxo wanted farms, not forests. The park is one of the few remnants of the Atlantic rain forest complete with rare specimens of brazilwood trees.

RAIN FOREST PHARMACEUTICALS: WHO SHOULD BENEFIT?

Knowledge of rain forest chemistry developed over the millennia through a process of observation and experimentation driven more by survival than by what would much later be called the scientific method. While the rain forest may be one of nature's storehouses, the identification of useful flora and their precise application depended on generations of forest dwellers. A long list of pharmaceuticals refined and synthesized in modern laboratories was derived initially from indigenous knowledge and practices. The value of such knowledge is not disputed. Scouring rain forests around the world and interrogating shamans and tribal members is one of the first steps to identify a new drug.

Clues to possible uses of indigenous knowledge come from a variety of sources, including anthropologists, missionaries, travel accounts, magazines, journals, and chance encounters. An example of the process of discovery involved a 1988 *National Geographic* magazine article on the Urueu-Wau-Wau tribe of the Amazon basin. One photograph in particular caught the attention of researchers at the pharmaceutical firm Merck. The photo showed a tapir bleeding to death from an arrow wound. The caption noted that the tip of the arrow had been coated with sap from the tiki uba tree, a natural anticoagulant. Researchers tested the bark and sap, identified the active agent, and began the process of developing a commercial product now used during heart surgery. In effect, the firm appropriated knowledge with no thought given to compensation and at very modest cost. Another example is the use of pilocarpine from the *Pilocarpus jaborandi* to treat glaucoma. The Guajajara Indians, who passed the knowledge to ethnobotanists, have become debt-ridden collectors of the fast-disappearing plant, while the government annually earns some $25 million by exporting it.

Bio-prospecting is not a new activity nor is it restricted to the drug industry. The search for new plants, fruits, grains, and a variety of natural products and knowledge about their use has been part of the discovery process for centuries. Marco Polo supposedly brought with him from a visit to the great Khan the procedure for making noodles. Today's scientists, backed by corporations and governments, have replaced wandering plant hunters. A gene bank stores plant data, turning the plant monopoly of tropical regions into a knowledge monopoly of advanced nations.

Modern intellectual property law, based on the presumed rights of individual creators of knowledge, does not recognize the collective intellectual property interests of tribal groups. The World Bank, in an effort to find a solution, pays for a team of patent lawyers to work with the Dhekuana tribe in Venezuela to safeguard their financial interests. It may be possible to classify indigenous knowledge as trade secrets, or a worldwide reworking of intellectual property law may be necessary.*

In the late 1980s pressure from nongovernmental organizations and international funding agencies intensified. Demands for preservation of the rain forest and the establishment of indigenous reserves, besides irritating officials, caused diplomatic unpleasantness and forced the government to address the issue. The difficulty of meeting conflicting demands for land, development, and forest preservation seemed exemplified by the relatively new state of Rondônia.

*Darrell Addison Posey, "Biodiversity, Genetic Resources and Indigenous People," in *Amazonia at the Crossroads: The Challenge of Sustainable Development*, ed. Anthony Hall (London, 2000), 188–204; José de Sousa Silva, "Plant Intellectual Property Rights: The Rise of Nature as a Commodity," in *Biotechnology in Latin America: Politics, Impacts, and Risks*, ed. N. Patrick Peritore and Ana Karina Galve-Peritore (Wilmington, DE, 1995), 57–68.

An agricultural state, still heavily forested, separated from Bolivia by the Guapore River and tied to the larger state of Mato Grosso by a highway network, Rondônia became an environmental frontline. Like Mato Grosso, the state produces soybeans for export along with lumber and cattle. During the military regime tax incentives and credit attracted developers and settlers. A haphazard land use pattern, with little attention paid to sustainable exploitation, characterized the early developmental history of the region.

With support of the World Bank, in 1988 planners launched the first large-scale land use zoning experiment in Rondônia and the neighboring state of Mato Grosso. In theory, the project represented a highly rational approach to land use. Technical information, soil samples, aerial and satellite mapping, and biodiversity inventories had to be gathered or made. The results of objective scientific research would then determine the proper use of land. Six zones, further subdivided into seven smaller units, blanketed the state. Zone one alloted 28 percent of the state already deforested to large-scale agriculture, livestock, and agri-forestry. Zone two, with 14 percent medium deforestation, appeared suitable for small-scale agriculture and mixed tree and crop farming. The next three zones, with low deforestation, could be exploited for sustainable fishing and forest collecting. Zone six, with very low deforestation (29 percent), became permanent forest and indigenous reserves. Variations of the land use zoning plan spread to other Amazon states.

Logging and ranching interests, in alliance with local politicians, consistently opposed the plan. Others ignored regulations against illegally burning the forest, hoping that if they deforested an area the zoning would be changed. Moreover, the technical experts ignored preexisting enterprises that did not fit into the scheme, including some *agrovilas* encouraged by INCRA. Planners succeeded in defining precise borders for indigenous reserves, thus making it easier to defend them legally. Over all, however, the scheme had little public support. Constant modification failed to establish a supportive constituency. Only the nongovernmental organizations and international agencies supported what might be characterized as a battle between social science and actual human behavior.

Changing the economic balance in favor of forests rather than cleared land appeared utopian. A combination of factors suggests that total pessimism may not be warranted. Increasingly widespread understanding of land use by settlers—knowledge gained the hard way—plays a role. The handwringing characteristic of the international reaction in the 1970s began to change in small ways in the 1980s as it became evident that poverty undercut any possibility of sustainable forests. The undeniable value of rain forests needed to be harmonized with individual economic needs. This goal required modernizing traditional forest collecting—not an easy task. Ben & Jerry's Rain Forest Crunch ice cream provided a tiny market but one that made a difference to forest collectors of Brazil nuts (Pará nuts). Forest fragrances used in natural products added yet another minor economic incentive to conserve. Ecotourism presented some intriguing possibilities, although fragile rain forests cannot carry large numbers of visitors without degradation.

The search for value relied upon imagination as well as knowledge. It dawned on researchers that what they previously believed to be natural landscapes in fact had been altered in various, almost imperceptible ways. Over time, a shaped environment emerged, which had been deliberately modified by fire, seeding, and selective cultivation. To indigenous people the forest provided medicines, shelter, and food, but not unassisted as outsiders assumed. Even the supply and species of nondomesticated animals or human-modified animals resulted from a type of forest husbandry. Artificial fish habitats planted with fish bait fruit is but one example of indigenous modification. This research insight represented a major perceptual breakthrough that shifted attention to what indigenous forest dwellers had always known and had practiced for their benefit.

Value, coupled with modified indigenous harvesting practices and international support, made it possible to devise a new sustainable logging method. A region is divided into sectors in which trees are cut, leaving selected mature specimens to re-seed and provide shade for the seedlings. The area is then left to regenerate over a thirty-year period after which the process is repeated. The extra costs are offset by a slightly higher price paid by the consumer for wood products that are certified to be the result of sustainable logging operations, in effect a chain beginning with modified indigenous methods and ending on an American or European showroom floor. It remains to be seen if this method will work in practice.

Another income source is forest knowledge itself. For centuries, Europeans dismissed indigenous knowledge as mostly folklore, in spite of having used medicinal plants almost as soon as they arrived in the New World. In the last several decades, a time of much more emphasis on intellectual property rights including the patenting of genes, forest lore has been recognized as valuable. Pharmaceutical companies bio-prospect the forests, but not before interviewing the local folk doctor and village experts. It takes millions of dollars to bring a new drug to market—a cost that is cut dramatically, in some cases by an estimated 40 percent, by relying initially on indigenous knowledge.

The solution to providing access to land and resources, while also preserving the forest, rests on monitoring and moderating the number of inhabitants and their immediate demands on the environment. Active economic exploitation often conflicts with preservation and sustainability goals. Social scientists, planners, and worldwide friends of the forests as yet do not have a controlling grasp of the problem from a political, psychological, economic, or social perspective. The point where deforestation and its negative environmental impact will stop and where a balance is achieved between the demand for land, development, and forested nature remains unclear.

Notes

1. See the tables in David Samuels, "Reinventing Local Government?" in Peter R. Kingstone and Timothy J. Powers, eds., *Democratic Brazil: Actors, Institutions, and Processes* (Pittsburgh, 2000).
2. Federal tax authorities announced in 2002 that professionals (lawyers, medical doctors, et al.) grossly underreported their incomes, while their actual expenditures exceeded the reported amount by twenty times or more. As a consequence, their actual tax rate amounted to 1.5 percent.
3. Benedita da Silva (Bené), elected Rio de Janeiro's lieutenant governor in 1998, assumed the higher office when the governor resigned to run for president in 2002. The first black woman to hold such a position, she subsequently failed in her bid to be elected governor in 2002.
4. Articles 182 and 183, *Lei Orgánica do Municipio de Belo Horizonte* (21 de Marzo de 1990).
5. Sidney Mintz noted the process of the spread of sugar consumption among members of the British working class, as they became aware of its use. It went from being a fashionable luxury to a necessary item with significant economic consequences. New forms of consumption resulted in important social change. *Sweetness and Power: The Place of Sugar in Modern History* (New York, 1986), 181.
6. Whether the state or private capital should operate radio stations became a major issue after World War I. Europe favored state ownership. The United States, initially ambivalent, decided on private capital. Washington believed that private ownership of radio would counter European control of information through their transatlantic cables. It also created a dynamic market for equipment manufacturers. The League of Nations' Washington Conference in 1927 allowed regional control of frequencies, much to the satisfaction of the United States.
7. Quoted in Bryan Daniel McCann, "Thin Air and the Solid State: Radio, Culture, and Politics in Brazil's Vargas Era" (Ph.D. diss., Yale University, 1999).
8. Editorial Abril, the country's largest magazine publisher, began distributing a Portuguese-language edition of *Playboy* in 1975. Brazil is the most profitable market for the magazine after the United States. Abril's first Latin American magazine was *Donald Duck* (*O Pato Donald*) in 1950. Amelia Simpson provides an exquisite deconstruction of Xuxa (see Bibliography).
9. Other British expatriates introduced the game to many countries, including to Argentina in 1867.
10. Similar problems are also evident in American baseball and European soccer.

CHAPTER SEVEN

Brazil in the New Century

Restructuring Poverty: Pentecostalism

In the 1990s one out of every six Brazilians belonged to a Protestant religious group. Forty percent of Latin American Protestants are Brazilian. Of that number over 75 percent are Pentecostals—approximately, twelve million in a country widely assumed to be historically and culturally Catholic. The roots of Pentecostalism in Brazil are barely a century old. It originated in the United States and in the poverty that afflicted the American working class in the Gilded Age of the late nineteenth century. The mad rush toward modernization and fabulous wealth that fell to those able to take advantage of that moment in American history left many behind, bewildered and in misery. One of those who struggled with the new reality, William Joseph Seymour, an African American preacher from Louisiana, provided the spark that eventually became a worldwide movement. He went to Los Angeles, California, in 1906 with his message of the gift of the Holy Spirit, speaking in tongues, and faith healing.

Two Swedish converts, Daniel Berg and Gunnar Vangren, believed they had been called to go to northern Brazil. They arrived in Belém in late 1910, dressed in their wool suits, ready to instruct and convert. By 1911 they had formed their own mission church and in 1918 formally established the Assembly of God (Assembléia de Deus, AD). For a while, Belém was the New Jerusalem. The AD remains the largest Pentecostal group in Brazil today. Farther south, an Italian, Luís Francescon, who had been converted in Chicago, founded the first Pentecostal church in São Paulo in 1910. Pastor Franciscon's church, the Christian Congregation (Congregação Cristã), initially catered to Italian immigrants but soon attracted Brazilian believers. In the 1930s missionaries made a conscious decision to nationalize the movement by turning pastoral functions over to the native-born.

Pentecostalism's success rests on its ability to respond to the social pathology of poverty. Mobility from poverty to riches is virtually impossible. The middle class has a degree of upward mobility, but it seldom extends to the lower classes. Cultural, economic, educational, and racial barriers constitute an almost impenetrable wall. Powerlessness is a constant psychological state that often leads to hopelessness, depression, alcoholism, domestic violence, and family abandonment. Pentecostal beliefs provide hope and an organizational method for one's daily life. Individual adherents have a direct connection with Jesus, in effect bypassing a structure that leaves them powerless. Speaking in tongues represents both a physical manifestation of the gift of the Holy Spirit and an implied spiritual fusion as well as a partnership with Jesus in every aspect of daily life. Life on the bottom can be made better, but escape from poverty will be a matter of degree. Lower-class believers have created a society apart from the hostile, unresponsive reality of poverty. The willingness of believers to tithe, in spite of abuses, may be directly related to their relief at being able to give rather than passively receive. They rally from below, turning inward to rescue themselves. In contrast to the Christian Base Communities, who hope to change state policy, the Pentecostals seek to change themselves.

Pentecostalism is assimilationist even as it rejects secular society. Racial tensions within the movement are much less pronounced than in society as a whole. Black pastors of racially mixed congregations are common. Believers express the desire to be treated with respect and on an equal basis with whites. While their desire is only partially met, the distinct possibility exists within the movement. It is accepted that blacks have the ability to come closer to God because of their humble circumstances and their alleged superior ability to speak in tongues. Afro-Brazilian healers also are more esteemed than white healers. Nevertheless, equality is uneven and riddled with lingering stereotypes recognized and resented by the Afro-Brazilians who make up some 50 percent of believers. It remains to be seen whether Pentecostalism will be swept by re-Africanization, perhaps leading to separation along racial lines.

In theory, Pentecostalism supports traditional gender and family roles. The family is considered a sacred institution ruled by a husband with a respectful, obedient wife and children. An important yet seemingly slight twist is that the family is the refuge and the only safe haven outside of the church. Those who because of work must navigate the streets are dealing with Satan at all times. There are two worlds—that of the Holy Spirit, and that on the outside of temptation and all the evil that follows for those who are seduced. Such a vision reinforces a moral segregation from the general society.

Believers are more prosperous and life is better. Drinking, gambling, drugs, and prostitution consume scarce resources—estimated

Middle-class apartment buildings in Copacabana with favelas in the background. Mudslides are a common hazard on unstable hillsides, and water and sanitation are often inadequate. Drug gangs are active in some of the favelas. *Courtesy of Tom André, photograph by Lisa M. Robinson*

at 30 percent of lower-class earnings. Sobriety makes it possible to hold down a steady job with a corresponding increase in earnings. A survey indicated that a large percentage of Pentecostal men work as security guards, presumably because of their reliability and honesty. Reorientation of expenditure means a better diet and fewer illnesses. The everyday utility of the Pentecostal lifestyle and its growing number of believers reinforce a sense of unity. So far this has not translated into effective political organization. The leadership, however, seems intrigued by the possibilities. A Pentecostal network, TV Record, could provide political access to the national audience far beyond its current programming.[1] The AD bureaucracy grew significantly in the postwar years and enabled the church to establish contacts with politicians, receive patronage, and develop political ambitions. Pentecostals have been elected to office at all levels. Nevertheless, the membership, as distinct from the leadership, is generally disinterested in mobilizing as a political group. Independent political power requires more active secular engagement, something believers avoid. Leadership is respected up to a point, but if the congregation feels that an error has been made they are quick to make it known, at times shouting down a pastor. The driving force remains the individual member, not the organization. Moreover, believers vote as they please rather than as their pastors might prefer.[2] Their perceived direct connection with Jesus bypasses the putative authority of pastors and church administrators, who can only plead for support.

Rethinking Politics

Party bosses prefer the current arrangement of weak political parties within a circumscribed federal system. The tools at hand to ensure their continued control are very effective. It is hard for the electorate to hold them accountable when representatives are not elected by districts. Elections of federal senators and deputies across a state and of local council officials in a large municipality require organizational skills and a permanent network. Political bosses have both, along with the ability to muster votes statewide. Who runs for office and at what level must be worked out in close consultation with political bosses if there is to be any chance of success. The system discourages mavericks who want to go it on their own. It is a male-dominated process. Consequently, in 2002 only 7 percent of congressional representatives are women, compared to Argentina's 31 percent.

Political bosses can create an almost tailor-made structure, including a party to meet any circumstance. Formation of short-lived political parties able to field a candidate for a particular election muddies the waters and fragments the vote. Only 101 voters need to sign a petition to register a new party provisionally. A permanent party registration is much more complex, but meanwhile the party has twelve months to use its provisional status for short-term tactical purposes. Party loyalty is fleeting and based on immediate shared needs. Individuals change parties for tactical purposes, sometimes changing back if a better deal is offered or the situation alters. The result is a weak system that makes coalition building a difficult task but one that appears to be inescapable.

Politics has traditionally been patriarchal and elitist. Mobilization of the lower classes invariably came from above, often to serve a purpose other than advancing lower-class interests. Vargas formed controlled unions during the Estado Novo and attempted to mobilize labor in his elected term. The rewards, while not insignificant, came down from above. Nevertheless, short-term concessions did not change the fundamental inequalities. The experience of the left in the postwar period, both positive and negative, forced soul searching and agonizing conclusions. Recourse to violence failed and, moreover, weakened the left politically and morally. Industrial strikes, such as the series of walkouts in São Paulo in the late 1970s, had limited goals unlikely to change the fundamental roots of poverty. International examples, such as the Solidarity movement in Poland, suggested that wider goals could bring about significant change. Luiz Inácio Lula da Silva (Lula), a prime mover of the 1970s strikes, proposed the formation of a workers' party to appeal to the lower class in general, not just union members. The Partido dos Trabalhadores (PT) officially formed in 1980. Several federal congressmen, including one senator, switched parties. The PT accepted the principles of democratic politics and the notion of *basismo*, or bottom-up organizing. Christian Base Communities, clerics, and others who endorsed grassroots movements lent support and at the same time provided a nominal party presence throughout Brazil. In the presidential elections of 1989, Lula almost won in the runoff against Fernando Collor de Melo. Subsequently, he lost to Cardoso, and in the president's run for a second term, Lula lost by a landslide. Nevertheless, by 1995 the party had five senators in addition to several state governors, and by 1998 some 750,000 members and a reputation for honesty and principle.

The growth of the PT coincided with the shift of political power to the local level. The Constitution of 1988 transferred revenue and power downward. Electing governors and mayors became as important as electing federal congressmen, if not more so. Broadening the party base to capture the presidency required a direct appeal to all voters. Yet the political rhetoric that built the party frightened the middle class. The PT sought to modify its former union militancy without losing its base support—not an easy task. Calls for capping or refusing to pay international debts and more social spending alarmed those who remembered the suffering inflicted by rampant inflation before the Real Plan. Renationalizing industries and utilities and restricting foreign imports in an era of market globalization would drive off the private investment and the revenue the country needed to address social needs. The PT appeared caught between demands for redistribution and the reality that the massive revenues required could come only from investment in increased development—the same dilemma faced by the military regime in 1964.

A move away from the negative image of shop floor politics reached a critical point in the person of Marta Suplicy. Middle-class concerns about the PT leader's lack of formal education and his radical background played a role in losing middle-class support for Lula's past presidential bids. At the last moment, voters who publicly favored the PT switched to other candidates. Marta Suplicy demonstrated that a middle-class professional could still support the PT and Lula. An energetic, attractive woman and well-known sex therapist, she had her own popular television show offering frank advice on sexual matters until she switched to politics. Running for mayor of São Paulo in 2000 on an anticorruption platform, as well as other everyday issues such as crime, homelessness, and street children, she won with 58 percent of the vote. As mayor of the most important city she exerted tremendous influence. Suplicy moved easily among the city's poor (estimated to be more than two million) and among industrialists and the upper classes. Dressed in elegant suits, exquisitely perfumed with perfectly groomed blonde hair, she charmed even her most hostile male critics. Politically, she bridged the social factions, and within the PT her presence indicated a move toward the more comfortable center. She describes her policies as "business-friendly socialism." Highly publicized romantic attachments may prevent her from reaching the top. Nevertheless, she presented a new, reassuring workers' party political model.

Nationwide the party steadily gained ground, with Lula finally winning the presidency in 2002. Yet it remains to be seen if the PT will be able to avoid the pitfalls—made almost inescapable by the Constitution of 1988—of fleeting party loyalty, weak and opportunistic coalitions, corruption, and political bosses. The constant switching of parties at all levels leads to a homogenized low level of ethics across the entire political spectrum. Whether the PT succeeds or fails, it has established a model sure to be adopted, adapted, and modified.[3]

President Cardoso also rethought the nature of Brazilian politics, but on a longer-term intellectual level. His books and articles left a trail that offers insight into the evolution of his ideas. An avid student of Karl Marx and Max Weber in his early academic career, he also embraced the need for empirical studies. In the conflict between theory and the way things are, he sided with reality rather than slip from theory into ideology. He studied sociology at the University of São Paulo under two internationally famous sociologists and taught there until forced out by the military regime. In exile he became a leading member of the dependency school, which posited a dynamic center and a struggling periphery of underdevelopment. His own unique version of dependency rejected simple historical inevitability and unchanging blocs. Like others of the school, he saw the proper context of analysis as the international system and underdevelopment as a location within the system, not stages of development. Nevertheless, when reminded of his previous academic opinions, he reportedly jokes, "Forget everything I said." In the end he settled on social democracy as a viable political structure able to redirect the country's historic patriarchal tradition. Cardoso critically scanned the world of the possible and allowed experience to influence his approach as president. As a result, he became a cautious and pragmatic reformer. Whether his realistic center-left model will have a lasting impact remains uncertain.

Crime, Drugs, and Public Order

The issue of crime and its causes is a complex one, involving many factors, including poverty, malnutrition, family instability, violence, illiteracy, uncertain values, and hopelessness. In a society that is rapidly adopting modern materialism, the limited ability of a significant proportion of the population to participate may encourage banditry, crime, and other illegal activities. The image of the good life presented on television and in movies reaches every class. Social expectations that certain groups engage in criminal activity may encourage such behavior by diminishing the notion of individual responsibility and at the same time justifying extralegal controls.

Expansion of the middle class, which is less able to pay for effective private security, presents more opportunities and accounts in part for the periodic public outrage. Fear of crime diverts resources to nonproductive uses (estimated at $3 billion in 2001) and distorts development in ways not immediately evident. The long-lasting social, psychological, political, and cultural consequences may be even more damaging. Extensive reliance on private security guards, estimated in 2001 at 500,000, is a concrete manifestation of the social pathology that afflicts the country. Nevertheless, few appear ready to deal with the symptoms or the root causes.

Drug usage, large amounts of illegal money, and turf battles compound the problem. Money supplies the means to organize criminal activity, and endless numbers of unemployed young men facilitate recruiting. The drug business is a labor-intensive industry and pays well. The wholesaler transports drugs from a market center, perhaps in the interior or across a convenient border, and sells them in bulk to the packager, who cuts the purity to the desired degree and then passes the drugs on to the *avião* (airplane) to retail the street product. A whole series of individuals, from the lookout (*olheiro*) to the runners, constitute a vertically organized industry. A young drug worker can earn from $7,000 to $30,000 per year with few skills other than his wits. Favelas provide the manpower and the ideal location for the industry. Ready customers can be found among both the affluent and the poverty-stricken.

Drug workers are associated with organized paramilitary groups with names that imply a political component. In Rio an organized crime army of some 10,000 (equivalent in size to the federal police) confronts a weak enforcement system. The two major groups are the Comando Vermelho (Red Command) and the Terceiro Comando (Third Command). All are well armed with the latest weapons and use cell phones, pagers, and all the other technology necessary to connect with their customers. Ill trained, poorly paid, underfunded, and disorganized, the police try to avoid direct confrontation whenever possible. As a result, the favelas are often ignored, except when the political authorities force them to provide a pretense of policing. Politicians frequently seek a tacit agreement with organized crime allowing them to establish their own sanctuary in return for avoiding open conflict and an obvious presence in certain zones. Gangs function as controlling political authorities in their own zones to the extent that they decree shop closings to honor their "fallen" comrades. An increasingly entrenched criminal interest group poses a potentially dangerous challenge to established authority. When Rio's governor Benedita (Bené) da Silva confronted organized crime's control of the favelas, gangs demonstrated their strength and disdain by ordering businesses in Copacabana and Ipanema to close in honor of one of their late members. The threat to previously uncontested upperclass zones shocked the city and played a role in Bené's unsuccessful bid for reelection in October 2002. A subsequent threat to disrupt elections caused some concern. The army and the police deployed in force to reassure voters, and the election went off without incident.

An unfortunate consequence is the negative impact on grassroots political organization within the favelas. In the first stage, the neighborhood associations and the drug operators coexist. But as the network expands, providing employment and money, its influence overshadows the role of the favela officials. For example, in Vidigal, drug operators threatened to kill the president of the association and his family in 1996 unless he petitioned the authorities to remove the police. In 1999 thugs physically threw out the elected president along with the board and installed their own. Finally, in January of the following year the imposed president's severed body parts washed ashore on Ipanema Beach. In 1994, Brazil's murder rate exceeded that of the United States. By 1996 it reached 24.8 per thousand compared to 10.1 in the United States. São Paulo in 1999 posted 9,000 homicides compared to 661 in New York.

The difficulty of dealing with urban violence and crime is compounded by organizational and political factors. The large number of police organizations and the lack of coordination among them is a problem. The federal police, with fewer than 10,000 men, in theory can be used to support the state enforcement structure, as can the federal highway police (Policia Rodoviária). The principal police forces are the Policia Militar (PM, Military Police)—not under military control but organized along military lines and functioning as an army reserve—and the investigative civil police. The PMs number around 400,000, more than in all branches of the military combined. Municipalities also rely upon Guardas Municipais to protect city property and employees. On occasion the army may be utilized. The whole system is highly bureaucratic on one level but largely unsupervised at the street level. Professionalism varies from state to state, ranging from ineffective to barely passable. A vivid demonstration of police incompetence occurred in June 2000, when 35 million viewers watched on television as police dealt ineptly with a bus hijacking. The gunman, captured alive, died of suffocation in the police van, and officers shot one of the hostages. The resulting outrage forced President Cardoso to quickly issue a "national public security plan," to spend more money on public safety.

In spite of the lack of police professionalism, and a low rate of solving crimes, Brazil's prisons are overcrowded. In 1997 the Organization of American States human rights commission censored Brazil. The Catholic Church called for releasing 70 percent of inmates, even suggesting a general amnesty in 1996. Amnesty International reported "terrifying" conditions in facilities for child offenders in São Paulo. Overcrowding and brutality combined to produce a state of constant tension.

São Paulo's Carandiru prison is Latin America's largest, making revolts inevitable. Brutal prison conditions contribute to a virtual state of siege. Riots, killings, and breakouts are common. An uprising in Carandiru in 1992 resulted in the killing of 111 prisoners by police. Colonel Ubiratan Guimarães, who issued the orders, subsequently received a sentence of 632 years in prison. Another prison rebellion in Carandiru in February 2001 almost became a national revolt. Inmates in São Paulo used cell phones to organize simultaneous uprisings in twenty-nine other prisons. In November 2001 the maximum-security facility at Rio's prison complex at Bangu experienced a takeover by 896 inmates armed with rifles, machine guns, and even grenades. A raid on Bangu I in 2002 by a special police force found a gang-operated telephone system able to set up conference calls worldwide. In most prisons, organized gangs function as a quasi-governing body allied with intimidated and corrupt prison administrators. Organized crime appears to control the states of Espírito Santo, north of Rio de Janeiro, and Acre in the far west.

A large part of the prison problem may be traced to ill-trained police, poor administrative practices (including inadequate record keeping), internal corruption, and overdue legal reform (including restructuring the court system, training judges, and paying them appropriately). Despite the political, financial, and cultural obstacles, complete overhaul of the criminal code appears necessary. In 2001 a panel of federal lawyers found 27,471 laws, many of them contradictory. It is not surprising that criminal law is unworkable. As Nagashi Furukawa, the beleaguered director of prisons of the state of São Paulo, observed, "I have come to the conclusion that prisons serve no purpose—the only thing they are good for is to make people worse." At the end of 2002 plans were announced to close Carandiru.

The treatment of prisoners and street children offers a glimpse into the political, cultural, and social psyche. Violence against street children stems from the widely held perception that they are vermin whose life of crime starts with minor theft, purse snatching, and crimes of opportunity and gradually turns to violent robbery and perhaps worse. The level of social hatred directed toward the street children appears to be a result of the psychological conflict between society's obligation to cherish and nurture the young, and the unwillingness or inability of the same society to address the conditions that lead to abandoned children. The results of a survey taken by the newspaper *Folha de São Paulo* in both Rio and São Paulo in 1993 demonstrated the moral and psychological contradictions. Taken shortly after the killing of eight children, the survey indicated that 46 percent of the respondents experienced fear when approached by a street child, and 83 percent felt pity.

Street children are in effect discarded as less than human. Extreme harshness toward them is justified by the belief that the court system does not function and that policing is ineffective. Merchants worry, with good reason, that the presence of street children keeps customers away from their stores. Storekeepers may have set the initial pattern of extralegal violence. The phenomenon reached a noticeable level in the 1960s. The continuing urban inflow of low-skilled labor, along with makeshift settlements, increased the number of poor children perceived to be a problem as well as the level of social desperation. In 1990, UNICEF estimated that 7.5 million children between the ages of ten and seventeen worked in the streets. In 2002, on any given night in Rio, 4,000 to 5,000 children huddle to sleep in doorways, tunnels, and other protected areas.

Going Global

The success of the Real Plan provided a financial foundation for economic expansion but did not ensure complete victory over inflation or budgetary stability. Weak federal control over financial institutions owned, or effectively controlled, by states and large publicly owned industrial corporations posed a potentially dangerous threat. Many of these entities had long ignored underfunded pension obligations and heavy debts. Hidden obligations that eventually became the Central Bank's problem constituted fiscal time bombs. Inevitably, overstaffed government enterprises served patronage needs. Inflated costs resulted in slim returns, if any, to the treasury. Government-owned banks served as devices for funneling money to various expensive, politically motivated projects. Borrowing money from banks for operating funds, wages, or construction projects resulted in constant bailouts. For example, in 1995, Banespa, the bank of the state of São Paulo, lent that state $15.5 billion, nine times the bank's net worth. Debts rolled over until an agreement could be worked out with the federal government to pay the bank's debt. In 1997 it required a bailout of $50 billion, the largest in the institution's history. Estimates of the amount of wasted resources by Banespa over the years range as high as $300 billion. Even private banks played the game. Expensive bailouts of insolvent banks undercut anti-inflationary policies. Their intimate connection with politicians at all levels made reform difficult and politically dangerous. The solution—to privatize—required dealing with politicians, unions, and bankers, all with fiscal skeletons in their vaults.

Privatization of banks began with smaller institutions before moving on to the major challenge of Banespa. Taken over by the Central Bank, Banespa went on the block in 1994. There were over sixty postponements before it could be sold. A Spanish bank, Banco Santander Central Hispano (BSCH), in November 2000 bought 60 percent of the voting stock for $3.7 billion. The new owners reduced the work force by 50 percent and increased returns on equity. Two other government banks, the Banco do Brasil and the Caixa Econômica Federal, posed similar problems. It remains to be seen just how successful bank privatization will be. Nevertheless, the sale of Banespa represented a fiscal milestone. In spite of fears that privatization would lead to foreign domination, publicly traded domestic banks are the major beneficiaries and control the financial services market, even to the extent of buying out foreign competitors. Of the country's six major banks, only one (BSCH) is foreign owned. Innovative product development, including offering accounts and credit cards to favela residents previously without access to credit, is characteristic of domestic banks. Unibanco makes its services available through some 5,000 post offices.

Telephone privatization proceeded relatively easily. Poor service, long waits for installation, and high costs guaranteed public support.

Moreover, most businesses recognized the need to use the new technology, including Internet access and cellular, if they hoped to stay competitive. Portugal's Telecom and Spain's Telefónica made substantial investments. The massive industrial network of the Companhia Vale do Rio Doce, at one time responsible for 90 percent of iron ore exports, went on the block as did aircraft manufacturer Embraer. Utilities also brought in money, and then raised rates to become profitable. Politically, privatization allowed the government to withdraw subsidies without a major battle.

The sale of domestic industry represented only one side of the process of globalization. Less well known is the creation of homegrown multinationals. Large Brazilian firms do business in the United States, Canada, Europe, and Asia with a work force drawn from many different nations. International construction firms based in Brazil work around the world. Itaú, a vast banking network, competes with Citicorp and others. Steelmaker Gerdau, with seven mills in the United States and two in Canada in addition to its domestic operations, is the world's twelfth largest producer. Orange juice companies have Florida production and distribution operations. In a similar fashion, American soybean farmers purchased properties in Brazil to take advantage of lower production costs and land prices. Brazilian corporations maintain networks and partnerships that link them with other multinationals. TV Globo in the 1990s marketed soap operas successfully in such unlikely spots as Eastern Europe. In a partnership with Mexico's Televisa, a series filmed in 2002 in Brazil in Spanish and aimed at the U.S. Hispanic population promises to capture a significant share of the advertising market. TV Globo used actors from all over Latin America to mirror the diverse origins of their American audience. An online chat room along with a choice of endings encourages viewer involvement. The existence of Brazilian multinationals, from large to small and engaged in every type of activity, perhaps spells the impending end of economic nationalism. Of all Latin American countries Brazil has the most registered companies (thirty-six) listed for trading in New York through depository receipts (ADRs). Nevertheless, it is only a small fraction of the number of ADRs traded.

The franchising of restaurant chains in the United States and Europe suggests a growing trend. The Fogo de Chão, one of the best *churrascaria* (barbecue) chains, with restaurants in São Paulo and Pôrto Alegre, has branches in Dallas, Houston, and Atlanta. The popularity of Brazilian food and beverages in the United States is indicated by the growing competition, such as Texas do Brazil with three restaurants in Texas and planned expansion to Memphis, Palm Beach, and Aruba. Other cities have attracted such enterprises, notably Miami and New York. The growing popularity of *cachaça* in the United States and Europe threatens the market for single malt scotch and tequila. The *caipirinha* made with *cachaça*, lime, or even passion fruit has become a trendy drink.[4]

Avança Brasil (Advance Brazil)

Development, with modernization as the objective, has been a remarkably consistent process in Brazil's history. While several different developmental visions are in play, in the end all agree on the objective. During the empire the advantages of port and transportation expansion, among other things, seemed beyond question to the elite. The parameters of development broadened with the establishment of the republic in 1889, changed dramatically with World War I, and continued to expand into the present. Through it all, development remained unbalanced with the lower classes reaping much less than the more favored elements of Brazilian society. Nevertheless, the need for semiskilled labor and the expansion of domestic markets and international trade inevitably increased the number of the workers, middle-class managers, and technicians as well as enterprises. With globalization a two-tier economy has developed, one restricted to the domestic market and the other functioning in both the domestic and international economies. Brazil's economic role in Latin America cannot be ignored. It has five times as many people as any other South American country and three times the GDP. Its economy is the largest in Latin America, followed by Mexico. If the city of São Paulo were an independent nation, it would be the third largest in Latin America. The southern state of Santa Catarina alone has an economy as large as those of Paraguay and Bolivia combined.

Multinational companies have a prominent public image, and many people assume that they dominate the economy. In reality, in 2000, approximately 98 percent of all enterprises were micro, small to medium concerns. Nevertheless, multinationals directed a significant percentage of exports (45 percent). While large industrial companies draw in smaller concerns as suppliers, the vast majority of firms have little contact with them and are not involved in exports. In addition, many multinationals sell to their subsidiaries in other countries rather than expanding export markets.

Exports in 2000 were concentrated in tight categories, products, companies, and regions. Twenty-five products represented 60 percent of exports, with seven nations receiving 56 percent of these items. Forty companies shipped 39 percent of exports from the south (Paraná, Santa Catarina, and Rio Grande do Sul), and the southeastern region

(São Paulo, Minas Gerais, Rio de Janeiro, and Espírito Santo) was responsible for 83 percent of exports. Industrial exports accounted for 57 percent, and 41.2 percent of exports came from agribusiness. On the positive side, markets remained diversified among the United States, Europe, and Asia. In 2001, Brazil ranked eleventh in bilateral trade with the United States.

A World Bank study in 2001 rated Brazil fifty-fifth out of sixty in facilitating the flow of trade, an indication that reforming internal procedures by itself would add significantly to exports. Brazil's external trade is only a small percentage of international commerce—far below its potential. Just a few percentage points would make a large impact on the GDP. Clearly, Brazil has not begun to engage fully its economy in world markets. When ad campaigns are used to boost exports, results are invariably good. In 2001 the Brazilian fruit campaign expanded exports of mangoes, papayas, melons, grapes, apples, and lemons 60 percent over 1998 levels. Chronically high interest rates reflecting perceived risk factors added 3.8 to more than 10 percent to production costs across every sector.

The overconcentration of industrial production in the city and state of São Paulo retards developmental momentum elsewhere. Inevitably, investments are attracted to the region because of its dynamic market, skilled work force, well-developed infrastructure, and effective transportation links. In 2001 the city received 42 percent of all external investments in the country. São Paulo contributes 35 percent to the republic's GDP and virtually the same percentage of exports. The challenge is to diversify across the nation without jeopardizing São Paulo's position as chief exporter. A major step in that direction is the opening of Ford's Camaçari industrial complex in the state of Bahia. The facility, surrounded by its parts suppliers, has the capacity to produce annually 250,000 vehicles and has generated 5,000 direct jobs. In 2001 the market absorbed just under one million cars. It remains to be seen what impact this growth will have in the northeast and whether other companies will follow Ford. The possibility of São Paulo becoming a heavy industry Rust Belt is a grim prospect. With this in mind, the Bank for National Economic and Social Development (BNDES) increased efforts to encourage smaller firms to export. While many indicated an interest, they lacked adequate knowledge of the global market and quality requirements, as well as the promotion and advertising skills necessary for success overseas. The realization that the country lacks such knowledge led to a flood of master's degree programs in business administration, most of doubtful quality but others up to international standards and likely to make a contribution. Bureaucratic paperwork barriers discourage inexperienced firms. The exporters' association (AEB) reported in 2002 that out of 100 first-time exporters, only twenty planned to do so again.

In order to encourage domestic producers to add an external component and to make exporting easier, the country's transportation system needs to be expanded and costs dramatically lowered. An expensive plan already under way includes improving ports, airports, railways, highways, and waterways. The Paraná River Hidrovía project is intended to create a second seacoast along the western border of the country. The project requires billions of dollars, most of which must come from foreign investors. The nation has barely utilized its rivers. Only an estimated 3 percent of navigable waterways are used. The potential for a vast river system is obvious. Realization that the country must attract ever more capital led to the creation in 2000 of an investment agency, Investe Brasil. The federal government's development plan for 2000–03, titled Avança Brasil, depends on attracting and holding global capital, perhaps in joint public and private enterprises.

Energy production has become a bottleneck made all too obvious by widespread blackouts across the country in 2001. A severe drought that suddenly dropped hydroelectric supplies below required levels caused a jump in prices for industry and consumers. Rationing of electricity became both a political and an economic issue. Accelerated development of natural gas resources and construction of pipelines, including extending the pipeline from Bolivia, along with a surge of new hydroelectric projects promises to relieve the energy shortage some time in the future.

An overlooked commercial asset is the Brazilian immigrant community in the United States, and to a lesser extent in other countries. Significant outmigration is often viewed as an indicator of discontent, that people have given up on the country. The return of some 225,000 Japanese-Brazilians to an uncertain welcome in Japan after several generations is a poignant reminder of the nation's failure to meet its people's expectations. Economic refugees make up a large percentage of those who leave. Yet there is a positive aspect to outmigration as well. Such enterprising people, many with experience in micro and small businesses, might have been lost to the nation in the nineteenth and most of the twentieth centuries, but not now. The ease of travel at an affordable price makes back-and-forth contact natural as well as ongoing. Telephone cards, sold at every convenience market, permit quick and economical voice communication. E-mail allows instant written and almost cost-free contact. Those who leave Brazil are not the old-type of immigrants who left the mother country behind to cross a seemingly endless sea and never to look back. Like other Latin American groups in the United States,

Brazilians have their immigrant networks. Brazilians in the United States number slightly under one million and have the potential to stimulate trade and commerce between the two countries. Their contribution is recognized already in the street signs of New York City's Little Brazil and in Atlanta, Boston, Miami, and New Orleans.

The Brazil Cost

A combination of actual negative realities and perceptual myths make up what is referred to aptly as the Brazil Cost, the international perception that the country may slip back into conditions of hyperinflation, unmanageable debt, and economic and political instability—ailments that afflicted the country between 1945 and 1964 and in the 1980s. The notion of extreme fragility underpins everything. As a result, the slightest hint of trouble is enough to set off a panic. When Russia defaulted in 1998, the real experienced a run, forcing a devaluation of the currency in the following year, even though Brazil's economic situation differed completely from that of the former Soviet Union. Fiscal problems in Argentina inevitably cast doubts about the country's financial health. Historically, Brazil has appeared vulnerable to financial disasters often not of its own making. Moreover, currency devaluation increases the debt burden. By 2000 the debt exceeded 50 percent of GDP. A 20.5 percent devaluation of the real pushed the debt to 61.9 percent of GDP in 2002. Interest on the debt is more than the total spent on education and health combined. With bad luck, it is possible to envision a debt burden equal to the GDP. A complex, often irrational tax system, which consumes approximately 33 percent of the national income while retarding economic growth, is in need of urgent reform.

The attractiveness of the country's market is diminished by the extremely poor distribution of wealth, which limits the buying power needed for medium- to high-value durable goods, as well as the attendant issues of crime, poverty, low educational attainment, malnutrition, and chronic health problems. Jean Ziegler, UN Special Representative for Nutrition Rights, after an extensive tour of the country in 2002, declared hunger in Brazil "an act of [state] violence."[5] Negatives such as widespread corruption, an inefficient and often hostile bureaucratic structure, and lack of legal and judicial transparency also deter investment. Labor expenses are inflated in spite of high unemployment because of government regulation that provides job tenure and social benefits. Estimated nonwage costs to business average some 102 percent of the actual wage. In 2001 the

World Bank rated Brazil forty-sixth out of fifty-nine countries in the amount of time wasted in dealing with bureaucrats and fifty-fifth out of sixty of those with efficient and transparent judicial systems.

When balanced against attractive investment opportunities, the Brazil Cost determines the degree of economic and political vulnerability and the point at which business will expand, flee, or settle into a static survival mode. Capital costs reflect the perceptual reality that serves inevitably as the actual reality, no matter how unjust. The cost in lost investment, tax revenue, technology transfer, and jobs is impossible to determine, but it could well be the difference between fiscal stability and constant crisis management. The possibility of a left-wing candidate winning the 2002 presidential election led to dire predictions and the downgrade of Brazil to third place on the scale of risk behind Argentina and Nigeria. Loose talk, not necessarily based on fact, had a negative impact. Lula, the candidate favored to win the presidency, intemperately called the proposed free trade zone as then envisioned an annexation of Latin America by the United States. U.S. Secretary of the Treasury Paul O'Neill's public grumblings in 2002 that taxpayer money would not be used to bail out Brazil devastated the country's bond market.

TOYOTA CONFRONTS THE BRAZIL COST

The subtle nature of the Brazil Cost makes it all but impossible to determine the economic loss. What does not happen, what investments are not made, what workers are not hired, what taxes are not paid, and other losses are real even though they cannot be tallied.

In the case of Toyota Motors, we have some indication of what might have happened, but did not. The company is the third largest automobile maker in the world. Toyota is also well known for its high-quality manufacturing and its ability to incorporate rapidly the latest technology long before the competition does. It is the type of company any country would be pleased to attract. Brazil's market of 174 million along with its reliance on cars and trucks should have been irresistible. Toyota tested the Brazilian market in 1952 when it imported 100 completely built units (CBUs). In 1958 it created a subsidiary to assemble completely knocked-down units (CKDs) in Brazil. The following year it introduced the Bandeirante Land Cruiser with 60 percent domestic parts. A separate, publicly held company— Toyota do Brasil, organized in 1961—raised capital to build an assembly plant in São Bernardo do Campo. By issuing shares the company delayed introducing its own capital. Subsequently, when financially prudent, the parent organization reincorporated the Brazilian company. Distribution depended on independent dealers who acted as the point of sale and provided service.

Toyota clearly shifted as much risk as possible to others, from shareholders of the Brazilian company to independent distributors. The explanation for its seemingly overly cautious approach, as noted in the company history, *Toyota, the First Fifty Years*, reflected the uncertainties of the Brazil Cost. According to the company, state interference and the absence of continuity in economic policies (read political instability) made long-range planning impossible. The company also experienced substantial losses over the years of massive inflation because of government price controls, which usually trailed the rate of inflation.

When Brazil liberalized its trade policies in 1990, making imported cars competitive, Toyota increased its imports of complete units rather than expanded production in Brazil. In 1994 the company decided to build a new plant in Argentina. Despite all of Argentina's political and economic problems, it appeared to be a better bet. Toyota counted too much on Mercosul and on Argentina's economic stability. In 1995, and again in 1997, Brazil imposed unilateral restrictions on cars imported from Argentina. The Brazil Cost has a long reach.

How much the company would have invested in Brazil under different circumstances is a matter of speculation. Fortunately, the relative economic and political stability of the Cardoso era made it possible for the company to make a major contribution in terms of jobs and exports. Toyota understood the potential of the Brazilian market and expanded its facility at Indaiatuba (São Paulo state) in 2002 to boost production to 57,000 units and also committed to increasing installation of local parts for the new Corolla to 70 percent. Much of the new production will be exported. The lesson is obvious: the government must put and keep its own house in order, and multinationals will respond to the benefit of all.

The perception of the country as politically unstable causes concerns that the government cannot rapidly and adequately address economic difficulties. Populist solutions embraced by disgruntled voters or even an authoritarian regime remain a perceived danger.[6] Capital flight occurs when investors lose confidence, whether justified or not. A 2001 poll showed little voter confidence in the country's institutions. The armed forces fared the best, with 24.2 percent in spite of dirty war incidents coming to light. At the bottom, the chamber of deputies received 3.4 percent and the senate 2.0 percent.

Toyota do Brasil's newly expanded manufacturing plant in Indaiatuba, São Paulo. Its opening was attended by 1,000 guests, including high government officials and President Fernando Cardoso. The larger facility will enable the company to export cars (the Corolla) to some twenty other countries. *Courtesy of Toyota do Brasil*

As the 2002 elections loomed, the possibility of a leftist candidate winning the presidency threw financial markets into a panic. An emergency $30 billion IMF loan to prevent a run on the country's foreign reserves once again demonstrated the negative impact of the Brazil Cost. The staged releasing of funds by the IMF indicated the level of apprehension about political instability, before and after the election—only $6 billion became available in 2002 with the rest reserved for after the election. The implications were clear. If the IMF did not approve of the incoming president's economic policies, it could reconsider both the terms and the amount of the loan.

Diplomacy in the New Century: Brazil and the United States

Brazil long perceived of itself as an imperial power within the South American context. In the twentieth century, Brazil consistently pressed for a respected role within the broader world community.

The army's long-standing interest in geopolitics stemmed from an understanding that diplomacy provided a shield behind which the nation could slowly gather strength. After World War II, relations with the United States cooled rapidly as interests diverged. Transfer of arms to Argentina in 1948 angered the government in spite of the fact that Brazil received 70 percent of all Lend-Lease allotted to Latin America. To show its collective displeasure the army declined to send a unit to fight in Korea in 1950. Alleged lack of respect and treating Brazil as inferior lay at the heart of the coolness. The veterans of the Brazilian Expeditionary Force (FEB), who provided the leadership for the military government in 1964, admired the methods and accomplishments of the United States but had no intention of accepting a dependent role.

The desire for self-sufficiency as well as appropriate international respect are related to both size and resources. The problem of ensuring sovereignty over a vast territory cannot be overestimated. Brazil's land border is 10,255 miles long and adjoins every South American country except Chile and Ecuador. The Amazonian border (6,804 miles) seems the most vulnerable. Underpopulated and weakly tied to the south, the region historically has been defined differently from the rest of Brazil by the international community. Its exotic impact on the early European explorers never wore off. The myth of a lush Garden of Eden filled with fantastic creatures, so green and hence so rich, triumphed over competing portrayals of the Amazon as a green hell. In recent times, international pressures intensified. The notion that drastic development will affect climate change far beyond Brazil's borders has become a major concern. A 1997 magazine article titled "They Want to Internationalize Our Amazon" cited alleged remarks by various world leaders on the fate of the rain forest. British prime minister John Major suggested that developed nations needed to extend the rule of law to regions considered the world's commons. Al Gore, a U.S. presidential candidate in 2000, declared in 1989 that "it [the Amazon] belongs to all of us." French president François Mitterrand reportedly stated that Brazil should accept relative sovereignty in Amazonia. Even Mikhail Gorbachev, the last leader of the Soviet Union, allegedly declared that Brazil should delegate responsibility for the preservation of the forest to competent international organizations. General Patrick Hughes of the U.S. Defense Intelligence Agency listed threats to the United States in 1998 as nuclear terrorism, the drug trade, scarcity of raw materials, and changes to the environment resulting in damage to other areas of the world.

Changing definitions of what constitutes grounds for war or intervention in the post–Cold War era have made it difficult to gauge international reaction. Actions or situations that previously would have been considered an internal affair now have the potential to become transnational issues. An implosion of power left the United States as the sole surviving superpower. In addition, overwhelming technical superiority coupled with economic might has reduced the relative actual cost of aggressive action. Admiral Mario César Flores sketched out the geopolitical reality in 1998 in the *Jornal do Brasil*, noting that others cannot hope for anything beyond a defensive posture, and even then success would be doubtful. An additional element, long an irritant, is the assumed moral superiority of the United States, which acts to rationalize its policy.

Drug production and illegal trade are seen as levers to reduce others to subordinate agents. Washington's plan to create a multinational antidrug center in Florida, use radar planes with the uncontested right to overfly Latin America, and coordinate police and military action against the trade resulted in Brazil's joining the less demanding UN antidrug agency. In 2000 an even more threatening project, Plan Colombia, combined a complex bundle of fears. The plan called for a $7.5 billion war on the drug-supported guerrilla groups in Colombia, with the United States supplying $1.3 billion and Europe and Colombia the remainder. Such a massive effort would push the contending forces across all borders and, of immediate concern, into the Amazon. Guerrilla war and drug money would enfeeble the army further, adding to Brazil's perceived weakness.

Bilateral trade issues are perhaps an inescapable source of aggravation. The roots of the conflict lie in attempts by the United States to protect politically sensitive industries in the face of worldwide competition. Antidumping laws and outright subsidies, particularly for agricultural commodities that Brazil produces inexpensively, are at issue year after year. At the same time, exports to the United States rose from 19 percent in 1998 to 24 percent in 2001. Nevertheless, Brazil claims that 60 percent of its exports have to contend with some sort of barrier. Two groups, the U.S.–Brazil Consultative Mechanism on Trade and Investment and the Four-plus-One Council on Trade and Investment (Brazil, Argentina, Paraguay, Uruguay, and the United States), attempt to negotiate trade issues.

Brazil's preferred option is a regional economic bloc (Mercosul) and construction of a political cocoon. Strengthening regional mechanisms offers a means to deal with issues before they damage relations, trade, or mutual confidence. South America under Brazilian leadership could then employ diplomacy to partially counterbalance the demands of the United States or Europe. If a hemisphere-wide free trade zone becomes a reality, South America could then negotiate a favorable deal. A high point in this strategy came with the meeting in 2001 of eleven South American heads of state in Brasília, chaired by President Henrique Cardoso. Brazil's leading news magazine, *Veja* (with the world's fourth largest circulation), featured on its cover an Uncle Sam figure dressed in Brazilian colors with the caption, "Brazil dressed in the clothes of a leader." Inside, it observed that the meeting represented the first step in putting together a South American bloc able to "confront American hegemony in the continent." Brazil has emerged as the economic engine of South America within the larger world system, a reality not entirely appreciated by its neighbors. Its market and industrial demands influence the politics and development strategies of South America as a whole—not always positively.

An episode in 2001 seems typical of Brazilian diplomacy. American president Jimmy Carter in 1976, under the International Security Assistance and Arms Export Control Act, limited weapons sales to Latin America, excluding expensive and sophisticated equipment. Carter and others argued that poor countries needed to direct resources to more pressing problems such as poverty. Subsequent American presidents continued the Carter policy. Washington used its implied protection, arms exports, and occasional exemptions from restrictions as a diplomatic lever when necessary, much to the irritation of Latin American governments and their militaries. Nevertheless, Latin America spent less on arms in the last several decades than any other region in the developing world. President Bill Clinton ended the policy, responding to complaints by, among others, manufacturing companies such as Boeing and Lockheed-Martin. Congress, however, continued to pressure U.S. companies not to sell advanced equipment to the region.

Worried that decisions made in Washington ignored legitimate security needs, officials turned to European suppliers such as Italy, Sweden, Russia, and France, who were more than willing to sell state-of-the-art military planes. Modernization of the air force appeared necessary because of the threat of the spillover of Colombian guerrillas and the drug war into the Amazon. As part of any deal, the planes must be manufactured in Brazil under license. A French company previously bought a 20 percent stake in the privatized aircraft manufacturer Embraer, making France a logical contender. To sidestep the United States in order to cut a deal would provide the equipment the air force wants, which could also be exported to others. Embraer is already the largest exporter of manufactured products and any deal would have a significant economic impact. Brasília is skillfully forcing an end to such restrictions. By breaking Washington's grip on arms sales, Brazil increases its own diplomatic influence. The maneuvering has aspects of the arms diplomacy discussed earlier, and the forcing of economic development such as the automobile industry after World War II. It remains to be seen whether Brazil will succeed in ending the Carter policy—if not at this time, it will attempt to do so in the future.

A mutually constructive interchange came with the signing of the Technical Safeguard Agreement (2000) making it possible for American companies to launch satellites from the Alcântara launch facility in Maranhão. The facility is 2.3 degrees south of the equator, which allows for heavier payloads and a 20 to 30 percent reduction in costs over launches at northern latitudes. A seaport and modern airport make access inexpensive. The agreement provides Brazil with substantial revenues and new technology. It also allows the United States to monitor Brazil's ballistic missile program. Profit, cost savings, advanced technical development, cooperation, and mutual suspicion are all wrapped up in the Alcântara agreement.[7]

A still troublesome issue is the threat posed by terrorist organizations in the trinational region, where the borders of Argentina, Paraguay, and Brazil come together. At the center is the northern protrusion of Argentina's province of Misiones, an isolated, ignored area perfectly situated for smuggling, gunrunning, drug trafficking, money laundering, and, most recently, terrorism. The problem first came to light with the bombing in 1992 of the Israeli embassy in Buenos Aires, followed two years later by the attack on the Jewish Community Center. A foiled plan to destroy the American embassy in Asunción, in 1996, indicated the potential danger. The First International Conference on Terrorism, held in Buenos Aires in 1997, uncovered more details about extremist Islamic groups in the region. Although the issue appeared to be of more concern to the United States, attacks on economic targets would have a devastating impact on the regional and national economy. São Paulo, a center of foreign investment, is within easy striking range. Some 85 percent of the top 500 U.S. companies have investments in the country. Large European and Asian firms have a similar presence. Any substantial attack would drive off investment and throw the country into economic crisis, with immediate domestic social and political consequences.

One gauge of the level of latent hostility to American hegemony is the reaction of prominent Brazilians to the terrorist events of September 11, 2001. President Cardoso, speaking before the French national assembly, equated the brutality of terrorism with that of perceived American global hegemony. Theologian Leonardo Boff regretted that only one plane had crashed into the Pentagon. Public opinion in general saw the attack as a fitting response to American arrogance. The resentment on the part of Brazilians for their yet unfulfilled ambitions at least temporarily swept away humanity, prudence, and political and economic common sense. American leaders have also been the source of insensitive and loose remarks. President Clinton, for example, had to apologize for comments made by high-ranking officials in his administration about the level of corruption in Brazil.[8] President George W. Bush's treasury secretary, Paul O'Neill, well known for speaking his mind regardless of bruised feelings, needlessly created counterproductive tension.

President Luiz Inácio Lula da Silva elevated the level of anxiety in Washington by questioning Brazil's adherence to the Nuclear Nonproliferation Treaty. In the event of Brazil's withdrawal the possibility of an expensive arms race between Brazil and Argentina and perhaps other South American republics once again loomed.

In spite of blunt and tasteless language and actions designed to counter American policy, it is important not to view the United States and Brazil as adversaries. The relationship is more like that between the United States and Britain in the second half of the nineteenth century. The need for investment, technology, loans, and markets did not stop the United States from contending, sometimes annoyingly, for status and economic standing. The goal is to achieve sovereign equality with the developed world. Meanwhile, Brazil and the United States are wary but friendly competitors. Relations between Washington and Brasília blow warm and cool, but never hot and cold.

The Itamaraty (diplomatic service) seldom misses an opportunity to point out how much Brazil and the United States have in common. While on occasion it may seem like diplomatic hyperbole, an element of truth underpins such assertions. The fact that the United States was the first country to recognize Brazil's independence at a crucial time is never forgotten, nor is Washington's enthusiastic reception of the creation of the republic in 1889. A publication (1998) of the Brazilian embassy in Washington, DC, titled *Brazil and the USA: What Do We Have in Common?* is one of the most recent, but certainly not the last such pamphlet.

Attempting to Fix the Future

Cardoso believed that he needed a second term in order to push through reforms. His first term mixed rhetoric with preliminary reform measures. For him to run again, however, congress had to pass a constitutional amendment, requiring a two-thirds vote by each house. The lack of credible alternatives, along with rumored bribes, provided the necessary constitutional change.

The second term proved much rockier than his first, perhaps because Cardoso intended to press for concrete results. While he felt politically stronger, he still had to deal with a coalition government that could be destabilized by an array of politically motivated events. The close connection between internal politics and problems elsewhere in Latin America continued to make not only the real but also the entire economy vulnerable in international financial markets. The willingness of some to bring the house down for their own interests perhaps is characteristic of a weak structure. The governor of the key state of Minas Gerais, former president Itamar Franco, threatened to default on that state's foreign debt, triggering a financial crisis. The subsequent attack on the real in international currency markets, while fought off, required a devaluation and help from international monetary agencies. The federal government can be plunged into a crisis by an array of actors and events beyond the control of the president.

In an attempt to avoid future debt problems the federal government crafted a fiscal responsibility law in May 2000 that imposed criminal penalties on officials, including the president, who spend beyond available revenues. The law prohibited the federal government from bailing out bankrupt states and cities and limited borrowing and payrolls. Officials who do not comply may be banned from holding public office or jailed. The law modified the definition of irresponsible behavior, but past debts remained a threatening problem. A complementary objective, tax reform and enforcement, posed an even more difficult challenge. Pension cuts and other reforms designed to deal with projected deficits called for near fatal political courage.

Fighting corruption in a government dependent on fragile coalitions placed the president in an awkward position. To pursue an investigation of a coalition member might well make it impossible to enact reform programs. Not to go forward with a congressional probe, however, might suggest that the president tolerated corruption. The dilemma surfaced in early 2001, when the leader of the Brazilian Democratic Movement (MDB), Jader Barbalho, won the powerful post of president of the senate. Opponents accused his party of raiding highway construction funds and draining the Amazon development agency (SUDAM). A preliminary audit suggested that $830 million had been diverted. A previous allegation of embezzling from a state bank had been dismissed under unusual circumstances. Senator Barbalho amassed a fortune during his career in politics, but to unravel the source of his wealth might undo many others. Cardoso's unsuccessful effort to stop a congressional probe of the affair in order to preserve the coalition appeared to be amoral and self-serving. Political scandals are treated like forest fires, to be snuffed out as rapidly as possible unless the governing party deems an inquiry useful.

Cardoso hoped that over his two terms all the philosophical foundations for a flourishing mass democracy presented in the Constitution of 1988 had been tested and made secure. Well aware of the ambivalence of the electorate toward democracy, he believed that the maturity of the system would make it impossible for one party or individual to govern without attention to complex interest groups, as is the case in modern developed countries. To be on the safe side, his handpicked successor, José Serra, a close friend, fellow exile during the military regime, and minister of health, shared his values and most of his political vision.

To complicate the presidential election and transition of power, Argentina's economic collapse in 2002 also engulfed Uruguay and Brazil and required IMF assistance. The Brazil Cost returned to life with a vengeance. Economic crisis threw into doubt Cardoso's neoliberalism. The Workers' Party presidential candidate, Lula, maintained his advantage in the polls leading up to the election of October 2002, in spite of international investors who warned of dire consequences. To avoid financial disaster he pledged to play by the rules of the game. Nevertheless, few in the international financial community believed he would be able to resist governing by ideology rather than by the pragmatism of the outgoing regime. The currency reflected their fear of debt default, steadily losing ground against the dollar, and inflation exceeded the limits set for 2002 and threatened to do the same in 2003.

The contrast between outgoing President Cardoso and his elected successor could hardly be more extreme. Cardoso, a cosmopolitan man by nature and circumstances, may have been one of the most cultured presidents in the country's history. His world extended far beyond Brazil both geographically and philosophically. His grasp of geopolitics and diplomacy forged both in the classroom and in exile equaled that of many career diplomats. Cardoso's relationship with ambitious interest groups, including the army, rested on a broad international vision of the nation's future. He mixed easily with world leaders, spoke their language, and shared many of their values. Understandably, they preferred Cardoso's handpicked candidate, José Serra, seemingly cut from the same cloth, to succeed him. Ironically, the ability of voters to select their representatives, rather than the reverse, is a sign of democratic strength. The rejection of Cardoso's choice to be the next president demonstrated the point. Mass democracy, notoriously ungrateful, constantly feeds on the future, not the past.

His successor, President Luiz Inácio Lula da Silva, represented a different Brazil.[9] His life experience mirrored the struggles and aspirations of the poverty-stricken and the modern working class. Born into a barely subsisting agricultural family of eight children in the northeast, Brazil's poorest region, he understood poverty. The entire family migrated to São Paulo where even a difficult existence promised more than survival in the northeast. At the age of ten he learned to read. As a child he worked the streets selling small items and shining shoes. Lula later was a beneficiary of President Kubitschek's drive to create a domestic automobile industry when he becam a skilled metal worker. In 1975, as the elected leader of the metal workers' union, he steered the union toward a more militant course in careful defiance of the military regime. Founding the Workers' Party in 1980 seemed to symbolize the trajectory of his own personal experience, from the depths of poverty to the modern industrial working class.

To the business community it all added up to a presidency with limited international experience and no prior governing responsibility. The extent to which the president had to rely upon the views of advisors worried many, while others appeared concerned that Lula would not surround himself with appropriate counselors. What appeared at stake—the future of economic liberalization, the free flow of foreign investment, default on the national debt with all its negative consequences, and failure to pursue inclusion in a U.S.-dominated hemisphere-wide free trade zone—placed a heavy burden on the future. Moreover, the president encountered an unsympathetic international political and financial community.

On the left, Lula faced a level of expectation that could not be met quickly or fully. Whether his constituents, with their own particular and at times conflicting interests, would be patient remained unclear. Finally, the fluid opportunism of party politics, switching parties, cutting deals, and corruption that stalled Cardoso's drive for reforms seemed likely to do so again. Nevertheless, Lula received a clear mandate for change, winning 46.44 percent on the first round of voting against Serra's 23.20 percent.[10] In the second round, Lula polled the largest percentage of any presidential candidate in the country's history with a decisive 61.4 percent.

Notes

1. TV Record is owned by the Igreja Universal do Reino de Deus (Universal Church of the Kingdom of God). It broadcasts commercial and secular programs during prime time and religious programs during off-hours.
2. The "evangelical bloc" in the chamber of deputies won 60 seats in the 2002 election representing 5.1 million voters, but distributed among eight parties. The largest contingent, 23 deputies, are members of the AD, followed by the Universal

Church of the Kingdom of God with 22. It should not be assumed that only religious believers voted for them.

3. The Federal Electoral Tribunal (TSE) decided that state coalitions must be the same throughout the republic in the election of 2002. This may result in less opportunism and more attention to actual shared interests if it remains a permanent feature.

4. *Cachaça* is made from distilled sugarcane juice, while rum is made from molasses.

5. Estimates of the population suffering from malnutrition range from 23 to 55 million. Ziegler quotation from *Brazil Focus*, March 16–22, 2002.

6. A survey conducted by Latinobarómetro in 2001 indicated that only 30 percent believed that democracy is the preferable form of government, down from 41 percent in 1995.

7. Brazil's missile program in the 1980s served as a counterbalance to a perceived Argentine threat. In the 1990s, Brazil agreed not to develop weapons of mass destruction.

8. Transparency International (Berlin) in 2002 rated Brazil 45 on its corruption scale compared to Mexico at 57, China at 59, the United States at 16, and Finland the least corrupt at 1.

9. Lula means squid (cuttlefish). He legally adopted the name.

10. To win in the first round a candidate must gain an absolute majority of all votes cast. Given the number of political parties, it is often necessary to go to a second round in which only the first and second highest vote winners face off.

CHAPTER EIGHT

The Historical Trajectory

The centrality of goal-directed economic development in Brazil's history is obvious. From the distribution of coffee trees in early nineteenth-century Brazil, to the ambitious waterway projects of our own time, state-directed goals characterize the process. Development is the means; modernization is the objective. Brazil continuously projects a fabulous future, much like a holograph visible in some fashion when held at an angle. Once the goal is achieved, yet another projected advance takes its place. Development is always being pushed forward.

Coupled with modernization is the well-established notion of national power and international prestige. Brazil's roots in a European monarchy made it possible to claim a type of South American uniqueness. An irritated British foreign secretary George Canning complained in 1825 shortly after independence that not only did Rio insist that it be regarded as an equal power but it also seemed to imply superiority. In spite of setbacks, the struggle for respect continues into the present. While recognized as a founding member of the League of Nations, Brazil nevertheless failed to secure a permanent seat on the League Council. Deeply disappointed, it withdrew altogether in 1926 to avoid what it viewed as unacceptable embarrassment.[1] After World War II the United States vaguely promised Brazil a permanent seat on the United Nations Security Council. In the end, it received only a rotating position. In 2001, Brazil again mounted a campaign for a permanent seat. Obviously, Brazil seeks respect and indeed deserves it.

Historical Stages

Brazil experienced several well-defined historical stages each ending with a redefinition of politics and economic and social relations. A process of adjusting continuity to immediate needs results in discernible change. The empire served the country well by sidestepping the problems of untested republican organization—while its neighbors in South America experienced endemic political confusion, geographical uncertainty, crushing debt, and a delayed sense of national identity. In addition, the imperial structure sheltered an archaic economic system long enough to allow it to make a transition to free labor. That it did so at the expense of a slave population denies it of any moral credit, yet the task of ending over three centuries of slavery should not be underestimated. The empire's organizational stability, less positively, permitted it to entertain territorial ambitions and engage in war. Ironically, the conflict with Paraguay accelerated the growth of a new class able to present an alternative to rule by an agricultural oligarchy, clearing the way for another transformation.

A commercial code, in spite of its incompleteness, laid the groundwork for business. The immigrant stream made it possible to end slavery with scarcely an economic pause and reinforced the growth of an urban ethos. The nineteenth century saw a shift in the balance of knowledge from the elite to the professional and working classes. Skill levels required using and maintaining machines, and the associated tasks of the nineteenth century fragmented the elite monopoly on knowledge beyond repair. Science and engineering technology demanded professionals. Railways, invented in 1827 on the heels of James Watts's steam engine, arrived in Brazil in the 1850s, less than a quarter-century after the first locomotive chugged across the English countryside on iron rails. Independent rail lines never developed into a national system. Yet the age of machines increased productivity and made new demands on workers, supervisors, merchant-distributors, shippers, and soldiers, among many others. The expansion of the knowledge classes became ever more necessary as complex urbanization added its demands. Development created an expanding urban core populated by literate managers, professionals, and workers amid a population still trapped in illiteracy, poverty, and misery.

The separation of knowledge from wealth created conditions for social change. Interdependence between the holders of wealth and those they employed to manage their assets required a change in status for both. The war with Paraguay, perhaps the first overwhelming demonstration of the vital importance of applied knowledge, foreshadowed the final end of slavery and the fall of the empire. A process of slow social and political absorption of the middle and working classes into the fabric of Brazil, dependent on economic development, became evident. Urbanization made it possible to increase the number of schools, directed attention to public health, and pushed science forward. That the cities, more attune to new ideas, provided the abolitionists seems quite natural. When slavery collapsed in 1888, followed by the end of the monarchy in 1889, the imperial system already had spent itself. During the second empire a republic grew in the shade of a legitimate and orderly empire, until it finally uprooted its parent.

The establishment of the republic represented a new arrangement of power and a redirecting of the country to meet the aspirations of an emerging military-middle class. Although that stage lasted only briefly, as the oligarchy reclaimed the presidency, time remained on the side of the emerging classes. The dropping of property qualifications in the Constitution of 1891, but not the literacy requirement, nevertheless meant an expansion of political participation for middle-class males. It excluded the lower classes and women from direct involvement in politics, but both groups continued to exert pressure in their own way. Women, because of gender-segregated education, established a professional base in teaching. From there a few elite women went on to professional schools, including medicine. The lower class had all the civil rights of citizens as well as the potential for males to become literate voters. Use of violence to make their views known remained an option, although subject to counterforce justified by the notion that they represented a dangerous barbarism. The inexperience of the military-middle class and the failure to broaden the electorate sufficiently opened the way for a return of the oligarchy, but one no longer completely agricultural and even less monolithic.

Nascent industrialization brought with it the problem of relations with industrial workers. Immigrant radicalism and the changing attitude of the Church created yet another group pressing for social and economic rights. The republic also grappled with the aftermath of slavery. Afro-Brazilians, desperately in demand in earlier times, after abolition became a surplus and marginal labor force, to be employed when alternatives could not be found. Downward pressure on all levels acted to reduce the size of the black artisan and shopkeeper class. The perception of their economic position, rather than the reality, influenced their social status. Allegedly degraded by slavery, the solution became genetic. Scientific racism promised to whiten the population in short order. While it failed to do so, it fixed a damaging ideal firmly in the minds of its proponents and their victims.

The counterrevolution that returned the oligarchy to power did not extinguish the still somewhat inarticulate demands of the emerging middle class. As a result, the 1920s became a time to protest both intellectually and physically. The centennial of independence in 1922 occasioned a national assessment. That year saw a fatal combination of ideas and military revolt. Modern Art Week, the Copacabana revolt and its shockingly bloody end, and the founding of the Brazilian Communist Party drained away legitimacy and threatened state order. The technological marvel of radio, still in its infancy and underestimated at the time, created broad access to information and suggested social and political alternatives. All of these tactics of discontent began to come together with the Prestes Column. While the dissident army marched, the urban middle class cheered it on from the cities.

The arrogance of the more powerful states led them to use their power to monopolize the government. They propped up coffee prices with expensive foreign loans and made no secret of their disdain for regions they considered hopelessly unproductive. They alienated what became a backward regional suboligarchy with little national power and no respect, all the while narrowing their political base. Eventually, São Paulo pushed every state aside. The old republic died from unsustainable politics.

Getúlio Vargas ushered in a time appropriately referred to as an era. Significantly, more books have been written on the Vargas period than any other in Brazilian history. President Vargas is frequently compared to his contemporary, American president Franklin D. Roosevelt. Both governed during trying times economically and politically. The two leaders used radio to their advantage and kept fragile societies together. Both seemed to be instinctive politicians with a muted authoritarian streak. Nevertheless, they rose to power under different historical imperatives.

President Vargas, propelled into office when the discontent of the old republic boiled over into violence, could have been a mere transitional figure were it not for several factors. His supporters had some coherent concrete ideas but lacked the confidence and experience to govern. They in effect pushed aside the elite, yet needed the political skills of the traditional governing class. In Vargas they found someone who understood the problems of the old republic and, moreover, appreciated that the country had to make good on the promise of the Constitution of 1891 and more. The essentially reactionary old republic had made the task urgent.

Vargas placed elite skills at the disposal of those intent, once and for all, on ending the power of the oligarchy. Like Roosevelt, many viewed him as a traitor to his class, while the middle, working, and lower classes saw him quite differently. The army almost instantly recognized the advantages offered by the president, while Afro-Brazilians and workers discovered in Vargas a protective paternalism absent since the fall of the empire. Significantly, throughout this period the army remained the most important of the three pillars of support. Their support, not immediately or often publicly apparent, nevertheless underpinned the stability of the regime. Vargas spent time and effort to align himself with the expectations of the army and wrapped it all the general notion of nationalism. In the end, when the army, particularly the FEB, endorsed democracy in 1945, he could not meet expectations. Even when he returned as an elected president in 1950, he could not put together a political base able to compensate for the absence of army support. Not surprisingly, the military pushed him out of office with personally fatal consequences.

The dysfunctional democratic period existed with the army standing off to one side, not helping but instead evaluating each president's performance on a moment-to-moment basis. When necessary, the army stepped in to force Vargas to dismiss his minister of labor, João Goulart, and then out of the presidency. Both Jânio da Silva Quadros and Goulart grappled with the army's intervention at crucial times. Only the first post-1945 president, General Eurico Dutra, had a free hand to govern. Juscelino Kubitschek survived in spite of military antipathy, only by rushing into the construction of Brasília and expanding industrial development. The military coup of 1964 represented an abrupt escalation of army involvement, not something out of the blue. Perhaps this explains the lack of public reaction the left had banked on. It also appeared to be a return of the Estado Novo military, without a Vargas or his equivalent.

Military activism between 1964 and 1985 focused on internal development—effective occupation of the national territory—and on mobilization of the industrial base to project influence on the international scene. The regime sought to remold the country in such a way as to make the nation modern and worthy of international respect. It did so keenly aware of the limited resources available. Recognized corporate entities, such as unions, became preferred forums for social negotiations over resources. Groups with concrete definable objectives did not threaten loss of political control. Moreover, limited resources distributed by corporate groups satisfied legitimate demands, roughly matching resources to social and political pressures. The hard choices fell on those unable to make an immediate contribution to developmental goals. Consequently, those elements already favored—the middle-class professionals and higher education—received the resources necessary to help plan, staff, and execute a development scheme. Social science planners and economists became the generals of development, while everyone else remained foot soldiers. The actual functioning of the government indicated a technological falling behind of the military and the triumph of specialized civilian technocrats. Just as the elite earlier had lost its hold on knowledge, so the army needed to draw in a vast number of civilians in order to govern a complex society.

When civilians returned to direct the top levels of government in 1985, they inherited an almost totally changed nation. They also faced an unsustainable debt burden. Old problems, still unresolved, mixed with new ones created by change itself, and others associated with globalism could not obscure the incredible transformation that had occurred. The country as it existed in 1964 could hardly be imagined. During the twenty-one-year period of the military regime, a long-term process arrived at the point of maturity. Materialism, in its most obvious form of consumerism—not only of goods but also of services, technology, music, and lifestyles—became a mass irreversible phenomenon, with implications for political and social expectations.

The crassness the elite had always feared and had associated with the United States triumphed, as did mass politics.[2] Urbanization and modern technology facilitated the process for all classes in differing degrees but moved relentlessly toward a mass market. During the 1970s, radio and later television fabricated a homogenized and national lifestyle requiring uniform consumption or at least desire. Historically, as consumer demands spread among the less affluent, they are met initially through contraband. Demand then broadens to include a wide array of goods, as is the case today. Even Bombril, a popular household steel wool, has its tax-free and cheaper smuggled counterpart. At a certain point, the legal and illegal economies come together, as the Italian experience suggests. Structural reforms are required to accommodate materialism's pressure on the state. Meanwhile, contraband raises the material standard of consumption at the bottom, but it is a short-term solution.

A trend that is now quite noticeable, but with at least nineteenth-century roots, is the growth of lower-class parallel organizations able to contend in varying degrees with those of the elite and middle class. A rallying from below, unencumbered by patriarchal controls or violent intimidation, became possible with urbanization and was intensified with modern communication technologies and the globalization of information. This is evident in virtually every area of activity, from Afro-Brazilian groups following 1888, to Carnival and samba clubs, soccer *torcidas*, radio fan clubs, Christian Base Communities, Pentecostals, unions, and the Movimento sem Terra, among innumerable other organizations. Collectively they push toward a mass democracy.

A declining birth rate, historically associated with urbanization, has plummeted even more dramatically because of the widespread use of birth control. By 2000 the birth rate fell to an estimated 1.3—below replacement level. With a falling birth rate, the work force becomes more valuable and wages increase accordingly. In the early

2000s, labor demands pulled in immigrants from Bolivia, Paraguay, and elsewhere in South America. Historically, immigrants displace natives from unskilled jobs and push them into tasks that require more education and a different wage level. Education has been shown to arouse expectations that require economic activity and generate an entrepreneurial momentum not directly dependent on government action. Smaller families mean higher income and increased consumerism. With all its alleged drawbacks, consumerism elevates the standard of living and unleashes expectations that politicians ignore at their peril.

At the middle- and upper-class levels, private schooling, literacy across many disciplines and the knowledge that surrounds every city dweller, radio, television, and newspapers all pull people into a different world. Education, directly linked to development needs, favored the middle class. The result was the inverse pattern of expansion of higher education and a stunted primary and secondary school system. Higher education accounts for some 60 percent of federal education spending—a legacy of the nation's directed developmental history.

The connection between education and the labor force becomes more evident as more value is placed on knowledge and technology than on physical strength. The driving element within society and the economy moved decisively to the knowledge class somewhere in the 1970s. Not surprisingly, educated Brazilians in 2001 were Latin America's most avid Internet users, watched the most television, and were likely to soon surpass others in the use of all forms of information technology. In 1993 cell phone subscribers numbered 400,000, and by 2001 there were more than 24 million. The rapidity with which new technology is adopted is startling. All indications suggest that the nation has moved into another stage, in which government-directed development will play a diminished role and knowledge workers will drive economic, political, and social development independently.

An example of the kind of important, fundamental change that has already occurred is the new civil code that replaced the outdated and largely ignored 1916 code. The code in force as of 2002 established legal equality between genders. It ended the centuries-old patriarchal authority of the husband and father to make unrestricted legal decisions for the family. The new code eliminated a husband's right to seek an annulment if it was determined that his bride was not a virgin at the time of marriage. The new code added a thoroughly modern provision, permitting a divorced husband to file for alimony from his former wife.

Confronting Residual Problems

Social connectivity between the classes is weak. Yet, paradoxically, lower-class responsiveness to elite expectations is high even when such expectations are negative and destructive. This may indicate a positive identification upward and a notion that such a move is possible or should be possible. It also has a connection with materialism's message that you are what you consume. Social mobility and the class connectivity it engenders are retarded by a flawed educational system. In spite of constitutional provisions, starting with the Constitution of 1934 and continuing to the present, that require a fixed percentage to be spent on education, public schools have failed. The current Constitution of 1988 mandates that states and municipalities spend 25 percent of revenues on education and that the federal government spend 18 percent. Unfortunately, legislators have not defined what constitutes a valid expenditure. The absence of any accounting review encourages corrupt practices. Schools are overadministered and understaffed at the classroom level. The Ministry of Education in Brasília has between 150,000 and 200,000 employees, a pattern copied by the states and municipalities. The educational bureaucracy, from the federal level down to that of individual schools, is a vital source of political patronage and contracts, needed or contrived.

The educational failure is most obvious at the primary level. Children attend school an average of only five years compared to nine years in Argentina and Chile. Teacher competence is a secondary consideration. In poor areas teachers are appointed or removed on political grounds. Undertrained, poorly paid teachers must deal with difficult social problems. Teachers in rural schools often do not have a primary school education. Recent attempts to require teaching certification may have some positive effect. Over 50 percent of first-grade students have to repeat the grade. Grade repetition has meant that approximately half of the students drop out at the primary levels. They learn little, leaving school functionally literate at best. Under these circumstances, those parents who can afford to do so send their children to private schools. A number of mechanisms designed to shift revenue to private schools also exhaust available resources. In view of Brazil's failure to publicly educate its citizens, this may be a rational response. The gap between supportive educational rhetoric and reality appears too great to last indefinitely.

Limited resources encourage constant shifting of funds from one worthy use to another, creating social and political expectations and bitter disappointment in equal measure. Once-completed projects are allowed to deteriorate until a crisis forces unplanned expenditure. The sudden electricity shortage in 2001, caused in part by natural forces but also by outmoded transmission lines and inadequate capacity, is just the most recent example. The mundane can turn into the critical virtually overnight. Moreover, an overwhelming desire to be modern leads to larger-than-life schemes and projects. A bold step into the future moves the country forward with a cutting-edge project based on a modest infrastructure, which may be outmoded and ill-maintained.

In a country with an ingrained patriarchal history, corruption may be inevitable. Attitudes toward corruption are conditioned by a sense of entitlement. Accountability at the top is limited to preserving status and a degree of public decorum in keeping with social position and presumed rights. Material success goes with position. While success in business is preferred, politics is an acceptable avenue because both quickly merge. Through politics come the resources and patronage that enable one to financially enter the elite. Corruption involving public funds drains the middle and lower classes, while creating potential wealth for the few. Paulo Maluf, active in politics during the military regime and into the 2000s, built a political machine in São Paulo that resulted in his election as governor and several terms as mayor as well as in making the careers of a number of deputies and senators. Construction projects provided the money for the machine and its principal members. Ironically, construction also provided the justification—"He steals, but gets thing done."[3] His personally chosen successor, the family accountant, Celso Pitta, proved an able student. Between them, they left one of the world's largest cities with an empty treasury, collapsing schools, and public transportation and health services in ruins. Celso Pitta prudently moved to a penthouse in Miami to write a tell-all book titled *The Trajectory of a Black in Brazilian Politics*.

The connection between corruption and development is a problem. It deprives the nation of useful projects in favor of others whose objective is to supply a source of graft. In early 2001 major scandals involving two large development agencies—SUDAM, the Amazonian development agency, and SUDENE, the agency for the impoverished northeast—provided the opportunity to reorganize and change the names of both of them. Businessmen and politicians defrauded the government of some $1.8 billion during the existence of the two agencies. Whether the changes will make a difference remains to be seen. The federal government has moved to open project management to public scrutiny, which may have some positive effect. Publication of cost data and other project information on the Internet promises to break new ground in efforts to promote government transparency. The task of disciplining politicians may shift from a weak presidency to the media and the area of public opinion. The Workers' Party has made honesty a plank of its platform, although the party has had its own share of scandals. The existence of coalition governments at the federal level makes it difficult to discipline politicians. This may change as the party structure strengthens.

Entitlement facilitates corruption at all levels, but it must be done with decorum. President Fernando Collor de Melo provided an example of corruption mixed with entitlement. In the end, he breached decorum and congress hounded him out of office. Judge Nicolau dos Santos, accused of organizing the embezzlement of $87 million during the construction of a São Paulo courthouse and the object of a supposed international police search in 2000, is another example. Claiming grave depression, he went from police custody to house arrest. Members of congress guilty of corruption may experience the same fate, but most escape criminal penalties. It is almost impossible to function effectively and remain untainted in a system in which corruption plays a significant role. Whatever changes are made, it is unlikely that the high court will impose harsh penalties on politicians.

Blanket congressional immunity extends beyond legislative matters. The sweeping nature of immunity rests on a sense of superiority and entitlement. An attempt in 2001 allegedly to restrict immunity provides for trial by the Federal Supreme Court (STF) even for common crimes. Nevertheless, a legislator may request suspension of proceedings if political persecution is alleged. In 1999 the high court ended immunity for former high officials, ruling, however, that it could be reestablished by congress. A desperate President Cardoso, worried about ambitious federal prosecutors anxious to file criminal charges against him once he was out of office, pressed congress to reestablish "judicial privilege" to make all former presidents, cabinet ministers, and members of congress immune from proceedings except for those of the STF.

The notion of office as a personal asset encourages practices that often go beyond the boundaries of what could be called acceptable. When a senator is forced out of office, an alternative, named at the time of his own election and unknown to the public, assumes the office. Only after the resignation of Senator Jader Barbalho, who was accused of massive corruption, did it become known that his eighty-two-year-old father, also implicated in the case, had been named the first alternative, followed by his private secretary. An individual under investigation and unsure of his fate might spend several months abroad until things are arranged or a deal cut. Time is on the side of those able to afford a good lawyer. The law allows for a new trial when a defendant has been sentenced to twenty years or more even if the sentence is upheld on appeal. Pressure to end such practices comes from the middle class,[4] while the lower classes complain but view themselves as powerless to effect change. The increase in the number of unionized workers and middle-class professionals has raised the issue to the political level, although still not to an effective degree. At the lower level (where voting is compulsory), an ill-educated and uninformed electorate casts a high proportion of blank and defective ballots. That corruption is such an issue, and embarrassing exposures are made with regularity, indicate that a new public ethic may be forming. In the voter poll noted earlier, the media are second to the military in public confidence in large part because of their aggressive reporting of wrongdoing at all levels. Meanwhile, insincere attempts to establish codes of ethics at least indicate that politicians are aware they have an image problem.

Distribution of wealth may hold one of the keys to Brazil's problems. According to the World Bank, income distribution in Brazil is worse than in India and South Africa. In the early 2000s, the country's Gini coefficient is well above the recognized international danger point of 4. Including hidden assets, it is probably at least 6, perhaps higher.[5] It is not simply a question of class greed or callousness. We know that the industrial revolutions of the eighteenth and nineteenth centuries in England created wide disparities in wealth. It will be recalled that Brazil's industrial revolution is largely a twentieth-century—actually a post-1945—event. In addition, in the latter part of the century a knowledge-high technology professional class emerged with intellectual capital able to create wealth and in the process gave rise to its own disparities.

Nevertheless, creation of a vast internal market is delayed by the problem of wealth in too few hands and the lack of adequate mechanisms for redirecting it to expand demand at the lower levels. Yet by itself redistribution is not enough; it must be linked to the constant creation of wealth and structural reforms to open the labor market. The redistribution of wealth is connected with other problems in ways hard to unravel. Brazil is essentially two nations—one modern, and the other still caught in the past, but with strong expectations of entering the twenty-first century.

The extremely poor distribution of wealth has encouraged an enclave society at all levels. The wealthy employ bodyguards and move around in bulletproof cars and helicopters to ensure their safety. At the end of the workday in São Paulo the well-to-do are carried off to another protected location. As the upper class is able to devise ever more effective security measures, the impact of crime moves down to the middle class, who must worry about robbery, street violence, and kidnapping in spite of their relatively modest means. Their apartment buildings are fenced and guarded at all hours. Newer buildings boast well-equipped workout rooms, lavish recreation facilities, and swimming pools to minimize the need to leave these protected complexes. The level of actual or perceived security drops at the lower rungs of society to become nonexistent at the bottom. In the favelas, both the police and criminal elements are to be feared. The varied impact of crime is estimated to reduce GDP by 10 to 13 percent. Resolving the distribution-of-wealth problem, along with an effective reorganization of law enforcement agencies, would benefit everyone.

Political violence, much like that which marred the old republic, continues to afflict the political system. Assassinations, in a crude way, circumvent the will of the electorate. Such acts indicate a desire for the fruits of power, yet exhibit little faith in politics. Over a five-year period, seventeen politicians across the nation, from Amazonas to São Paulo, have been killed. Bomb threats and menacing e-mails are commonplace. In 2002 the mayor of Santo André (state of São Paulo), taken from an SUV by thugs, turned up dead on a dirt road with his face mutilated and shot by seven bullets. He had been reelected three times, most recently with 70 percent of the vote. The Workers' Party has suffered the most, but other parties have lost elected officials to violence as well.

A long-delayed issue is the rationalization of the role of the army. Every constitution, from 1891 on, including that of 1988, acknowledges the military as the guarantor of the constitution. In effect, the army functions both above and within the constitution. This demands military attention to and involvement in politics at times of real or perceived crisis. Rather than a last resort, force quickly becomes an option. Moreover, the role of the military as guarantor relieves civilian politicians of responsibility and impedes the elaboration of a constitutional tradition of review by the country's Supreme Court rather than by the senior officer corps. Within the army itself, constitutional issues promote factionalism among the officer corps and serious lapses of discipline in the ranks.

Racism is a difficult problem and a sensitive issue. In the competition for jobs it is used as a tool to secure advantage. Understandably, over 200 terms to denote racial variations are employed in an attempt to circumvent racial discrimination. President Fernando Henrique Cardoso, after his election in 1994, formally declared racial democracy a myth. In addition to voicing his personal and academic convictions,[6] the president was responding to mounting political pressure. The new attitude at the cultural and political levels may indicate movement toward embracing a long-delayed and tired ideal. Irrational racial attitudes can collapse quickly.

The absence of formal segregation, as in the American South after the Civil War, makes change at the national political level easier. By not introducing formal segregation, the state avoided placing itself in the position of punishing a large segment of the population. The only charge can be that the state did little to defend the black and Afro-Brazilian population against hardening social attitudes. Society devised a system of informal, unequal treatment supposedly based on an individual's class, not race. Placing the issue in a class rather than race context made it possible for Brazil to claim to be a racial democracy. National self-delusion nevertheless encapsulated an ideal. The re-Africanization movement may reinvigorate efforts to add enforcement to the law and substance to the rhetoric. Success and its financial rewards have some impact on social attitudes but the underlying core rejection of equality remains evident. Folk wisdom observes that "money whitens." Nevertheless, a wealthy Afro-Brazilian elite circulates largely within separate social enclaves. In 2002 the administration and congress discussed various schemes to open universities and government positions on a quota basis to Afro-Brazilians, as well as preparatory schools for those hoping to persue higher education. One senator declared that 46 percent of the population might be eligible. In the months before the 2002 presidential election, President Cardoso announced (on May 13, Abolition Day) a comprehensive human rights package of some 518 proposals for affirmative action quotas in government service for Afro-Brazilians, women, and the disabled, nutrition rights, and councils for older citizens. The proposals also provided for legalization of same-sex unions, child welfare programs, and other social reforms. Cardoso submerged race as one element among many. The discussion appears to indicate changing social attitudes in addition to political considerations. When a degree of cultural equality or respect is achieved, perhaps the merging of cultures will continue on a more constructive basis.

Taking a longer view, from independence to the new millennium, the changes seem quite incredible despite the still heavy burden of history. One statistic illustrates the extent of the transformation—in 2001 coffee constituted only 5 percent of exports, down from 75 percent in 1900. It is obvious that in spite of all the problems chronicled in this work, and those yet to be faced, Brazil has emerged as a well-defined nation with a strong sense of national identity. Although many areas retain a strong sense of regional identity, they exist within a national context. Brazil is no longer fearful of coming apart or worried about its neighbors. In fact, it seems to have moved beyond territorial questions to embrace the benefits of interdependent economies. Internal complexity and globalization have made it difficult, perhaps impossible, for any one group to establish political or economic hegemony. The 2002 presidential election saw every serious candidate, including Luiz Inácio Lula da Silva, touring Europe and the United States to reassure foreign governments and investors of their moderation. The selection process for the presidency is a long one, which winnows out many pre-candidates and often brutally dumps a frontrunner. It is life or death with each poll. The very number of polling organizations and the frequency of their surveys tend to provide an accurate assessment allowing politicians to adjust to voter expectations. Social coalitions reflected in political parties are necessary to govern complex societies—a reality that acts to modify extreme positions. This may explain the readiness to make public the country's needs, problems, and national failings. The existence of the recognized Brazil Cost is significant. The negative elements appear drawn together for all to contemplate. The obstacles in the way of trade, investment, work force expansion, education, housing, public health, race, crime, and environmental issues are evident and clearly, if not easily, surmountable. The election of President Lula da Silva, the country's first working-class president, represents a milestone in mass democracy. Whether he succeeds or fails, it is an important historical moment.

Brazil's struggle for modernity, respect, and a place within the global system explains much. Yet the details of history provide the human drama. Modernization and outside influences have not transformed Brazil into a mirror image of France or of the United States, as some desired and others feared. Over the course of history, the republic has evolved into something much more distinctive, invariably recognized by even casual visitors. Brazil is to a large extent its own creation.

Notes

1. Spanish America, particularly Argentina, resented what it saw as the Brazilians' pretensions and the apparent willingness of the world body to humor them.
2. The tendency to associate crassness with the United States has deep roots. When Pedro II visited the United States in 1876, he commented in a personal letter that "it is huge [the Centennial Exposition] as everything is here. Good taste is what is almost always lacking." Quoted in Roderick J. Barman, *Citizen Emperor: Pedro II and the Making of Brazil, 1825–1891* (Stanford, 1999), 279.
3. Paulo Maluf's bank accounts in Switzerland and on the Isle of Jersey became the focus of official investigation in 2001.
4. The Movimento Humor pela Cidadania (citizens' humor movement) in São Paulo provided an example of middle-class resentment. Used in connection with the 2000 municipal elections, the organization distributed posters picturing a fat politician with a footprint on his bottom and U.S. dollars flying from his pockets with the caption, "Corrupto Bota Fora" (Boot out the crook).

5. A statistical gauge indicating equality. 0 is perfect equality and 10 is the opposite extreme. An alternative scale runs from 1 to 100.
6. Cardoso's Ph.D. dissertation was published as *Capitalismo e Escravidão no Brasil Meridional o Negro na Sociedade Escravocrata do Rio Grande do Sul* (São Paulo, 1962).

Selected Bibliography

The following selected works in English offer a vast fund of knowledge about Brazil. All of them have been consulted to construct this history and have influenced my own interpretation. Between them they provide topic-oriented bibliographies to facilitate an in-depth examination of a particular subject with bibliographic links to related studies.

Information and concise essays on historical periods, movements, people, and events are found in the multi-volume *The Encyclopedia of Latin American History and Culture*, edited by Barbara A. Tenenbaum (New York, 1995); and *The Cambridge Encyclopedia of Latin America*, 2d ed. (Cambridge, 1992). The multi-volume *The Cambridge History of Latin America*, edited by Leslie Bethell, is extremely useful. Separately published works on Brazil drawn from it are available.

The *Handbook of Latin American Studies*, edited by the staff of the Hispanic Division of the Library of Congress, reviews the current literature on a two-year sequence. The *Handbook* includes articles and books in English, Portuguese, and other languages. An extremely useful newsletter, *Brazil Focus*, edited by David Fleischer in Brasília (fleischer@uol.com.br), provides weekly information.

Modern histories of Brazil in English, each with its own particular emphasis, are Joseph Smith, *A History of Brazil, 1500–2000: Politics, Economics, Society, Diplomacy* (London, 2002); Thomas E. Skidmore, *Brazil: Five Centuries of Change* (Oxford, 1999); Robert M. Levene, *The History of Brazil* (Westport, 1999); E. Bradford Burns, *A History of Brazil*, 3d ed. (New York, 1993); and Ronald M. Schneider, *"Order and Progress": A Political History of Brazil* (Boulder, 1991). Rollie E. Poppino, *Brazil: The Land and the People*, 2d ed. (New York, 1973); and Donald E. Worcester, *Brazil from Colony to World Power* (New York, 1973), are dated, but still useful. An interpretative study by Marshall C. Eaken, *Brazil: The Once and Future Country* (New York, 1997) interestingly complements the histories noted above. The almost encyclopedic works of John W. F. Dulles, not all of which are listed in the bibliography, collectively constitute a multi-volume source of Brazilian history in the middle period of the twentieth century.

Jan Rocha has written two short useful country studies that do not shy away from dealing with difficult subjects—*Brazil in Focus: A Guide to the People and Culture* for the Latin American Bureau (London,

2000); and *Brazil: The Background, the Issues, the People* (Oxford, 2000) for Oxfam.

Alden, Dauril. *Royal Government in Colonial Brazil.* Berkeley, 1968.
_____, ed. *Colonial Roots of Modern Brazil.* Berkeley, 1973.
Andrews, George Reid. *Blacks and Whites in São Paulo, Brazil, 1888–1988.* Madison, 1991.
Bacchus, Winfred A. *Mission in Mufti: Brazil's Military Regimes, 1964–1985.* Westport, 1990.
Barman, Roderick J. *Brazil: The Forging of a Nation, 1798–1852.* Stanford, 1988.
_____. *Citizen Emperor: Pedro II and the Making of Brazil, 1825–1891.* Stanford, 1999.
_____. *Princess Isabel of Brazil: Gender and Power in Nineteenth-Century Brazil.* Wilmington, 2002.
Bello, José Maria. *A History of Modern Brazil, 1889–1964.* Stanford, 1966.
Bethell, Leslie, ed. *Brazil: Empire and Republic, 1822–1930.* Cambridge, 1989.
Blount, John Allen. "The Public Health Movement in São Paulo, Brazil: A History of the Sanitary Service, 1890–1918." Unpublished Ph.D. diss., Tulane University, 1971.
Borges, Dain E. *The Family in Bahia, Brazil, 1870–1945.* Stanford, 1992.
Brown, Diana DeG. *Umbanda: Religion and Politics in Urban Brazil.* New York, 1994.
Chandler, Billy Jaynes. *The Bandit King: Lampião of Brazil.* College Station, 1978.
Chesnut, R. Andrew. *Born again in Brazil: The Pentecostal Boom and the Pathogens of Poverty.* New Brunswick, 1997.
Conniff, Michael L. *Urban Politics in Brazil: The Rise of Populism, 1925–1945.* Pittsburgh, 1981.
Conrad, Robert. *The Destruction of Brazilian Slavery, 1850–1888.* Berkeley, 1972.
Crook, Larry, and Randall Johnson, eds. *Black Brazil: Culture, Identity, and Social Mobilization.* Los Angeles, 1999.
Cruz Costa, João. *A History of Ideas in Brazil: The Development of Philosophy in Brazil and the Evolution of National History.* Berkeley, 1964.
Davies, R. E. G. *Airlines of Latin America since 1919.* London, 1984.
_____. *A History of the World's Airlines.* London. 1964.
Davis, Darien J. *Avoiding the Dark: Race and the Forging of National Culture in Modern Brazil.* Aldershot, 1999.
_____, ed. *Slavery and Beyond: The African Impact in Latin America and the Caribbean.* Wilmington, 1995.
Dean, Warren. *Brazil and the Struggle for Rubber.* Cambridge, 1987.
_____. *The Industrialization of São Paulo, 1880–1945.* Austin, 1969.
Della Cava, Ralph. *Miracle at Joaseiro.* New York, 1970.
Dulles, John W. F. *Carlos Lacerda, Brazilian Crusader.* 2 vols. Austin, 1991–1996.
_____. *Castello Branco: The Making of a Brazilian President.* College Station, 1978.
_____. *President Castello Branco: Brazilian Reformer.* College Station, 1980.
_____. *Vargas of Brazil: A Political Biography.* Austin, 1967.
Dunn, Chistopher. *Brutality Garden: Tropicália and the Emergence of a Brazilian Counterculture.* Chapel Hill, 2001.

Flory, Thomas. *Judge and Jury in Imperial Brazil, 1808–1871: Social Control and Political Stability in the New State.* Austin, 1981.

Franko-Jones, Patrice. *The Brazilian Defense Industry.* Boulder, 1992.

Gay, Robert. *Popular Organization and Democracy in Rio de Janeiro: A Tale of Two Favelas.* Philadelphia, 1994.

Gill, Anthony. *Rendering unto Caesar: The Catholic Church and the State in Latin America.* Chicago, 1998.

Goertzel, Ted G. *Fernando Henrique Cardoso: Reinventing Democracy in Brazil.* Boulder, 1999.

Graham, Lawrence S. *Civil Service Reform in Brazil: Principles versus Practice.* Austin, 1968.

Graham, Richard. *Britain and the Onset of Modernization in Brazil, 1850–1914.* Cambridge, 1968.

Graham, Sandra Lauderdale. *House and Street: The Domestic World of Servants and Masters in Nineteenth-Century Rio de Janeiro.* Cambridge, 1988.

Green, James N. *Beyond Carnival: Male Homosexuality in Twentieth-Century Brazil.* Chicago, 1999.

Greenfield, Gerald M. *Latin American Urbanization: Historical Profiles of Major Cities.* Westport, 1994.

Guimarães, Robert. *The Ecopolitics of Development in the Third World: Politics and the Environment in Brazil.* Boulder, 1991.

Hanchard, Michael, ed. *Racial Politics in Contemporary Brazil.* Durham, 1999.

Hanher, June E. *Civilian-Military Relations in Brazil, 1889–1898.* Columbia, 1969.

———. *Emancipating the Female Sex: The Struggle for Women's Rights in Brazil.* Durham, 1990.

Haring, C. H. *Empire in Brazil: A New World Experiment with Monarchy.* Cambridge, 1958.

Hilton, Stanley E. *Hitler's Secret War in South America, 1939–1945.* Baton Rouge, 1981.

———. *Brazil and the Soviet Challenge, 1917–1947.* Austin, 1991.

Holloway, Thomas H. *Immigrants on the Land: Coffee and Society in São Paulo, 1886–1934.* Chapel Hill, 1980.

———. *Policing Rio de Janeiro.* Stanford, 1993.

Huggins, Martha. *Political Policing: The United States and Latin America.* Durham, 1998.

Karasch, Mary C. *Slave Life in Rio de Janeiro, 1808–1850.* Princeton, 1987.

Kraay, Hendrik, ed. *Afro-Brazilian Culture and Politics: Bahia, 1790s to 1990s.* Armonk, 1998.

Lang, James. *Portuguese Brazil: The King's Plantation.* New York, 1979.

Levi, Darrell E. *The Prados of São Paulo, Brazil: An Elite Family and Social Change.* Athens, GA, 1987.

Levine, Robert M. *The Vargas Regime: The Critical Years, 1934–1938.* New York, 1970.

———. *Vale of Tears: Revisiting the Canudos Massacre in Northeastern Brazil, 1893–1897.* Berkeley, 1992.

Love, Joseph L. *São Paulo in the Brazilian Federation, 1889–1937.* Palo Alto, 1980.

Luebke, Frederick C. *Germans in Brazil: A Comparative History of Cultural Conflict during World War I.* Baton Rouge, 1987.

Macaulay, Neill. *Dom Pedro: The Struggle for Liberty in Brazil and in Portugal, 1798–1834.* Durham, 1986.

_____. *The Prestes Column Revolution in Brazil.* New York, 1974.

Marchant, Anyda. *Viscount Mauá and the Empire of Brazil: A Biography of Irineu Evangelista de Sousa, 1813–1889.* Berkeley, 1965.

Mariz, Cecilia Loreto. *Coping with Poverty: Pentecostals and Christian Base Communities in Brazil.* Philadelphia, 1994.

Maxwell, Kenneth. *Conflicts and Conspiracies.* Cambridge, 1973.

_____. *Pombal, Paradox of the Enlightenment.* Cambridge, 1995.

Maybury-Lewis, Biorn. *The Politics of the Possible: The Brazilian Rural Workers' Trade Union Movement, 1964–1985.* Philadelphia, 1994.

McCann, Bryan Daniel. "Thin Air and the Solid State: Radio, Culture, and Politics in Brazil's Vargas Era." Unpublished Ph.D. dissertation, Yale University, 1999.

McGowan, Chris, and Ricardo Pessanha. *The Brazilian Sound: Samba, Bossa Nova, and the Popular Music of Brazil.* Philadelphia, 1999.

Meade, Teresa A. *"Civilizing" Rio: Reform and Resistance in a Brazilian City, 1889–1930.* University Park, 1997.

Page, Joseph A. *The Brazilians.* New York, 1995.

Pang, Eul-Soo. *Bahia in the First Brazilian Republic: Coronelismo and Oligarchies, 1889–1934.* Gainesville, 1979.

Parker, Phyllis R. *Brazil and the Quiet Intervention, 1964.* Austin, 1979.

Penglase, Ben. *Final Justice: Police and Death Squad's Homicides of Adolescents in Brazil.* New York, 1994.

Pereira, Anthony W. *The End of the Peasantry.* Pittsburgh, 1997.

Peritore, N. Patrick, and Ana Karina Galve-Peritore, eds. *Biotechnology in Latin America: Politics, Impacts, and Risks.* Wilmington, 1995.

Perlman, Janice E. *The Myth of Marginality: Urban Poverty and Politics in Rio de Janeiro.* Berkeley, 1979.

Place, Susan E., ed. *Tropical Rainforests: Latin American Nature and Society in Transition.* 2d ed. Wilmington, 2001.

Plank, David N. *The Means of Our Salvation: Public Education in Brazil, 1930–1995.* Boulder, 1996.

Prado, Caio, Jr. *The Colonial Background of Modern Brazil.* Berkeley, 1967.

Purcell, Susan Kaufman, and Riordan Riott. *Brazil under Cardoso.* Boulder, 1997.

Schwoch, James. *The American Radio Industry and Its Latin American Activities, 1900–1939.* Urbana, 1990.

Simpson, Amelia. *Xuxa; The Mega-marketing of Gender, Race, and Modernity.* Philadelphia, 1993.

Skidmore, Thomas E. *Black into White: Race and Nationality in Brazilian Thought.* New York, 1974.

_____. *Politics in Brazil.* Oxford, 1967.

_____. *Politics of Military Rule in Brazil.* New York, 1988.

Smith, Thomas Hunter, III. "A Monument to Lazarus: The Evolution of the Leprosy Hospital of Rio de Janeiro." Unpublished Ph.D. dissertation, Texas Christian University, 1999.

Stam, Robert. *Tropical Multiculturalism: A Comparative History of Race in Brazilian Cinema and Culture.* Durham, 1997.

Stepan, Alfred. *Rethinking Military Politics.* Princeton, 1988.

_____, ed. *Democratizing Brazil.* Oxford, 1989.

Stepan, Nancy. *The Beginning of Brazilian Science.* New York, 1967.

Stewart, Douglas Ian. *After the Trees: Living on the Transamazon Highway.* Austin, 1994.

Summ, G. Harvey. *Brazilian Mosaic: Portraits of a Diverse People and Culture.* Wilmington, 1995.

Topik, Steven. *The Political Economy of the Brazilian State, 1889–1930.* Austin, 1987.

Toplin, Robert Brent. *The Abolition of Slavery in Brazil.* New York, 1972.

Toussaint-Samson, Adele. *A Parisian in Brazil.* Wilmington, 2001.

Viotti da Costa, Emilia. *The Brazilian Empire: Myths and Histories.* Rev. ed. Chapel Hill, 2000.

Walters, Vernon A. *Silent Missions.* Garden City, 1978.

Warren, Michael A. *Ordem e Civilização: The Modernization of Brazilian Naval Yards in the Nineteenth Century.* Unpublished Ph.D. dissertation, Tulane University, 1997.

Weinstein, Barbara. *The Amazon Rubber Boom, 1850–1920.* Stanford, 1983.

Wells, Alan. *Picture-tube Imperialism? The Impact of U.S. Television on Latin America.* Maryknoll, 1972.

Wirth, John D. *The Politics of Brazilian Development, 1930–1954.* Stanford, 1970.

Zimmermann, Eduardo, ed. *Judicial Institutions in Nineteenth-Century Latin America.* London, 1999.

INDEX

Acre, 207
Advertising, 76–79, 175–76, 177–78, 181
Afro-Brazilians, 40, 45–46, 67, 80, 168–73; and Carnival, 183–84, 232; Frente Negra Brasileira (FNB), 96, 169; Movimento Negro Unificado (MNU), 169; and Pentecostalism, 200; prejudice/discrimination against, 13, 65–67, 111, 168, 169, 170, 172, 182, 200, 229, 238–39; in Rio, 170; in São Paulo, 45, 46, 170, 171; and sports, 171, 178, 179, 180–81, 182; and state governments, 170–72; and television, 178, 179; Vargas supported by, 95–96, 169, 230. *See also* Slavery
Agriculture: cacao, 18; coffee, 18, 21, 22, 23, 26, 27, 40–41, 42–43, 47, 60, 62, 76, 77, 86, 88–89, 108, 122, 129, 230, 239; CONTAG, 151; cotton, 26, 27, 28, 89, 116; INCRA, 152–53, 195; and public health, 72; rubber, 18, 62–64; and rural unions, 150–51; sugar, 1, 26, 27, 28, 192; Taubaté Convention, 62; tobacco, 1–2, 78. *See also* Economic conditions; Economic policies
Air France, 91
Alagoas, 13–14
Alcântara launch facilities, 221
Alfonsín, Raúl, 187
Aliança Nacional Libertadora (ANL), 98–99
Amazonia, 25, 93, 94, 155, 191–97, 218; Amazon development agency (SUDAM), 223, 235; Manaus, 63, 152, 153, 174; and Plan Colombia, 219, 220; policies of the military in, 149, 152–54, 189, 195; and rain forest pharmaceuticals, 193–94, 196; Rondônia, 194–95

American School. *See* Colegio MacKenzie
Anarchism, 64, 65, 75–76
Andrada e Silva, José Bonifácio de, 4, 8, 10
Andrade, Mario de, 81
Andrade, Oswaldo de, 81–82
Angela Maria, 177
Angola, 158–59
Angra dos Reis, 157
Antarctica (beer maker), 77
Apprentice Sailor School, 25
Aragão, José Joaquim de Moriz de, 109
Aranha, Oswaldo, 111
Arena Riocentro incident, 144
Argentina, 65–66, 117, 174, 215; air connections with, 90, 93; Corrientes province, 14; dirty war in, 160; economic conditions in, 214, 224; education in, 234; Entre Ríos province, 14; fiscal problems in, 214; Misiones province, 221; relations with Bolivia, 107, 108; relations with Brazil, 11, 34–35, 84, 107–8, 113, 120, 164, 186, 187–88, 216, 218, 219, 222; relations with Paraguay, 34, 35, 107, 108, 219; relations with United States, 108, 188, 218, 219; relations with Uruguay, 219; terrorism in, 221; Toyota Motors in, 216; and War of the Triple Alliance, 35–36; women in, 202
Argentine-Brazilian Economic Integration Program (ABIP), 187
Army. *See* Military, the
Art, modernism in, 77, 79–82
Asociación Latinoamericana de Integración (ALADI), 187
Assembly of God (AD), 199, 201
Automobiles and automobile industry, 78, 129–33, 212, 215–16, 221, 225; knocked-down units (CKDs), 129, 131, 215